MILESTONES

THEATRE

Milestones in Musical Theatre tracks ten of the most significant moments in musical theatre history, from some of its earliest incarnations, especially those crafted by Black creators, to its rise as a global phenomenon.

Designed for weekly use in musical theatre courses, these ten chosen snapshots chart the development of this unique art form and move through its history chronologically, tracking the earliest operettas through the mid-century Golden Age classics, as well as the creative explosion in directing talent, which reshaped the form and the movement toward inclusivity that has recast its creators. Each chapter explores how the musical and its history have been deeply influenced by a variety of factors, including race, gender, and nationality, and examines how each milestone represents a significant turning point for this beloved art form.

Milestones are a range of accessible textbooks, breaking down the need-to-know moments in the social, cultural, political, and artistic development of foundational subject areas. This book is ideal for diverse and inclusive undergraduate musical theatre history courses.

Mary Jo Lodge is Professor of Theater at Lafayette College in Easton, PA, the current Producing Artistic Director for the Lafayette Theater Department and an active director/choreographer and musical theatre scholar.

Milestones Series

Milestones are a range of accessible textbooks, breaking down the need-to-know moments in the social, cultural, political and artistic development of foundational subject areas. Each book maps out ten key moments in the development of its subject, from the emergence of an academic discipline or the chronology of a period in history, to the evolution of an idea or school of thought.

The *Milestones* books are ideal for undergraduate students, either as degree primers or classroom textbooks. The ten key moments make them an ideal fit for weekly class reading and easily digestible for individual study.

Milestones in Dance History
edited by Dana Tai Soon Burgess

Milestones in Dance in the USA
edited by Elizabeth McPherson

Milestones in Asian American Theatre
edited by Josephine Lee

Milestones in Musical Theatre
edited by Mary Jo Lodge

For more information about this series, please visit: https://www.routledge.com/Milestones/book-series/MILES

MILESTONES IN MUSICAL THEATRE

Edited by Mary Jo Lodge

Routledge
Taylor & Francis Group

LONDON AND NEW YORK

Designed cover image: Multi-colored lighting equipment by SFROLOV / Shutterstock; Theatre Seats by Jack Q. / Shutterstock; *West Side Story* Playbill from the The New York Public Library (https://digitalcollections.nypl. org/items/7715284d-9474-5dfd-e040-e00a1806474d); "I'm just wild about Harry": fox trot song from the musical *Shuffle Along* from the The New York Public Library (https://digitalcollections.nypl.org/items/510d47da-4d59-a3d9-e040-e00a18064a99).

First published 2023
by Routledge
4 Park Square, Milton Park, Abingdon, Oxon OX14 4RN

and by Routledge
605 Third Avenue, New York, NY 10158

Routledge is an imprint of the Taylor & Francis Group, an informa business

British Library Cataloguing-in-Publication Data
A catalogue record for this book is available from the British Library

Library of Congress Cataloging-in-Publication Data
Names: Lodge, Mary Jo, editor.
Title: Milestones in musical theatre / edited by Mary Jo Lodge.
Description: [1.] | Abingdon, Oxon ; New York : Routledge, 2023. |
Series: Milestones | Includes bibliographical references and index.
Identifiers: LCCN 2022060775 (print) | LCCN 2022060776 (ebook) |
ISBN 9781032188287 (hardback) | ISBN 9781032188263 (paperback) |
ISBN 9781003256458 (ebook)
Subjects: LCSH: Musicals--History and criticism. | Musical theater.
Classification: LCC ML2054. M52 2023 (print) | LCC ML2054 (ebook) |
DDC 782.1/409--dc23/eng/20221223
LC record available at https://lccn.loc.gov/2022060775
LC ebook record available at https://lccn.loc.gov/2022060776

ISBN: 9781032188287 (hbk)
ISBN: 9781032188263 (pbk)
ISBN: 9781003256458 (ebk)

DOI: 10.4324/9781003256458

Typeset in Bembo
by KnowledgeWorks Global Ltd.

For my father, Paul J. Lodge, who helped me meet all of my milestones

For my daughters, Ciara & Lily, as I help them to meet theirs

Contents

Contents

Contributors

Paige Allen is a theatre-maker, writer, and researcher. She has written for the *Oxford Review of Books*, *The Oxonian Review*, *The Daily Princetonian*, and Perlego. Allen has presented research on musical theatre with "Barricades: A *Les Mis* Convention' and the Association for Theatre in Higher Education and presented research on Gothic literature at Oxford and Cambridge. She earned an MSt in Women's, Gender, and Sexuality Studies with Distinction from the University of Oxford and an A.B. in English, magna cum laude, from Princeton University with minors in Theater and Music Theater. She received the Pyne Prize, Princeton's highest undergraduate honor.

Virginia Anderson is an associate professor of Theater at Connecticut College where she teaches courses at the intersection of performance and culture and directs for the main stage. Much of her scholarly work concerns the on- and off-stage history of Broadway theatre and the AIDS epidemic; recent essays include "Choreographing a Cause: Broadway Bares as Philanthroproduction and Embodied Index to Changing Attitudes Toward HIV/AIDS," "Performing Interventions: The Politics and Theatre of China's AIDS Crisis in the Early Twenty-First Century" and "'Something Bad [was] Happening': *Falsettos* as an Historical Record of the AIDS Epidemic." Additional essays concerning musical history appear in the *Routledge Companion to Musical Theatre* and *Media and Performance in the Musical*. To learn more, see www.virginialanderson.com.

Barrie Gelles is a theatre scholar, director, and educator. She writes about the aesthetics of musical theatre, Jewishness, and Broadway musicals, and approaches to pedagogy and practice within the academy with a focus on accessibility in classroom and production practice. Barrie is a doctoral candidate at The Graduate Center, CUNY and an adjunct instructor at Baruch College, Marymount Manhattan College, and NYU Steinhardt School of Culture, Education and Human Development. She directs theatre in New York City with a focus on new musicals, rarely produced musicals, and re-envisioned revivals of musicals. For more information, please visit www. barriegelles.com.

Eric M. Glover is an assistant professor adjunct at the David Geffen School of Drama at Yale University where he practices dramaturgy and dramatic criticism. Previously, "Billy Porter (Pittsburgh, Pennsylvania, 1969-)" and "In, But Not Of" were both published in *Fifty Key Figures in Queer US Theatre* and *Troubling Traditions: Canonicity, Theatre, and Performance in the US*. Eric will also work as a production dramaturge at Yale Repertory Theatre for playwright Christina Anderson's *the ripple, the wave that carried me home*.

Olaf Jubin is currently a primary researcher for a study by the Paris-Lodron University Salzburg on how the musical represents European history; the four-year project is sponsored by Austrian Science Fund (FWF). He is also associate lecturer on the BA and MA in Musical Theatre at Goldsmiths, University of London. For 17 years, he worked at Regent's University London where he was a Professor of Musical Theatre and Media Studies. He is a co-author of *British Musical Theatre since 1950* (Bloomsbury, 2016) and co-editor of *The Oxford Handbook of the British Musical* (OUP, 2016) as well as of the forthcoming *The Oxford Handbook of the Global Stage Musical* (OUP, 2023). In 2017, his monograph on *Into the Woods* appeared as part of the Routledge Fourth Wall series. He recently edited *Paris and the Musical: the City of Light on Stage and Screen* (Routledge, 2021) and is preparing a book on the dramaturgy and lyrics of Tim Rice.

Raymond Knapp is distinguished professor of Musicology and Humanities at UCLA, where he directs the Center for Musical Humanities and chairs the Department of Musicology. His books include *The American Musical and the Formation of National Identity* (winner, Nathan Award for Dramatic Criticism), *The American Musical and the Performance of Personal Identity*, *The Oxford Handbook of the American Musical* (co-edited with Mitchell Morris and Stacy Wolf), and *Making Light: Haydn, Musical Camp, and the Long Shadow of German Idealism*. He is currently co-editing *The Oxford Handbook of the Television Musical* with Jessica Sternfeld.

Paul Laird is professor of musicology at the University of Kansas School of Music, where he also holds a courtesy appointment in the Department of Theatre and Dance. He has published widely on the topic of the American musical. His recent books include co-editing with Mary Jo Lodge *Dueling Grounds: Revolution and Revelation in the Musical* Hamilton (Oxford University Press), his own *West Side Story, Gypsy, and the Art of Broadway Orchestration* (Routledge), both published in 2021, and co-writing *West Side Story in Spain: The Transcultural Adaptation of an Iconic American Show* with Gonzalo Fernández Monte.

Mary Jo Lodge is professor of Theater at Lafayette College in Pennsylvania, and is a theatre performer, director, choreographer, and scholar. She is also the Producing Artistic Director for Lafayette College's Theater Department season. She has published numerous articles and book chapters on the musical and has directed and choreographed a wide range of professional, college, and summer stock productions. She was a Fulbright scholar in London researching the musical and teaching at the University of Roehampton. She co-edited, with Paul R. Laird, the collection *Dueling Grounds: Revolution and Revelation in the Musical Hamilton*, which was published by Oxford University Press in May of 2021.

Holley Replogle-Wong teaches in the Department of Musicology at UCLA and is the Program Director of the UCLA Center for Musical Humanities. Holley also lectures for LA Opera Connects and sings for the occasional film soundtrack. Publications include contributions to *The Oxford Handbooks of the American Musical* (2011) and *The Television Musical* (2022), and *The Routledge Companion to the Contemporary Musical* (2019).

Colleen Rua is assistant professor of Theatre Studies in the School of Theatre and Dance at the University of Florida with a specialization in Latinx Theatre. Recent publications include "El Poder y Educación: Bilingualism and Translation in the American Musical," in Delos Journal of World Literature and Translation, and the forthcoming "Defiant Joy and Care-Based Solidarity in Puerto Rican Theatre" in *Performance Research*. Recent directing credits include *Marisol, ...And Jesus Moonwalks the Mississippi* (UF); *The Skin of Our Teeth, Gypsy, Assassins,* and *Conference of the Birds* (Bridgewater State University); *Red Bike, Pantomime, The Crossing,* and *In the Time of the Butterflies* (BSU's Latin American and Caribbean Studies Staged Reading Series); *A Crossover Dream* (KC/ACTF Region I); and the

English language premiere of *Nosotras que los queremos tanto* (Suffolk University's Modern Theatre). Her forthcoming book is under contract with Routledge. Dr. Rua's current field research focuses on community-engaged theatre practice in Puerto Rico.

Rina Tanaka is assistant professor at the Faculty of Cultural Studies, Kyoto Sangyo University and was a visiting fellow at the Department of Music Sociology at the University of Music and Performing Arts Vienna. Her research interests include the sociocultural history of musical between German-speaking countries and East Asia since the twentieth century. In 2019, she was awarded the Helsinki Prize from the International Federation for Theatre Research. She received her Ph.D. with a dissertation titled "Wiener Musicals and their Developments: Glocalization History of Musicals between Vienna and Japan."

Stacy Wolf is professor of Theater and American Studies at Princeton University. She is the author of *A Problem Like Maria: Gender and Sexuality in the American Musical*; *Changed for Good: A Feminist History of the Broadway Musical*; and *Beyond Broadway: The Pleasure and Promise of Musical Theatre Across America*, which was selected as a finalist for the Best Book of 2020 Award by the Association for Theatre in Higher Education. Wolf also co-edited (with Raymond Knapp and Mitchell Morris) *The Oxford Handbook of the American Musical* and has written numerous articles about women in musical theatre.

Acknowledgments

Special thanks to Laura MacDonald, Doug Reside, the New York Library for the Performing Arts, and the scholarly musical theatre communities at the Association for Theater in Higher Education and the Song, Stage, and Screen conferences for inspiring this volume. Research Support was provided by the Excel Scholars program at Lafayette College. Research assistance was provided by Matthew White. Publication support was provided by Lafayette College. The index was created by Sara McClure.

Introduction: Setting the stage for musical theatre milestones

Mary Jo Lodge

In 2020, *A Strange Loop*, with music, **lyrics**, and a book by Michael R. Jackson, won the Pulitzer Prize for drama, the most recent musical of just ten in the history of the form to win the coveted award. The show follows a young writer, pictured in Figure 0.1, "in a fat, Black, queer body" who aspires to create "a big, Black, queer-ass" musical on Broadway, which the show calls a "cis-het all-white space."[1] Jackson's groundbreaking work, which wrestles with identity, sexuality, creativity and the legacy of whiteness on Broadway, and his historic win, the first for a Black writer of a musical, is a landmark in the development of the musical, which has grappled with many of the same issues that *A Strange Loop* confronts head-on. The recognition of *A Strange Loop* shows, in some ways, how far the musical has come in its 150-year history, though the content of the show reiterates the challenges that remain for the genre.

A Strange Loop, despite its awards, which include a Tony win for Best Musical, closed in January of 2023, and after opening in April 2022, ran on Broadway for less than a year, often a marker of a show's relative success. Perhaps Broadway audiences were not ready for its innovations and blunt truths, though, throughout its history, the success of musicals has been challenging to predict and understand, except through the lens of time and distance. Certainly, the popularity of the musical has ebbed and flowed throughout its history, from when the world could not get enough of *The Merry Widow* (1907) or *My Fair Lady* (1956) to when musicals seemed to be going the way of the silent film in the late 1980s and early 1990s. Musicals roared back in the 2000s, however, and despite the global pandemic which shuttered theatres and silenced

DOI: 10.4324/9781003256458-1

Figure 0.1: From left, James Jackson Jr., Jason Veasey, John-Michael Lyles, Jacquel Spivey, L. Morgan Lee, John-Andrew Morrison, Antwayn Hopper. Spivey (center, in dark gray), who plays Usher, is surrounded by the ensemble, who play his Thoughts, in *A Strange Loop*. Photo by Marc J. Franklin

shows worldwide starting in 2020, are being performed live once again. The global musical theatre boom the world was experiencing prior to 2020 seems destined to continue in 2023 and beyond, even if certain shows, like *A Strange Loop*, don't experience the long runs their accolades seemed to herald.

To understand the journey of the musical from its earliest incarnations to *A Strange Loop* requires a careful examination of its past. *Milestones in Musical Theatre* explores the history of the musical, the creative artists who make musicals, and the changing structure musical theatre has employed. In particular, this text examines ten significant events in musical theatre history that changed the trajectory of the form, and range from its early days, when the musical was struggling to break free from the legacy of the racist minstrel show, to today, when women and artists of color like Jackson are carving out a more inclusive space for creators of the musical. For the purposes of this volume, a milestone denotes a moment of change for the musical, as a whole, in terms of either what a musical is (or can be) or how a musical is made (including where and by whom it was made) or how a musical's success is ultimately measured. Using these broader criteria ensures that this volume moves beyond being simply a genius narrative, as many extant musical theatre history books are, focused almost exclusively on the achievements of a select group of creators, mostly white men, during the so-called Golden Age, dating from the mid-1940s through the mid-1960s, and just after. Since so many significant developments in musical theatre exist beyond that limited range and criteria, this text strives to be more inclusive.

MAKING THE MUSICAL

Before examining the history of the musical, it is helpful to understand some key terms and features of the art form, and to know more about the roles of those involved in bringing the musical to life. Richard Kislan, writing initially in the 1980s in his book *The Musical*, included a detailed description of the musical which has stood the test of time:

> Musical theater is *total theater*—an artistic system that not only encourages the use of techniques beyond the spoken word for projecting dramatic ideas but makes nonliteral dramatic revelation a priority in the creative and artistic process. Musical theater is the most collaborative form in all the arts. To measure a work accurately means to weigh the contributions of the librettist, composer, lyricist, director, choreographer, actors, singers, dancers, and designers of scenery, costume and lighting.[2]

First, it is useful to understand the term *total theater* in the above, an artistic idea often associated with German **composer** and theorist Richard Wagner, who championed the German concept of **Gesamtkunstwerk**, which translates to Kislan's term total work of art (or total theater), which Wagner used in two famous essays on art in 1849. Wagner's idea that all of the arts come together in one complete work (he was writing with opera in mind at the time) has become a governing principle for how musicals are presented today. Musicals can contain rich scenic designs, grand compositions, and complex dances and their overall effect is a result of the collaborative efforts of the many artists involved.

"Techniques beyond the spoken word," as Kislan calls them are, for musicals, primarily singing and dancing (and today, possibly even playing an instrument or doing all those things at the same time), which are ways of communicating which convey "dramatic ideas."[3] These ideas may be revealed in a "nonliteral" way–such as when the female heroine Laurey in Rodgers and Hammerstein's famous musical *Oklahoma!* (1943) works through her feelings about her two suitors via dance in the show's famous **dream ballet**, or, earlier in the same show, when Laurey and cowboy Curly sing "People Will Say We're in Love," a hypothetical love song which makes clear to the audience that the two characters are meant to be together, even if they don't know it yet.

As Kislan reveals in his long list of contributors to the musical, shows are successfully created only when the individual creative artists skilled in each aspect of the form come together and collaborate on a project. It is helpful to understand each of their contributions to better understand the musical. First, in the modern musical, the story is often of primary importance, though as the chapters in this volume reveal, that was (and is) not always the case. The **libretto** is another word for the book or story of the musical and the **librettist** is the person who writes the libretto. The libretto of a musical, particularly when it is adapted from a pre-existing source like a novel, as in the case of *Show Boat*, requires simplification of its source material so that the main ideas can be presented musically and lyrically, at the high point of each scene. Librettos, like all good stories, need characters, a plot (or a series of situations), dialogue & a theme or concept. Most musicals have at least one subplot. The libretto provides a basis for the music and lyrics that grow out of a musical's story. The end of one scene in a musical should propel the next scene forward. The end of one act of a musical should compel the audience to return for the second act to see what happens next.

The **lyricist** writes a musical's lyrics (the words to the songs), which often convey the show's theme. Lyric writing involves elements of meter or timing; the words for a song must fit its music, both structurally and thematically. Lyric writing, like poetry writing, often involves rhyming. The composer creates the music or the **score** for a musical. Typically, composers and lyricists work as a team, though some individuals, like Frank Loesser, who wrote

Guys and Dolls and Michael R. Jackson of the aforementioned *A Strange Loop*, write both music and lyrics, and can thus work on their own. The songs in musicals typically appear when words alone are not enough to express the emotional content of a scene. Theatre songs usually fill a dramatic function, such as "I want" songs, which typically reveal a principal character's objective in the show, and often propel a musical's action, and "I am" songs, which communicate details about a character or situation.

A musical's **director** is the creative artist in charge of uniting all of the elements of the show together. The director stages the show and interfaces with the design team to create a cohesive vision, which may revolve around a central concept. The director may stage musical numbers, otherwise, the **choreographer**, originally called the dance director, creates musical staging and dance numbers. The musical director differs from the overall director of a musical as he or she is the person who supervises the musical elements of the show, from teaching the songs to the performers, to sometimes conducting the orchestra, though that position may separately be filled by a conductor. Many musicals feature a chorus, a group of actors, singers and or dancers who support the main action and may play multiple roles in the show. In older musicals, the chorus functions as a cohesive group, with few characters having individual identities (they might, for instance, all also wear the same costumes). Today, the chorus is usually treated as a group of individuals.

MILESTONES BEFORE THE MILESTONES

Examining the components of musicals and the creative artists who make them can illuminate the art form, but it is also useful to explore the roots of the modern musical by looking back in history at its important antecedents, and its more recent predecessors. The four important landmarks on the road to the development of the musical listed below paved the way for the milestones examined in greater detail in this text and ultimately, for *A Strange Loop*. Of note, early musicals (prior to about 1940) were typically called musical comedies, as musical dramas really didn't exist until *Show Boat* premiered in 1927, so several of the below antecedents relate specifically to the comic lineage of early musicals.

First, the musical finds its roots in several places where music, dance, and acting were intertwined, but its earliest and most enduring antecedents are found in ancient Greek theatre, dating from about 500–400 BCE. Historian John Kenrick argues that "in ancient Greece," the first dramas were musicals that used dialogue, song and dance as integrated storytelling tools," while Denny Martin Flinn makes a case for Greek comic playwright Aristophanes, the only playwright of Greek Old Comedy whose works survive today, as a writer of "comic musical theatre."[4] What survives today from these ancient works is a focus on dialogue combined with music and dance and the use of a singing and dancing chorus actively involved in the production. In fact, today, only musicals and operas still employ a chorus; it has largely disappeared from modern non-musical dramas but remains integral even to new musicals.

Second, and much later, opera is an important historical forerunner of the musical. While grand opera (also called opera seria), the dramatic form involving singing, acting, and possibly some dancing united with the serious subject matter and often large-scale **spectacle**, was exceptionally popular in the 1700 and 1800s, it was intended for court audiences and even royalty, while comic operas, which were structurally the same, enjoyed wider appeal. Operetta, a term Flinn and others credit to composer Mozart (meaning "little opera"), developed later, but was popular well into the 1900s.[5] Flinn suggests operettas descended from both comic operas in Europe and from ballad operas which emerged in England in 1728 when John Gay **interpolated** (or took from other sources) opera melodies and existing popular songs (all usually by different composers), but set them with new, often satirical lyrics in a new, opera-like story. *The Beggar's Opera* influenced both operetta and later musical comedy because, as Flinn argues, "it was popular and funny and dealt with contemporary society," all of which became the hallmarks of both later forms, which like their predecessors also included music, dance, and spectacle.[6]

While these first two antecedents developed across the ocean from Broadway, the next precursors of the musical were the uniquely American entertainments that developed in the United States: minstrel shows and vaudeville. Minstrel shows were deeply racist entertainments that emerged in America as early as 1815, and then rose to prominence starting in the 1840s in New York City. They featured white performers who used blackface makeup to play exaggerated Black characters who present an "idealized, genteel version of American slavery" and "plantation life" that never existed.[7] Minstrelsy was, for a time, a wildly popular entertainment in America and even in Europe, and it survived long enough that early films included blackface performers, but it rightly eventually fell out of favor with audiences. Knapp argues that its central feature of a line of performers with two "End Men" known as Tambo and Bones at each end, survives "in the singing-dancing chorus line that supports a central 'star.'"[8] Vaudeville, popularized in New York in the 1860s by impresario (all around showman and **producer**) Tony Pastor, offered a wide range of acts on one bill, but Pastor's successful innovation was that he offered a more respectable version of what other American forms, like variety and **burlesque**, already did, in order to attract audiences with some women and even families. The musical emulated this more family friendly approach and continues to employ it, to some degree, today.

Finally, it is helpful to begin a discussion of the musical by introducing the first musical, but as historian Katherine Preston notes, musical theatre scholars do not agree on what the first musical is; she cites the most frequently identified options as "*The Black Crook, Little Johnny Jones, Evangeline, Show Boat, The Beggar's Opera* (and) *The Wizard of the Nile.*"[9] Likely the most often cited "first musical" is *The Black Crook*, which premiered in New York City in 1866 and famously came to be when a struggling burlesque performance included a French ballet troupe in the production after they were stranded as the result of a fire at the theatre where they had been meant to perform. The ballet was not the highbrow artform it is now, and the scandalous spectacle of the French dancers in tutus and tights captivated audiences, who supported the haphazard production with periodic runs over the next forty years, making it far and away the most successful early musical. Of the other shows Preston lists, *The Beggar's Opera* stands as the first ballad opera, while the later *Show Boat* was the first musical drama, but many musical comedies preceded it. *The Wizard of the Nile* was the first successful opera composed by Victor Herbert in 1895, while *Evangeline*, which premiered in 1874, was the first musical with a fully original score (but was eclipsed in popularity by *The Black Crook*). *Little Johnny Jones*, the first show created by

7

and starring the multitalented George M. Cohan, was a great early success with a cohesive score and book, both created by Jones, but happened years later than the musicals mentioned above.

TEN MILESTONES IN MUSICAL THEATRE

The chapters in this volume build on the history discussed above, and while they do explore the major works like *Show Boat, Oklahoma,* and *West Side Story* that are the focus of other musical theatre history texts, they focus more specifically on milestones—often shows, but sometimes trends or even creators that denote moments of transition for the musical as an artform. Taken together, these milestones paint a rich picture of the development of the musical in America and around the world over the last one hundred and fifty years and provide the foundation for future milestones in musical theatre.

The first milestone, explored in Chapter 1, acknowledges the great debt the musical owes to its pioneering Black artists. Eric Glover prioritizes Black musicals as formative in the creation of the musical, with a particular focus on *In Dahomey*, from 1903, and *Shuffle Along,* 1921. The second milestone, discussed in Chapter 2, explores the musical's early successes in its quest to be considered a legitimate art form. Paul R. Laird uses *HMS Pinafore* (1878), *Show Boat* (1927), *Of Thee I Sing* (1931) & *South Pacific* (1949) to examine how musicals transformed into serious art, worthy of such prestigious acknowledgments as the Pulitzer Prize. Chapter 3 includes the third milestone, which considers the way musicals, once derided as frivolous, came to embrace political content and even political activism. Virginia Anderson uses *Pins and Needles* (1937), *The Cradle Will Rock* (1937), and later shows like *La Cage Aux Folles (1983)* and *Falsettos* (1992) to explore the ways musicals might embrace or assist activist causes, either through their depiction on stage or through the actions of their creators and casts outside of their performances.

In Chapter 4, I examine the fourth milestone, the rise to prominence, and even dominance, of the director and the **director/ choreographer** of the musical, and the related rise of the concept musical. I discuss the Golden Age of musical theatre direction, which ran from the mid-1950s through the 1980s, and use such shows as *West Side Story* (1957), *Company (1970),* and *A Chorus Line* (1975) to examine influential directors of the musical including Jerome Robbins, Hal Prince, and Michael Bennett. Chapter 5 traces the next milestone, which examines how rock music's arrival on the Broadway stage dramatically changed the intended audience for musicals. Barrie Gelles explores teen and youth-oriented musicals like *Hair (1968), Rent (1996),* and *Spring Awakening* (2006), which reshaped the musical for a new generation. In Chapter 6, Holley Replogle-Wong and Raymond Knapp examine the next milestone, the phenomenon of worldwide hit musicals, especially more recent shows with very long runs. They look at productions like *Les Misérables (1987)* and *The Phantom of the Opera (1988),* spectacle driven musicals from the era of the **megamusical** which have been running successfully around the globe for, in some cases, over thirty years.

In Chapter 7, Olaf Jubin explores a milestone related to, but distinct from the previous one, in that it focuses on popular, long-running musicals, but more specifically ones that have found success in many corners of the globe but have not been hits on Broadway. He examines the wildly successful German production of *Starlight Express (1984),* as well as the Canadian hit *Anne of Green Gables (1964)* and the Austrian smash *Elisabeth (1992)* as examples of when musicals are the biggest hits in a particular country (other than the United States) and often nowhere else. The eighth milestone, examined by Colleen Rua in Chapter 8 moves from the questions of geography and length of run above to inclusivity, specifically in regard to representations of Latinos in musicals on Broadway. Rua looks at musicals including *The Capeman* (1998), *In the Heights* (2008), and *On Your Feet* (2015) to explore how the portrayals of Latinx characters in musicals have evolved, particularly recently, in musicals created by Latinx writers. In Chapter 9, Rina Tanaka explores the current explosion of interest in musicals in Asia by examining the production that started that boom, the 1963 version of *My Fair Lady* performed by the Tōhō Company in Japan. Tanaka examines how that production opened the door for the later megamusicals of the 1980s and beyond that played with great success in the Asian market. Finally, in Chapter 10, Paige Allen and Stacy Wolf examine the tenth milestone, which is the increased participation of women in creative teams for Broadway musicals. Broadway, since its inception, has been overwhelmingly dominated by all-male (and typically all-white) creative teams; however, in 2015, the musical *Waitress* had an all-female creative team. Allen and Wolf explore how recent advances by women working behind the scenes on Broadway musicals may mark a transitional moment for future creative contributions by women and female identifying artists.

Taken together, these ten milestones, and the historical antecedents that lead to their development, organize the messy and complex history of the musical into a cohesive story, one which is more inclusive in its consideration of who made the musical and which is more expansive in its consideration of where, how and for whom musicals are made. What a musical is and can be has changed significantly over time and indeed, musicals like *A Strange Loop* reveal that the form continues to grow, change, and progress.

NOTES

1 Michael R. Jackson, "Intermission Song," *A Strange Loop: Original Broadway Cast Recording*, 2019.
2 Richard Kislan, *The Musical: A Look at the American Musical Theater* (New York, NY: Applause, 1996), 4.
3 Kislan, 4.
4 John Kenrick, *Musical Theatre: A History*, 2nd (London, UK: Bloomsbury Publishing, 2017), 7, & Denny Martin Flinn, *Musical!: A Grand Tour* (New York: Schirmer Books, 1997), 10.
5 Flinn, 59.
6 Flinn, 59.
7 Raymond Knapp, *The American Musical and the Formation of National Identity* (Princeton, NJ: Princeton Univ. Press, 2006), 50.
8 Knapp, 53.
9 Katherine K. Preston, "American Musical Theatre Before the Twentieth Century," in *The Cambridge Companion the Musical*, 3rd ed. (Cambridge, UK: Cambridge University Press, 2017), pp. 21–50, 21.

CHAPTER 1

Early successful shows on Broadway by Black creators and the movement away from minstrel stereotypes

Eric M. Glover

Early Black musicals archive the vestiges of anti-Black racism and white supremacy with which early Black musical theatre writers contended on stage and off. In his book, *Black Manhattan*, a cultural and social history of Black people in New York, James Weldon Johnson counted the ways that Black people advanced the form of the US musical, "Beginning as a mere butt of laughter, he [the Negro in the theatre] has worked on up through minstrelsy and the musical-comedy shows to become a creator of laughter; to become a maker of songs and dances for the people."[1] The history of Black musicals starts with Black people performing in blackface and continues with Black people resisting the offenses of the minstrel show. When white vaudeville promoters Jules Hurtig and Harry Seamon presented *In Dahomey* in 1903 on Broadway, the Black musical built on a foundation of stage work by Will Marion Cook, Robert ("Bob") Cole, and others. The success of the later musical *Shuffle Along* extended to providing producers evidence that musicals by and about Black people were and remain a commercially viable enterprise. *In Dahomey* and *Shuffle Along* derived out of the artistry of Black designers, directors, performers, and writers working at the highest levels of theatre on and beyond Broadway in the twentieth century.

DOI: 10.4324/9781003256458-2

PRODUCTION HISTORIES

Jules Hurtig and Harry Seamon presented *In Dahomey* (1903), subtitled *A Negro Musical Comedy*, at the New York Theatre, New York, in February 1903. Written by composer Cook, lyricist Paul Laurence Dunbar, and writer of the dialogue Jesse A. Shipp, the musical comedy in three acts starred Aida Overton Walker, George W. Walker, and Bert Williams. *In Dahomey*, having already played Stamford in September 1902, ran 53 performances and transferred to the former Shaftesbury Theatre, central London, in May 1903. In 1903, a tour of England, Scotland, and Wales followed the original central London production, and in 1904, a tour of Portland, San Francisco, and St. Louis followed the revival on Broadway. British monarchs Edward VII and Alexandra had *In Dahomey* play Buckingham Palace in 1903.[2]

Cook's music and Dunbar's lyrics, of the Black-authored scores that were published in the 1900s, was the only musical comedy that was nearly complete; it was unusual for writing teams back then to do original musicals all on their own.[3] Cook and Dunbar were credited by themselves, but William J. Accooe, John H. Cook, Al Johns, James Weldon Johnson, Cecil Mack, Benjamin L. Shook, and James J. Vaughan's songs were also interpolated: "It [*In Dahomey*] was also the first African-American show that synthesized successfully the various genres of American musical theatre popular at the beginning of the twentieth century—minstrelsy, vaudeville, comic opera, and musical comedy."[4] *In Dahomey* also made rising stars out of its opening night cast and production staff, particularly Overton, and popularized the cakewalk, a Black social dance. Directed by Shauneille Perry and choreographed by Chiquita Ross Glover nearly one hundred years after the original, *In Dahomey* was remade in June 1999 Off-Off-Broadway at the Harry De Jur Playhouse, New York. Woodie King, Jr., founder of the Henry Street Settlement's New Federal Theatre of New York, produced and Shirley Verrett, an internationally renowned opera singer, starred.[5]

Nikko Producing Company presented the original Broadway production of *Shuffle Along*, which opened at the 63rd Street Music Hall, New York, on May 23, 1921. Written by performers Aubrey Lyles and Flournoy Miller and lyricist Noble Sissle and conducted by composer Eubie Blake, Walter Brooks and Laurence Deas directed and choreographed the musical comedy in two acts. Blake presided at the piano while Lyles and Miller performed their roles Sam Peck and Steve Jenkins, respectively, and Sissle, political boss Tom Sharper. Even though *Shuffle Along* (1921) spawned subsequent revivals in 1933 and 1952 on the Main Stem, none were as successful with New York audiences and critics alike as the original Broadway production. The 2016 original musical *Shuffle Along or the Making of the Musical Sensation of 1921 and All That Followed*, by director George C. Wolfe and choreographer Savion Glover, told the story of the making of the musical.

Blake, Lyles, Miller, and Sissle were born and raised one generation removed from slavery and freedom, the children of parents both emancipated and freeborn. Although the Thirteenth Amendment to the Constitution of the United States of America only ratified the abolition of slavery in December 1865, Black people made significant advancements on stage and off after. The authors of *Shuffle Along* sought to distinguish themselves from the stereotype of the shuffling and slow-witted Negro that came to define their parents. The original Broadway production also anticipated the blossoming of Black culture known as the Harlem Renaissance, about which many argue that *Shuffle Along* shuffled along ironically in New York in the 1920s. The Black people going to the theatre to see *Shuffle Along* are also credited with desegregating and integrating the orchestra seating of the theatre.

THE WORLDS OF THE MUSICALS

Today's Black musicals owe as much to Cook, Dunbar, and Shipp's *In Dahomey* as they do to Blake, Lyles, Miller, and Sissle's *Shuffle Along*. If you were to look at imagery, language, structure, style, symbolism, themes, and tone in *In Dahomey*, "a full-length musical comedy … created and performed almost entirely by African-Americans," then you would also see the ways in which Walker and Williams subverted the minstrel show dramaturgically.[6] Walker and Williams applied burnt cork to critique the supremacy of whiteness and evaded a caste system intent on discriminating against Black people legally. One of the major plot points in *In Dahomey* concerns the Black characters emigrating

13

to Dahomey from whence captive Black Africans were taken by effort and force in the transatlantic slave trade. These Black characters' mobility, much like Walker and Williams's mobility in real life, breaks away from their white supremacist captors and escapes their values.

Act 1 of *In Dahomey* opens outside of an intelligence service where Dr. Straight, a street fakir, peddles his preparations to passersby in Boston. One of Dr. Straight's cosmetic salves, Oblicuticus, transforms a Black person's skin from Black to white; another of Dr. Straight's cosmetic salves, Straightaline, transforms a Black person's hair from kinky to straight. Gainesville's Cecil Lightfoot, president of the Dahomey Colonization Society, solicits by mail Boston's George Reeder, proprietor of the intelligence service, to recover lost property. Unwittingly, Reeder recruits con men Shylock Homestead (Williams) and Rareback Pinkerton (Walker) to recover Lightfoot's property: a silver strongbox with a cat on the outside and a cat's eye on the inside. Homestead and Pinkerton, members of an organized crime syndicate, trick Dr. Straight, Hustling Charley (a professional criminal with links to organized crime), and Reeder into making money on Lightfoot's property in Gainesville.

Act 2 of *In Dahomey* opens on the exterior of the Lightfoot garden and home where audiences learn more about Lightfoot's family in Gainesville. The Dahomey Colonization Society, much like the American Colonization Society that argued that Black people cannot be integrated into white America, seeks to transport emancipated and freeborn Black people "back" to Africa. Lightfoot plans to vacate the home his former enslaver gave Lightfoot's family and settle his family in the historical kingdom of Dahomey (present-day Benin). One of Lightfoot's children, troublesome daughter Rosetta (Overton) who is born free status, aspires to climb to the top and make it on Broadway in "I Wants to Be a Actor Lady." Homestead and Pinkerton arrive in Gainesville to eat the nouveau riche Lightfoot out of house and home at the end of the act.

Act 3 of *In Dahomey* confused many audiences and critics so much subsequent revivals and remakes of the musical made act 3 a prologue. When Pinkerton finds out that Homestead is richer than

Lightfoot, the target of their organized crime syndicate, Pinkerton seeks to defraud Homestead, making money on Homestead's, instead of on Lightfoot's, life savings. The Cannibal King appoints Homestead and Pinkerton honorary West African chiefs after they give him barrels of whiskey as a token of their appreciation. Just when Homestead and Pinkerton find Lightfoot's property, a silver strongbox with a cat on the outside and a cat's eye on the inside, Lightfoot announces his departure and also his disappointment. "On Emancipation Day" and "That's How the Cakewalk's Done" conclude the musical in Dahomey (present-day Benin) and last no less than twenty minutes combined.[7]

A musical comedy is different from an integrated book musical in that the former's dancing, dialogue, and songs are loosely connected by the plot. In 1903, Overton introduced the song "I Wants to Be a Actor Lady," written by lyricist Vincent Bryan and composer Harry Von Tilzer, for the London stop of *In Dahomey* and after.[8] Bryan and Von Tilzer and pictured in Figure 1.1, both white men, arose in show business centered in Tin Pan Alley in the late nineteenth and early twentieth centuries. "I Wants to Be a Actor Lady" is important because it is metatheatrical, as the character Rosetta and the "actor lady" playing her sing about wanting to make it big on Broadway: "In her rendition of the song, Walker revealed her ability to inhabit material not expressly written for 'colored performers,' reanimating the song to fit and reflect the oft-invisible desires of black and particularly black female performers who longed to 'star in the show ... no back row shady.'"[9] Overton's rendition of the song as a Black woman pointed out the limited chances for employment that were available to her at the time.

Overton's character Rosetta is an ingenue who possesses qualities, such as innocence and naivete, that were rarely afforded to Black women in musical theatre. "I Wants to Be a Actor Lady" occurs in act 2 after Cicero Lightfoot and Mose Lightfoot exit, just when Rosetta enters with both a looking glass and a wheelbarrow in tow. Rosetta sings "I Wants to Be a Actor Lady" to herself as she looks intently at her reflection in the looking glass in hand. It is not known how Overton's rendition related to elements of the mise-en-scène and staging, but Overton's stage business with her looking glass was said to be popular with audiences and critics.[10] Overton as Rosetta, instead of seeing through a looking glass

Figure 1.1: Wood mounted sheet music cover for "I Wants to Be a Actor Lady," date stamped 1902 (prior to the Broadway opening)

darkly, self-actualized in song and dance and got to star on and beyond Broadway.

The song's lyrics reference persons, places, and things that audiences at the Shaftesbury Theatre for the London stop of *In Dahomey* would have recognized. For example, the song's **refrain** references Mrs. Leslie Carter, nicknamed "the American Sarah Bernhardt,"

Clyde Fitch (whose popularity as a playwright would not outlive his death), Laura Jean Libbey, and William Shakespeare:

> I wants to be a actor lady
> Star in the play,
> Upon Broadway
> Spotlight for me, no back-row shady.
> I'm the real thing,
> I dance and sing.
> Miss Carter she may play "Du Barry"
> But she can't sing "Good Morning, Carrie."
> I wants to be a actor lady too,
> Indeed I do![11]

Bryan references "Good Morning, Carrie" (1901), written by Elmer Bowman, R. C. McPherson, and Chris Smith, and introduced and performed by Walker and Williams. By drawing a connection in the lyrical content between Mrs. Leslie Carter and "Good Morning, Carrie," Bryan showcases a shift in how he wants his audience to understand the singer's performing body. Overton showed that, as a performer of great versatility, she adapted and was adapted to many different functions in everyday life and live performance.

In Dahomey, in addition to being haunted by the legacy of blackface minstrelsy, is haunted by the legacies of black-on-black minstrelsy and class warfare. In his book Love and Theft: Blackface Minstrelsy and the American Working Class, Eric Lott argues that blackface minstrelsy made a white man American and Anglo in the eyes of white supremacists, "The black mask offered a way to play with collective fears of a degraded and threatening—and male—Other while at the same time maintaining some symbolic control over them."[12] A white man performing in blackface minstrelsy performed a figurative mastery over that which he was not, Black men and boys, reinforcing his whiteness. When ethnic Irish, Italian, and Jewish male members of the US working class performed in blackface minstrelsy, ethnic Irish, Italian, and Jewish men assimilated into white America discursively and gesturally, for example. Ethnic Irish, Italian, and Jewish men who were considered Black men by the metrics at the time were made white men materially and psychically.

Theatre and performance studies scholars have also accepted that blackface minstrelsy is to white men performers what black-on-black minstrelsy is to Black men performers. In his book *The Last "Darky": Bert Williams, Black-on-Black Minstrelsy, and the African Diaspora* (2006), Louis Chude-Sokei argues that black-on-black minstrelsy rejected US definitions of Blackness that failed to acknowledge diasporic Blackness:

> his [Bert Williams's] performance as a West Indian mimicking an African-American (or, more precisely, as an African-American stereotype which he hoped to both ennoble and differentiate from himself via that comic mimicry) is argued to signify not only a nationalist reclamation of a black 'soul' obscured by white minstrelsy but also a critique of a black modernism that was hardening its own racial borders.[13]

Williams performing Homestead in *In Dahomey* also performed a figurative mastery over that which he was not, African-American men and boys, reinforcing his Caribbeanness. Although Williams and Walker introduced "Two Real Coons" with Williams in blackface and Walker without blackface, originally Williams was supposed to play the straight man without blackface and Walker the fool in blackface. The light-skinned Williams and the dark-skinned Walker changed clothes, played against type, and ended up challenging how theatrical Blackness looked as well as sounded.

Imagery, language, structure, style, symbolism, themes, and tone that surfaced in *In Dahomey* resurfaced in *Shuffle Along* eighteen years later either consciously or unconsciously. Mrs. Sam Peck, a suffragette, and Tom Sharper, a political boss, hire Jack Penrose, a detective, to spy on Steve Jenkins, a mayoral candidate, and Mrs. Sam Peck's husband, Sam, respectively. Penrose ends up finding Jenkins robbing Peck and vice versa and another character robbing both of them at the end of act 2. Penrose harkens back to Homestead, Pinkerton, and Reeder in *In Dahomey*, all of whom Lightfoot hires to recover and bring his property, a silver strongbox with a cat on the outside, home. So too Pinkerton robs his ace Homestead and Lightfoot in *In Dahomey* just as Onions robs his employers Jenkins and Peck in *Shuffle Along*.

The musical's setting (Jimtown in Dixieland) and subjects (Election Day, participatory democracy, and voting rights) had also surfaced in *In Dahomey* eighteen years earlier. As Robin D. G. Kelley and Earl Lewis in their book collection *To Make Our World Anew: A History of African-Americans since 1880* (2005) remind us, Black people thrived without white interference: "African-American men and women founded all-black towns such as Mound Bayou in Mississippi, or Langston and Boley in Oklahoma, and imagined a promised land free of white terrorism."[14] Jimtown imagines one such city where citizens, settling the states in the southeast constituting the Confederate States of America, give the Confederacy the finger. The Dahomey Colonization Society, the back-to-Africa governmental authority in *In Dahomey*, seeks to settle the country, therefore, enacting against Black Africans on the Dark Continent what the transatlantic slave trade hath wrought. These casts of Black characters rehearsed and performed an autonomy that Black people cannot take for granted outside of the worlds of these musicals.

The song "I'm Just Wild about Harry" is one of the most popular songs that survives the original Broadway production of *Shuffle Along* (1921). Although Blake wrote the song to be performed by Lottie Gee and a chorus as a waltz, Gee and Sissle convinced Blake that his composition would work much better as a "one-step."[15] This foxtrot, a dance number in 4/4 time with an alternation of two slow steps and two fast, is drawn from ragtime with a syncopated rhythm. In *Shuffle Along or the Making of the Musical Sensation of 1921 and All That Followed* (2016), George C. Wolfe and Savion Glover re-create Gee and Sissle ragging it to Blake's liking. Ragtime and tap are the forms evident in Wolfe and Glover's *The Making Of* which moves the song to the end of act 1.

Gee's character Jessie is forbidden by her father, Proprietor of Jimtown Hotel Jim Williams, from getting married to Harry lest Harry is elected mayor. "I'm Just Wild about Harry" occurs in act 2 after Jessie renews her vow to wed Harry despite his losing his election and before he is declared the rightful mayor of Jimtown. The relationship between the music and the lyrics in the song continues to be harmonious, and Jessie and the Syncopating Sunflowers build the harmony by dancing until the end of the song. *The Making Of* revives and remakes the song, a solo, into a pedagogical duet for Gee (Audra McDonald) and Li'l Baby C (Curtis Holland).

Blake (Brandon Victor Dixon) is teaching Gee (McDonald) "I'm Just Wild about Harry" on the deck of the Music Hall prior to opening night. Blake thinks that his music for "I'm Just Wild about Harry" has got to feel and sound like Blake belongs on Broadway to fit in, but Sissle (Joshua Henry) reminds him that "[y]ou don't belong by trying to belong; you belong by being who you are."[16] Gee drafts Li'l Baby C, a tap dancer, into helping her line "I'm Just Wild about Harry" out by providing her melodic line syncopation. The main drape closes and when it reopens, it is opening night on Monday, May 23, and the company, dressed in white costumes, sings and dances the act 1 finale:

> I'm just wild about Harry
> And Harry's wild about me.
> The heav'nly blisses of his kisses
> Fill me with ecstasy.
> He's sweet just like chocolate candy.
> And just like honey from the bee.
> Oh, I'm just wild about Harry
> And he's just wild about
> Cannot do without,
> He's just wild about me.[17]

McDonald playing Gee playing Jessie scats her music, in the dance break to the instrumental accompaniment, and substitutes the lyrics for improvised nonsense syllables.[18]

THE CREATIVE TEAMS OF *IN DAHOMEY* AND *SHUFFLE ALONG*

Jesse A. Shipp (dialogue for *In Dahomey*/Hustling Charley) was born free in Cincinnati, approximately 21 months before enslaved Black people were emancipated, and he died in Queens in 1934. Shipp got his start as a performer and a stage manager, working on productions of *Uncle Tom's Cabin* circa 1894–1895, John William Isham's *Oriental America* (1896), and *In Dahomey* as Hustling

Charley. Bob Cole and Billy Johnson hired Shipp to serve as their stage manager for the original Broadway production of *A Trip to Coontown* (1898).[19] Shipp's aspirations as a writer took him to Chicago where theatre impresario Robert T. Motts named him playwright in residence at Chicago's Pekin Theatre which attracted and catered to Black constituent audiences. Shipp was noted for his more sophisticated development, relative to the early Black musical theatre on and beyond Broadway, of Black character and of plot.[20]

Will Marion Cook (music for *In Dahomey*) was born in Washington, DC, in 1869 to free parents and he died in New York in 1944 from pancreatic cancer. Cook's father, John Hartwell Cook, was a graduate of Oberlin College and Cook followed in his father's footsteps by matriculating at Oberlin Conservatory of Music where Cook studied violin in his youth. Cook undertook advanced study at the National Conservatory of Music of America, New York, where he studied under Antonín Dvořák and John White in 1894–1895. Cook, by turns a composer, a lyricist, a musical director, and a performer, wrote the music that accompanied Paul Laurence Dunbar's lyrics in 1898 for *Clorindy or the Origin of the Cakewalk*. Cook was married to Abbie Mitchell who originated the role of Clara in George Gershwin's *Porgy and Bess* (1935) and sang the song "Summertime" solo.[21]

Paul Laurence Dunbar (lyrics for *In Dahomey*) was born in Dayton in 1872 to parents who were formerly enslaved and he died in Dayton in 1906 from tuberculosis. Known for his poetics and poetry and for nonfiction prose and prose fiction internationally, Dunbar is considered the first Black person in the United States to make a living as a writer exclusively. Dunbar wrote poems set in standard English while it was Dunbar's poems in African-American Vernacular English that brought him acclaim all over the world. Given that readers associated the mechanics of African-American Vernacular English with the mechanics of blackface minstrelsy, Dunbar struggled to free himself and to free his poems from white people's expectations of Blackness. Dunbar's lyrics for *In Dahomey* evinced his ability to outwit the limits that the theatre imposed while experimenting with content as well as form.[22]

George W. Walker (Rareback Pinkerton in *In Dahomey*) was born the son of a policeman in Lawrence, Kansas, in 1873 and he predeceased his wife, Aida Overton, in 1911. Before performing the straight man to the fool Bert Williams played in blackface as "Two Real Coons," Walker participated in medicine shows and minstrel shows as a child performer in a traveling troupe. Walker formed The Frogs, a Black men's benevolent society organized to give money to and help out professionals in the entertainment industry in 1908. "Tom" Brown, Bob Cole, "Sam" Corker, Jr., James Reese Europe, J. Rosamond Johnson, R. C. ("Cecil Mack") McPherson, Alex Rogers, Shipp, Lester A. Walton, and Williams helped Walker organize The Frogs. Walker and Williams's production company "The Williams and Walker Company" also protected and furthered the care and the superintendence of the fine arts concurrently.[23]

Egbert ("Bert") Williams (Shylock Homestead in *In Dahomey*) was born in Nassau, the Bahamas, in 1874 and he died in New York in 1922 after a bout with pneumonia. W. C. Fields (1880–1946) with whom Williams was credited in the Ziegfeld *Follies of 1915* and the Ziegfeld *Follies of 1917*, the first and only Black performer, said Williams was "the funniest man I [Fields] ever saw and the saddest man I ever knew." Williams earned more than $1,000,000 total in today's dollars performing in Florenz Ziegfeld, Jr.'s **revues** while experiencing microaggressions from many of his colleagues. When colleagues, including those in the Ziegfeld *Follies*, went on strike in 1919 against Actor's Equity Association, none of Williams's castmates and crewmates let him know they were doing so, for example. Williams, himself a composer and a lyricist, wrote "Jonah Man" (*In Dahomey*) and "Nobody" (*Abyssinia* [1906]) which became his signature songs in his repertoire.[24]

Aida Overton (Rosetta Lightfoot in *In Dahomey*), also known as the Queen of the Cakewalk, was born in Richmond, Virginia, in 1880 and died in New York in 1914. Overton joined John William Isham's production company "Isham's Octoroons" at age fifteen and then Matilda Sissieretta Jones's production company the "Black Patti's Troubadours" where Overton met her husband, Walker, the vaudeville comedian. Overton originated the role of Rosetta in *In Dahomey*, singing Vincent Bryan and Harry Von Tilzer's "I Wants to Be a Actor Lady" solo. The original Broadway production of *In Dahomey* interpolated the cakewalk, a Black social dance for which Overton was known, derived from enslaved people mocking their white plantation owners' walk-ing figures and steps. Overton experienced even greater success when she as Salome danced Salome's *Dance of the Seven Veils* at the Victoria Theatre, New York, in 1912.[25]

Aubrey Lyles (1884–1932) (dialogue for *Shuffle Along*/member of Nikko Producing Company/Sam Peck) originally wanted to practice medicine when he matriculated at Fisk University except Lyles pursued a career in live performance with Flournoy Miller. Lyles and Miller, members of the vaudeville team "Miller and Lyles," wrote the dialogue and James P. Johnson and Cecil Mack wrote the music and the lyrics, respectively, for *Runnin' Wild* (1923). Lyles and Miller performed in the musical *The Great Temptations* (1926) and they directed the musical *Rang Tang* (1927) together with director Charles Davis. The musical *Keep Shufflin'* (Daly's 63rd Street Theatre, 1928) with lyrics by Henry Creamer and Andy Razaf and music by James P. Johnson, Clarence Todd, and Thomas ("Fats") Waller kept Lyles shuffling. The musicals in which Lyles took his final bow were Vincent Youmans's *Great Day* (Cosmopolitan Theatre, 1929) and Johnson's *Sugar Hill* (Forrest Theatre, 1931).[26]

James Hubert ("Eubie") Blake (1887–1983) (member of Nikko Producing Company/music for *Shuffle Along*/musical director), the surviving child of formerly enslaved Black parents, was born in Baltimore where he studied organ starting at age four. In 1981, the Presidential Medal of Freedom was bestowed on Blake by the US President Ronald Reagan for contributing to the culture of the United States and opening doors for future Black fine art-ists. The US Congress, both the House of Representatives and the Senate, passed a joint resolution designating 7 February as Eubie Blake Day in 1984. *The Eighty-Six Years of Eubie Blake*, which reunited Blake and Sissle, was nominated for a 1969 Best Jazz Instrumental Album GRAMMY Award and inducted in 2006 in the US National Recording Registry. A postage stamp, the fifth time a Black musical theatre writer was so honored, was issued by the US Postal Service in September 1995.[27]

Flournoy Miller (1887–1971) (dialogue for *Shuffle Along*/member of Nikko Producing Company/Steve Jenkins) was born in Columbia, Tennessee; he matriculated at Fisk University where he and Aubrey Lyles started performing as "Miller and Lyles." When in 1905 theatrical impresario Robert F. Motts named them playwrights in residence at Chicago's Pekin Theatre, Miller and Lyles introduced the characters Steve Jenkins and Sam Peck, respectively, in a skit. Jenkins and Peck's skit *The Mayor of Dixie*, in which Miller and Lyles appeared in burnt cork, formed the basis for *Shuffle Along* (1921). Miller and Lyles inspired the white comedic duo Charles Correll and Freeman Gosden, known for creating the *Amos 'n' Andy Show* (1928) radio program, to repeat and revise Miller and Lyles's style. The television program *Amos 'n' Andy* (1951–1953), derived from blackface minstrel shows and trafficking in racial stereotypes, is considered one of the first sitcoms.[28]

Noble Sissle (1889–1975) (lyrics for *Shuffle Along*/member of Nikko Producing Company/Tom Sharper) was born in Indianapolis where he showed early promise as a fine artist, first as a soprano, then as a tenor. In 1916, Sissle met James Reese Europe, leader of the 369th Infantry Regiment of the United States Army band, where Sissle served simultaneously as Europe's lead vocalist and also as his sergeant-at-law. Sissle and Blake had met in Baltimore in 1915 and continued working together with Europe's army band, nicknamed "Harlem's Hellfighters," and on their own. Sissle and Blake formed the "Dixie Duo," making them one of the first Black acts in the United States to perform without darkening either of their faces in the style of blackface minstrelsy. Sissle died in Tampa in 1975 and left his legacy as a band leader, a civic official, a lead vocalist, and a lyricist behind.[29]

THE RELEVANT CRITICISM

Literary critic Houston A. Baker, Jr.'s *mastery of form* and *deformation of mastery* help to understand *In Dahomey* and *Shuffle Along* as political protests. Baker in his book *Modernism and the Harlem Renaissance,* argues that in the New Negro Harlem Renaissance Black people invented new ways of seeing and hearing themselves and their statuses as subjects. These Black people, known as New Negroes, replaced stymieing notions of Blackness by representing the race over and against anti-Black racism and white supremacy. *Mastery of form* and *deformation of mastery* are two of the approaches to representing the race by which a Black person complemented and complicated the canon according to Baker in his book:

> The mastery of form conceals, disguises, floats like a trick-ster butterfly in order to sting like a bee. The deformation of mastery, by contrast, is Morris Day singing 'Jungle Love,' advertising, with certainty, his unabashed badness—which is not always conjoined with violence. Deformation is a go(uer) rilla action in the face of acknowledged adversaries.[30]

I contend that Black people working in Black musical theatre, then, exemplified both *mastery of form* and *deformation of mastery* by performing their musicals.

Literary critic Lindon Barrett's *singing voice* also helps us to under-stand the ways in which *In Dahomey* and *Shuffle Along* created and maintained representational visibility. Barrett in his book *Blackness and Value: Seeing Double,* argues that vocal sound is the register in which a Black person seeks and finds both who they are and what they want: "It [the singing voice] provides one important means of formalizing and celebrating an existence oth-erwise proposed as negative and negligible."[31] In western civiliza-tion, where the ability to write is associated with whiteness, the ability to sing, to be and become, is associated with Blackness. A Black person's *singing voice* introduces and reintroduces via song and dance "disturbing social, verbal, and bodily performances into the most intimate and minute domains of civic and personal identity formation," then.[32] Song and dance exemplify a hierar-chy of affects in which a Black person accords value to themself by dint and virtue of their being.

Literary critic Daphne A. Brooks's *spectacular opacity* helps us understand the ways in which a Black person invalidates claims made upon Black people epistemologically. Brooks in her book *Bodies in Dissent: Spectacular Performances of Race and Freedom, 1850–1910* (2006), argues that Black people self-fashioned via gesture and speech to undermine traditional categories of race and sex: "In what we may refer to as a 'spectacular opacity,' this cultural phenomenon emerges at varying times as a product of the performer's will, at other times as a visual obstacle erupting as a result of the hostile spectator's epistemological resistance to reading alternative racial and gender representations."[33] Material properties and visual technologies, by animating their scripts and executing their visions, helped these Black people represent the race via gesture and speech. When Black people resorted to performing in blackface, as was the expectation of white people going to the theatre, Black people changed the joke and slipped the yoke on white people instead. They recognized a Black person's ability to levy dissent in material properties, *spectacular opacity*, and visual technologies against claims being made on them epistemologically.

Shipp, Cook, Dunbar, the Walkers, Williams, Lyles, Blake, Miller, and Sissle as designers, directors, performers, and writers realized their dreams of representing the race. Even as the practice of the theatre discriminated against Black people working on and beyond Broadway, they mastered the form of the US musical to deform the mastery of the narrative genre. They accepted their singing voices countered dominant ideology and insisted on staking a claim for Black people's humanity amid anti-Black racism and white supremacy. By understanding the affective and cognitive powers of representational visibility over Black people, Black musical theatre writers therefore "reveal the gaps, erasures, and ellipses in dominant visual narratives and their underlying ideology."[34] These Black artists, repeating and revising the conventions of blackface minstrelsy, continued to challenge both what was stated explicitly and what was really meant.

NOTES

1 James Weldon Johnson, *Black Manhattan* (New York: Alfred A. Knopf, 1930), 224.
2 Daphne A. Brooks, *Bodies in Dissent: Spectacular Performances of Race and Freedom, 1850–1910* (Durham: Duke University Press, 2006), 280.
3 James V. Hatch and Ted Shine, eds., *Black Theater USA: Plays by African-Americans, 1847 to Today* (New York: The Free Press, 1996), 63.
4 Hatch and Shine, *Black Theater USA*, 65.
5 "In Dahomey," Home of Woodie King Jr.'s New Federal Theatre, accessed August 15, 2022, www.newfederaltheatre.com/production/in-dahomey/.
6 Thomas L. Riis, ed., *The Music and Scripts of In Dahomey* (Madison: A-R Editions, 1996), xiii.

7 Hatch and Shine, *Black Theater USA*, 83.
8 Hatch and Shine, *Black Theater USA*, 73.
9 Brooks, *Bodies in Dissent*, 261.
10 Hatch and Shine, *Black Theater USA*, 73.
11 Riis, *The Music and Scripts of* In Dahomey, 70.
12 Eric Lott, *Love and Theft: Blackface Minstrelsy and the American Working Class* (New York: Oxford University Press, 1993), 25.
13 Louis Chude-Sokei, *The Last "Darky": Bert Williams, Black-on-Black Minstrelsy, and the African Diaspora* (Durham: Duke University Press, 2006), 12.
14 Robert D. G. Kelley and Earl Lewis, eds., *To Make Our World Anew: A History of African-Americans since 1880* (New York: Oxford University Press, 2005), ix.
15 "10 Little-Known Facts about Sissle and Blake's Shuffle Along | OUPblog," OUPblog | Oxford University Press's Academic Insights for the World, accessed August 15, 2022, blog.oup.com/2020/12/10-little-known-facts-about-sissle-and-blakes-shuffle-along/.
16 Marco Dog, "A new number to end Act I," YouTube video, December 18, 2016, www.youtube.com/watch?v=Ziv9a8ylKYA/.
17 "Shuffle Along," The New York Public Library, accessed August 15, 2022, static.nypl.org/MOTM/ShuffleAlong/ShuffleAlong.html.
18 Marco Dog, "A new number to end Act I."
19 Con man Jim Flimflammer (Johnson) attempts to con the unsuspecting Silas Green out of a $5,000 pension, but Willie Wayside (Cole appearing in whiteface), a white vagabond, stops Flimflammer in the end.
20 Henry T. Sampson, *Blacks in Blackface: A Source Book on Early Black Musical Shows* (Lanham: The Scarecrow Press, 2013), vii-1446.
21 Marva Carter, *Swing Along: The Musical Life of Will Marion Cook* (New York: Oxford University Press, 2008), 3–128.
22 Gene Andrew Jarrett, *Paul Laurence Dunbar: The Life and Times of a Caged Bird* (Princeton: Princeton University Press, 2022), 1–460.
23 Sampson, *Blacks in Blackface*, vii-1446.
24 Sampson, *Blacks in Blackface*, vii-1446.
25 Sampson, *Blacks in Blackface*, vii-1446.
26 Sampson, *Blacks in Blackface*, vii-1446.
27 Ken Bloom and Richard Carlin, *Eubie Blake: Rags, Rhythm, and Race* (New York: Oxford University Press, 2020), vii-376.
28 Sampson, *Blacks in Blackface*, vii-1446.
29 Sampson, *Blacks in Blackface*, vii-1446.
30 Houston A. Baker, Jr., *Modernism and the Harlem Renaissance* (Chicago: University of Chicago Press, 1987), 50.
31 Lindon Barrett, *Blackness and Value: Seeing Double* (Cambridge: Cambridge University Press, 1999), 57.
32 Barrett, *Blackness and Value*, 86.
33 Brooks, *Bodies in Dissent*, 8.
34 Nicole R. Fleetwood, *Troubling Vision: Performance, Visuality, and Blackness* (Chicago: University of Chicago Press, 2011), 30.

RECOMMENDATIONS FOR ADDITIONAL RESOURCES

Blake, Eubie. *Sissle and Blake Sing* Shuffle Along, 2016. Noble Sissle. Harbinger Records HCD 3204, compact disc.

Harbinger Records' album is the original 1928 archival record of Eubie Blake's score as it was performed by cast and crew on opening night. Although the album is not an "original Broadway cast recording" in the traditional sense of the phrase, *Sissle and Blake Sing* Shuffle Along features performances by Blake, Sissle, and other participating artists.

Bloom, Ken, and Richard Carlin. *Eubie Blake: Rags, Rhythm, and Race.* New York: Oxford University Press, 2020.

This is a recent, full-length study of James Hubert Blake and of his life and times as the composer of the 1921 musical comedy *Shuffle Along.* Bloom and Carlin won the 2017 GRAMMY Award for Best Album Notes at the 59th Annual GRAMMY Awards for the liner notes that accompany Harbinger Records' *Sissle and Blake Sing* Shuffle Along.

Carter, Marva. *Swing Along: The Musical Life of Will Marion Cook.* New York: Oxford University Press, 2008.

This is a full-length study of Will Marion Cook and of his life and times as the composer of the 1903 musical comedy *In Dahomey.* Cook's experience at National Conservatory of Music of America and at Oberlin Conservatory of Music is addressed among his experience in the Clef Club, for Black musicians, and the Southern Syncopated Orchestra.

Gaines, Caseen. *Footnotes: The Black Artists Who Rewrote the Rules of the Great White Way.* Naperville: Sourcebooks, 2021.

This is a cultural and social discussion of the authors of *Shuffle Along,* the relevant criticism, the script's production history, and the world of the musical. The original Broadway production of *Shuffle Along* is re-created from a treasure trove of audio recordings, clippings, financial and legal papers, personal correspondence, personal papers, printed ephemera, professional correspondence, and vertical files.

Jarrett, Gene Andrew. *Paul Laurence Dunbar: The Life and Times of a Caged Bird.* Princeton: Princeton University Press, 2022.

This is a recent full-length study of Paul Laurence Dunbar and of his life and times as a musical theatre writer, a playwright, and a poet. Even though he made a living as a professional writer, the first US Black person to do so, Dunbar grew to resent the use of African-American Vernacular English that made him famous.

CHAPTER 2

The musical goes legit
From *H.M.S. Pinafore* to *South Pacific*

Paul R. Laird

When does a work of musical theatre in the Anglo-American tradition move from the status of commercial art and entertainment
for a given moment to something with lasting meaning? Certainly,
not all shows are similar in terms of what they offer to posterity.
Those that enter the permanent repertory usually include elements
that enhance their relevancy to later generations, such as especially
popular songs or a book that captures the public's imagination. A
musical need not be serious to achieve such status. *Show Boat*, *South
Pacific*, *West Side Story*, and *Hamilton* are examples, but so are *H.M.S.
Pinafore*, *Guys and Dolls*, and *Hello, Dolly!*. Looking at the genre's
history, one notes how shows move into this "legit" status, bear-
ing traits that have helped deepen the musical as an institution and
bringing greater weight and significance to the entire genre. Gilbert
and Sullivan wrote hugely popular and enduring comic operas in the
late nineteenth century. The high quality of their librettos and music
combined with their single team authorship (at a time when many
works had multiple contributors) and enforcement of their copy-
rights strengthened the concept of the "work" in the light musical
theatre as an entity worthy of admiration, like a play or opera. A
generation later in the 1910s, Jerome Kern and his collaborators P. G.
Wodehouse and Guy Bolton wrote several musical comedies for the
tiny Princess Theatre in New York City, imbuing the pieces with a
sense of integration between plot and score and profoundly influencing the next generation of musical comedy writers. Kern later wrote
Show Boat (1927) with Oscar Hammerstein II, a show that many
identify as the first musical play, where most elements of the production help to render the serious plot. *Of Thee I Sing* (1931) and *South
Pacific* (1949) were the first two musicals to win the Pulitzer Prize for
Drama, recognition that these shows had achieved sufficient *gravitas*
to compete with plays. *Of Thee I Sing*, with its score by George and

DOI: 10.4324/9781003256458-3

Ira Gershwin and book by George S. Kaufman and Morrie Ryskind, achieved its greater weight from brilliant political satire. As J. Brooks Atkinson wrote after the premiere: "They have fitted the dunce's cap to politics and government, and crowded an evening with laughter."[1] Rodgers and Hammerstein's *South Pacific*—which included Joshua Logan's substantive contribution to its book—was a serious musical play that included a frank portrayal of American racism. This chapter offers consideration of these creators and works that helped bring maturity and depth to Anglo-American musical theatre.

GILBERT AND SULLIVAN

The names of the teams that write musicals help form the genre's pantheon: Rodgers and Hammerstein, Lerner and Loewe, Kander and Ebb, Lloyd Webber and Rice, and Schönberg and Boublil. The earliest figures in this hall of fame whose works still come to the stage are Gilbert and Sullivan, whose 14 shows premiering over a quarter-century between 1871 and 1896 defined the British comic opera for their period and influenced later works. Several of their creations were just as popular in the United States and other countries as in the United Kingdom. Beyond their works, however, librettist W. S. Gilbert (1836–1911), composer Sir Arthur Sullivan (1842–1900), and their producer Rupert D'Oyly Carte (1844–1901) played an important role in defining the significance of authorship and the integrity of an individual work in musical theatre. Contemporary American copyright law did not allow foreign nationals to register their works for protection in the United States. Once Gilbert and Sullivan published a piano/vocal score of a work, any theatrical producer in the United States could use that as a basis for a production, including with orchestra if they wanted to pay for the score's orchestration. Gilbert and Sullivan earned nothing from these productions and deemed them acts of piracy. After *H.M.S. Pinafore* opened in London on May 25, 1878, it was playing within a year in eight theatres in New York City and in over a hundred all over the United States.[2] D'Oyly Carte's efforts to stem the tide on *Pinafore* in the United States failed, but he had brought Gilbert and Sullivan with him and insisted that they finish *The Pirates of Penzance* for a New York premiere, which took place on December 31, 1879. D'Oyly Carte arranged a quiet premiere of *Penzance* in tiny Paignton, England two nights before by one of his *Pinafore* touring companies to ensure the show's simultaneous copyright in England, but they were unable to enforce a US copyright because Gilbert and Sullivan were foreign nationals.[3] The producer, however, was not easily deterred. After *The Mikado* premiered in London on March 14, 1885, they learned of plans to produce the show in New York with a fresh orchestration based on the published piano/vocal score. As they had done with *Princess Ida*, the authors and D'Oyly Carte hired an American to write the piano accompaniments for the piano/vocal score, allowing him to defend that copyright in an American court as a US citizen. (Besides this American publication, no other materials from *The Mikado* had yet appeared in print.[4]) *Princess Ida* was not popular enough in the United States to justify bringing a legal case, but that was not the case with *The Mikado*. D'Oyly Carte snuck a company into New York under assumed names and opened before his competition, soundly trouncing the other production at the box office, but at first, they lost in court even with their American arranger holding the copyright.[5] However, in *Carte v. Evans*, decided in their favor in the United States Court for the Massachusetts District, they won the right to collect royalties on their work in the United States with the court noting that hiring an American arranger had cleverly used the American copyright law to their own advantage: "All steps taken to secure the copyright, and vest it in the plaintiff, were authorized by our statute. Undoubtedly the plan adopted displayed great ingenuity, and the effect is to vest in these foreign authors valuable American rights in their work, but there is nothing of evasion or violation of the law."[6] D'Oyly Carte's legal battle intrinsically increased the perceived worth and prestige of authorship in the musical theatre, a patina then transferred to others working in the genre.

Gilbert and Sullivan, of course, also added value to their authorship because of the outstanding quality of their works, including both Gilbert's inspired lunacy in his comic situations and brilliant lyrics and Sullivan's ability to present those lyrics comprehensibly while also writing memorable tunes and parodying the opera repertoire. Writing in 1925, critic Hermann Klein eloquently stated the team's accomplishment as experienced in their second show, which premiered in 1877:

> ... *The Sorcerer* made manifest what skill and dexterity could do with clever people who were not stars; with actors who

were not too 'distinguished' to be moulded into their parts or to yield to the fancies of tutors who knew exactly what they wanted, odd and unusual as these fancies might seem to them. [...]

For until then no living soul had seen upon the stage such weird, eccentric, yet intensely human beings...[.] Their strangeness was disconcerting but irresistible; they conjured into existence a hitherto unknown comic world of sheer delight. The novel fascination and attractiveness of what they said and sang, whether in solo, ensemble, or chorus, fell upon the ear with a tickling lilt or a soothing balm that was irresistible.[7]

Such "tickling lilt" or "soothing balm," however, are not easy to come by, and Gilbert and Sullivan managed such moments with remarkable frequency, as may be appreciated in the show that first made them popular in the United States, *H.M.S. Pinafore.* Gilbert provided Little Buttercup with a naïve opening number describing herself and the goods that she sells, showing her simple nature and easy manner with the sailors, set by Sullivan to a cloying waltz, mostly diatonic but with enough chromaticism to make the audience perhaps wonder where her character might take the show, and in the end, she is the solution to every problem.[8] The audience meets the ingenue Josephine in her hopeless ballad "Sorry Her Lot Who Loves Too Well," an ABAB number redolent of many such operatic arias that includes Gilbert's evocative but plain lyrics, setting the situation while perhaps also parodying such sentimentality:

Heavy the sorrow that bows the head
When love is alive and hope is dead?[9]

Sullivan charges right into the material and offers an expert imitation of such numbers in countless operas, with the A sections in F minor and B sections in the parallel major, lovely and lyrical while simultaneously an over-the-top sentiment solved outrageously in this comic romp. This humorous musical smorgasbord continues directly with the entrance of Sir Joseph Porter, Lord of the Admiralty, on his barge with his "Sisters, Cousins and Aunts." The women sing a silly, if characteristic, barcarolle on "Over the Bright Blue Sea" with Gilbert arrogantly introducing the show's foolish baritone in a leadership position with a mention of his Knight Commander of the Bath, a military award:

> Shout o'er the bright blue sea
> For Sir Joseph Porter, K. C. B.[10]

The following chorus, "Sir Joseph's Barge Is Seen," features the men's and women's choruses each singing a ditty, musical ideas that Sullivan later combines. We are assured that the sailors are "sober men and true,/And attentive to our duty," while the women are "Gaily tripping,/Lightly skipping," affects that Sullivan artfully captures in the music.[11] Following his greeting to the *Pinafore* ("Now Give Three Cheers"), Sir Joseph sings (or often speaks) his song "I Am the Monarch of the Sea," where the Lord of the Admiralty, painfully admits:

> But when the breezes blow,
> I generally go below,
> And seek the seclusion that a cabin grants...[12]

This is answered by Hebe, Sir Joseph's first cousin, "And so do his sisters and his cousins and his aunts," an inane refrain parroted by the female chorus in the fashion that Gilbert and Sullivan used so often, an influence on later writers, as noted below. After this short number, Sir Joseph immediately launches into "When I Was a Lad," a satire on the British political system that sometimes allowed unqualified Parliament members to occupy high positions. Sullivan set the lyrics to a bright march, and Gilbert provided such witty snippets as:

> I grew so rich that I was sent
> By a pocket borough into Parliament.
> I always voted at my party's call,
> And I never thought of thinking for myself at all.
> Chorus: He never thought of thinking for himself at all.[13]

These lines still cause rueful smiles if one lives in a country with a legislative body within the national government, and there are countless other moments in Gilbert and Sullivan's output that still ring sufficiently true today for these nineteenth-century works to remain popular with a slice of the musical theatre audience.

Show Boat (1927)

The works of Gilbert and Sullivan were still wildly popular in the
United States in the late 1920s, when *Show Boat* became recognized as an American musical play of serious importance, but there
are several significant contributions to the notion of the musical
"going legit" that should be recognized in the interim. About the
time that the famed British team stopped writing new works in
1896, operettas conceived in the United States were becoming
more popular, as were some foreign works of great international
fame. Representative shows include *Robin Hood* (1891) by Reginald
De Koven and Harry B. Smith and *Naughty Marietta* (1910) by
Victor Herbert and Rida Johnson Young, the latter being one of
several popular works by Herbert, a prominent Irish American
composer and conductor. Another musician/composer with notable credentials in other musical disciplines who wrote stage music
was John Philip Sousa, whose operetta *El Capitan* (1896, libretto
by Charles Klein and Tom Frost) played on Broadway for several
months. The presence of such well-known musical figures working in musical theatre helped add heft to the notion of a score
being written by a single composer. Herbert furthered this cause
by being the first Broadway composer to insist in his contracts that
there should be no "interpolations"—songs by other authors often
inserted in shows by stars or producers—in his scores, and Herbert
was at the forefront in the fight for better copyright recognition,
resulting in new legislation in 1909.[14] Herbert also played a major
role in founding the American Society of Composers, Authors
and Publishers (ASCAP) in 1914, again trying to help composers and lyricists to secure the right to own and profit from their
works. One must also consider the importance of a hugely famous
international show like *The Merry Widow* by Franz Lehár (*Die lustige Witwe*; Vienna, 1905; London and New York, 1907), which
became an industry on its own in terms of productions and the sale
of related merchandise, making a musical theatre work one of the
time's most significant entertainment properties. In the following decade, composer Jerome Kern collaborated with book writer
Guy Bolton and lyricist P. G. Wodehouse in the creation of several
musical comedies for the 299-seat Princess Theatre. They strove
for more realistic plots with approachable songs in everyday idioms
that were more carefully integrated into the stories.[15] Important
examples included *Very Good Eddie* (1915), *Oh, Boy!* (1917), and

Oh, Lady! Lady! (1918). These shows helped to raise the quality of musical comedies, influencing several of the most important writers in the genre during the 1920s and beyond, increasing the relative importance of the work and its score in this genre.

Show Boat, therefore, burst on the scene when audiences had been conditioned to celebrate a show's authors and with some interest in a score and plot that complemented each other rather than working at cross purposes. (There were still many shows where this was not the case, but carefully conceived operettas and musical comedies helped birth the musical play.) Based on a best-selling novel by Edna Ferber, *Show Boat* was only the second Broadway musical created from a novel.[16] Rodgers and Hart's *A Connecticut Yankee in King Arthur's Court*, based on the Mark Twain novel, opened on November 3, 1927, but it was a satire, whereas *Show Boat*, which premiered on December 27, was a serious musical play that addressed issues of racism in a way that was unusual in American culture at the time. Compared to contemporary standards, the writers worked deliberately as they adapted the property's complicated, dramatic story. Composer Jerome Kern secured the rights for a musical adaptation of Ferber's novel in November 1926 and the next month he and writer Oscar Hammerstein II each signed contracts with producer Florenz Ziegfeld, calling for them to deliver a script in the next three weeks, due January 1, 1927, with an opening planned before April 1.[17] While it is true that books for musicals tended to be written quickly, Kern and Hammerstein could not have been thinking that this was possible with this adaptation, and Ziegfeld clearly had no idea what they had in mind. In fact, the public first saw *Show Boat* at the National Theatre in Washington on November 15, 1927, and the musical went through extensive changes as out-of-town try-outs continued in Pittsburgh, Cleveland, and Philadelphia. The hard work paid off when *Show Boat* took Broadway by storm and was immediately recognized as something special. In the *New York Times* the next day, the anonymous critic gave Ziegfeld the most credit for the show, labeling him the "maestro" and reporting that advance word from the try-outs had suggested that *Show Boat* might be "Mr. Ziegfeld's superlative achievement."[18] The review continues: "It would be difficult to quarrel with such tidings, for last night's performance came perilously near to realizing the most fulsome of them."[19]

The critic praised Hammerstein for his "adaptation of the novel that has been intelligently made" and Kern for "an exceptionally tuneful score," but this of course only scratches the surface of what made *Show Boat* a show that for many represented a new era in the musical theatre.[20]

Figure 2.1: Sheet music cover for "Make Believe" from *Show Boat* (1927)

Stephen Banfield has enumerated the often-cited, critical themes that demonstrate why *Show Boat* was ground-breaking: it marks the genre reaching its point of "first maturity"; the first scene, which includes Magnolia and Gaylord singing "Make Believe" (pictured in Figure 2.1) is an early example of a successful **musical scene** with "an unprecedented continuity of musical thought in terms of integrated songs, character motifs, and thematic transformation";[21] the sympathetic treatment of racial issues that seems unusual for 1927; and the show's lengthy and complicated production history. In the same list, Banfield notes the show's somewhat disappointing second act—not a reason for celebration—but an implicit recognition of the utterly extraordinary first act. Krueger has also noted that *Show Boat* presents the character Magnolia, "... the first protagonist in a Broadway musical to mature from a seventeen-year-old innocent to a strong, independent adult as do characters in novels or straight drama."[22] Krueger references the show's chorus that included whites and African Americans singing onstage together, another new sight in a Broadway musical. The musical also featured real commentary about race decades before the Civil Rights Movement, as the plot included Julie, a mixed race woman passing for white who is in an interracial marriage, and the song "Ol' Man River" sung by Joe, which included lyrics about how hard African Americans work.[23] That was merely one song in the show that boldly added to the drama and developed the characterizations. Soon thereafter, Julie joins in singing "Can't Help Lovin' Dat Man" with the African American servants, a song that those characters believe to be only known by members of their race, marking Julie as perhaps not what she seems.[24] There are numerous moments in *Show Boat* where the music delineates the drama, a trait revisited in a satire four years later.

Of Thee I Sing

The first musical ever to win the Pulitzer Prize for Drama, *Of Thee I Sing*, benefited handsomely from the pointed satire in the book by George S. Kaufman and Morrie Ryskind and from George and Ira Gershwin's witty score, which carried a similar punch and included some of the longer musical sequences heard in Broadway musicals to that point. Despite worthy plays during the 1931–1932 season from Eugene O'Neill, Robert E. Sherwood, and Philip Barry, the prize committee at Columbia University decided the following concerning this "musical play":

> Not only is it [the show] coherent and well knit enough to class as a play, aside from the music, but it is a biting and true satire on American politics and public attitude toward them. Its effect on the stage promises to be very considerable, because musical plays are always popular and by injecting genuine satire and point into them a very large public is reached.[25]

The award went to Kaufman, Ryskind, and Ira Gershwin; music was not part of the citation. (When *South Pacific* became the next musical to win the Pulitzer in 1950, by then the prize committee had decided that music had something to do with the show's success; Richard Rodgers also received that award.) This recognition for *Of Thee I Sing* was a ground-breaking moment for the musical theatre, confirming the genre's potential for dramatic power and fine writing.

These four writers had tried political satire before in *Strike Up the Band*, which closed out-of-town in 1927 with a book by Kaufman, but later Ryskind revised it, and the show had a successful Broadway run of 191 performances in the first half of 1930. This experience inspired the men to create another satire together, their first idea being the two political parties competing to champion the best national anthem, but they later decided that it needed romance and love became the campaign theme as one party nominates bachelor John P. Wintergreen for the presidency, holds a beauty contest in Atlantic City to choose a first lady, and uses the campaign song "Love Is Sweeping the Country." Wintergreen, however, falls in love with the pageant secretary, Mary Turner, and the unsuccessful beauty queen Diana Devereaux makes trouble, leading all the way to Wintergreen's impeachment. He is saved by Mary's pregnancy because the Senate will not impeach an expectant father. France backs their descendent Devereaux and later threatens war, but, in the end, she marries Vice-President Alexander Throttlebottom, who fills in for the president, and harmony reigns. As one commentator wrote, the writers were "… debunking the smug hypocrisy, the charlatanism, the essential absurdity of much that passes for political thought and action in these States."[26]

Kaufman and Ryskind provided a book that combined rapier-sharp wit with inspired silliness while satirizing American politics and its dependence on public relations and stunts, the fatuousness of some politicians, obsessions with beauty and other superficialities, and finding humor in American political institutions. With his lyrics, Ira Gershwin joined in the spirit, producing whimsical images and rhymes that pursued many of the same ends while also tickling the ear with delightful surprises. His brother brought his usual winning tunes spiced with syncopations and cross-accents, the kinds of melodies that stay in one's head for hours. In contrast to a musical comedy like *Girl Crazy*, which opened the previous year, *Of Thee I Sing* included few potential hits because the songs had to serve the satire and dramatic moment in a stricter manner than was the reigning pattern. This forced the Gershwin brothers to extend themselves through more attention to the plot and character development, a matter complicated through musical sequences that were both much longer than was expected from the musical comedies of the day and more involved with the storytelling. They include solo songs, recitatives, choruses, **underscoring**, and non-stop music.[27] The score enhances the show's ridiculousness with frequent inclusion of choruses based on a common effect made famous by Gilbert and Sullivan, with material just sung by a soloist immediately repeated chorally, underlining the inanity of a situation.

A good example of one of these sequences is the Act 1 Finale, which includes Wintergreen's inauguration, his marriage to Mary Turner, his second confrontation with Diana Devereaux, and the Supreme Court's determination that Mary's corn muffins (which she carries with her) really are more important than Devereaux's search for justice after winning the beauty contest.[28] The scene opens with the Supreme Court marching out, counting off to a loony whole-tone scale and then launching into a comic description of their governmental function: "Only we can take a law and make it legal!"[29] Wintergreen comes on with a fanfare and responds to the invitation for his inaugural address with a verse assuring us that there are serious issues he values (repeated by the ensemble), but instead, he will say farewell to other women in Gershwin's AABA song, "A Kiss for Cinderella," a diverting soft-shoe which the chorus joins with counterpoint as Wintergreen repeats two A sections with new text. Wintergreen admits in the B section that he never knew these women, and the chorus trolls him with "All the girls he didn't know so well..."[30] Mary comes in with her own fanfare and sings briefly of her happiness asking if she might be dreaming, the ingenue who is a lyric soprano against Diana the belter. The chief justice administers the hilarious oath of office and marriage vows, spoken over underscoring, and the newlyweds sing Mary's entrance music as a duet. Diana rudely interrupts and explains her objections, punctuating her disappointment after the beauty contest with a descending whole-tone scale on "All my castles came tumbling down..."[31] The fickle judges and chorus first upbraid Diana for a "communistic plot!"[32], but after Wintergreen sings in recitative about his true love, everyone objects in brief, punchy statements, ending with telling the new president "... you're a dirty, dirty name."[33] In recitative, Mary assures John of her eternal love and Diana asks why Mary wears the ring. Wintergreen **reprises** the short song "Some Girls Can Bake a Pie," already used to explain himself after the beauty pageant because it concludes with his praise for Mary's corn muffins. Diana and the chorus quickly react, raising the question, "Which is more important? Corn muffins or justice?"[34] Mary again bears samples, the Supreme Court tries them as evidence, and they quickly rule in Mary's favor. Diana has a fast quatrain to assure everyone that she will spread her story all over the country, and the act quickly closes with a bit of the title tune over a triumphant orchestration. Love and corn muffins have triumphed, and as the audience went off to intermission, perhaps some were aware that they had just witnessed a most unusual scene for the American musical theatre in 1931–1932.

South Pacific

Recipient of ten Tony Awards and the second musical to win the Pulitzer Prize for Drama, *South Pacific* might be the most persuasive argument for the joint genius of Richard Rodgers and Oscar Hammerstein II. It opened on April 7, 1949, and ran for 1,925 performances, one of numerous plays and films that both interpreted and capitalized upon the American experience in World War II, but in this case not through empty patriotism or a glorified tale of sacrifice and valor. This storied team of writers placed their finest skills and theatrical instincts at the service of a story that laid bare the innate racism of white Americans, making the Tonkinese people (Vietnamese workers the French brought to Pacific islands) encountered by American forces in the South Pacific stand-ins for African Americans. One American, Navy nurse Nellie Forbush, overcomes the racism that she learned growing up in Little Rock, Arkansas, while another, Joe Cable, falls deeply in love with the Tonkinese Liat but cannot bring himself to marry her because he knows what she will face back home in Philadelphia. Like many shows from an earlier time, *South Pacific* includes what are now problematic issues of representation and perception, but that does not change the care and depth of knowledge that Rodgers and Hammerstein brought to its creation. Joshua Logan, the show's director, co-wrote the book with Hammerstein, bringing with him military experience that the other man lacked and helping to make the show ring true to the many Americans that had recently spent time in uniform.

Hammerstein and Logan adapted *Tales of the South Pacific* by James Michener, a volume of short stories based on the writer's wartime experiences.[35] They used characters from throughout the volume but based their work mostly on the stories "Our Heroine," about Nellie Forbush and the French planter Emile de Becque, and "Fo' Dolla'," concerning Bloody Mary, Joe Cable, and Liat. They created a taut play that proceeded from bored Seabees, Marines, and nurses killing time on an island not yet involved in the war to one mobilizing for combat, with numerous believable, multi-faceted personalities. The main characters—Nellie, Emile, Joe, and Bloody Mary—come leaping off the stage. Liat is less well-drawn, mostly because she does not speak or sing, but Luther Billis is a schemer allowed to have a tender side because he is protective of Nellie. Even Captain Brackett of the minor characters shows more than one side, albeit briefly. Music is crucial to character development throughout.[36] "Dites-moi" is a sweet song for de Becque's children, showing them to be a happy family.[37] Nellie emerges as a prototypical American woman by singing songs that sound like contemporary popular fare—"A Cockeyed Optimist," "I'm Gonna Wash That Man Right Outta My Hair," and "A Wonderful Guy"—but each also narrates her journey as a character and tells us important things about her.

Emile's identity as an exotic Frenchman a generation older than Nellie is colored substantially by "Some Enchanted Evening" and "This Nearly Was Mine," and his cinematic duet with Nellie, "Twin Soliloquies," sets up a major romantic moment in the first scene after we hear their thoughts, a clever solution for two singers that could not sing a major duet because of inherent balance problems between an operatic bass and a Broadway belter. Bloody Mary's songs both thrust the plot forward: the exotic "Bali Ha'i" successfully tempts Cable to the nearby island to meet Liat and "Happy Talk" is a seductive number in which Mary tries desperately to convince Cable to marry her daughter. (In the original production, director Logan had Betta St. John, playing Liat, participate in the song with charming sign language while her mother sang.) Cable sings the sweet "Younger Than Springtime" to Liat upon meeting her before they make love, and then in Act 2, he offers the ironic "You've Got to Be Carefully Taught" to Emile, a condemnation of racism ironically set to a delightful tune. It deepens Cable's character, indirectly explaining that it is such American racism that has prevented him from believing that he could marry Liat, a situation that plagues him. The male chorus of Seabees and Marines sing two energetic numbers: "Bloody Mary," introducing her character; and "There Is Nothin' Like a Dame," confirming that they are men who crave female companionship. The show's only other major song is "Honey Bun," a play-within-a-play number that concludes the Thanksgiving show for the people on the base. Brief reprises of at least eight songs make fourteen appearances in *South Pacific* (not including encores that follow shortly after a first performance), perhaps most memorably in three places: Emile teases Nellie with a bit of "I'm Gonna Wash That Man Right Outta My Hair" after the party toward the end of Act 1, a song she did not think he had heard (tacit admission that the song is part of the story); Joe sings a tortured reprise of "Younger Than Springtime" after Liat leaves him, the text now in the past tense; and Nellie sings part of "Some Enchanted Evening" when she worries that Emile will not survive his mission after Joe has already died. The show's plot is unthinkable without these many musical moments providing depth and momentum. The skill with which Rodgers and Hammerstein worked their songs into the fabric of the powerful, ground-breaking musical play demonstrates how the musical theatre as a genre could carry a serious dramatic load.

CONCLUSION

A more "legit" status in the musical theatre forged over about seven decades between about 1880 and 1950 was the product of an increased prominence of shows authored by noted teams of writers, burnishing the image of those shows and the creators through greater legal protection of their rights to own their works, and a growing recognition of the ability of these writers to both offer superior value in terms of entertainment and handle serious material. Gilbert and Sullivan adroitly offered humorous situations and lyrics that nearly defined the English-speaking musical theatre in their times and remained popular for more than another century, while Kern and Hammerstein challenged audiences with the first adaptation of a serious novel into the world of the musical comedy, writing about a dysfunctional family and commenting about race in the United States. Kaufman, Ryskind, and the Gershwin brothers successfully melded sparkling political satire with the musical comedy. Rodgers and Hammerstein did more than most Broadway writers to define the musical play for the postwar era while again addressing American problems with race. These writers and others helped bring the luster of artistic creation to a commercial medium, materially changing the Anglo-American musical theatre for those who followed in their footsteps.

NOTES

1 J. Brooks Atkinson, "THE PLAY: Fitting the Dunce's Cap on Politics in a Musical-Go-Round by Kaufman, Ryskind and Gershwin," *The New York Times*, December 28, 1931, 21.
2 Alexander P. Browne, "Sir Arthur Sullivan and Piracy," *The North American Review* 148, no. 391 (June 1889): 750.
3 Caryl Brahms, *Gilbert and Sullivan: Lost Chords and Discords* (London: Weidenfeld & Nicolson, 1975), 91–92.
4 Browne, 756–757.
5 Brahms, 154–155.
6 Browne, 760.
7 Hermann Klein, *Musicians and Mummers* (London: Cassell & Co., 1925), quoted in Arthur Jacobs, *Arthur Sullivan: A Victorian Musician*, 2nd ed. (Portland, OR: Amadeus Press, 1992), 117.

8 W. S. Gilbert and Sir Arthur Sullivan, H.M.S. Pinafore *in Full Score*. New Edition by Carl Simpson and Ephraim Hammett Jones (Mineola, NY: Dover Publications, Inc., 2002), 30–33.

9 Gilbert and Sullivan, 52–55, quotation on p. 53.

10 Gilbert and Sullivan, 57.

11 Gilbert and Sullivan, 58–68.

12 Gilbert and Sullivan, 69–72, quotation on pp. 71–72.

13 Gilbert and Sullivan, 73–86, quotation on p. 82.

14 For a fine biography on Victor Herbert, see: Neil Gould, *Victor Herbert: A Theatrical Life* (New York: Fordham University Press, 2008).

15 Stephen Banfield, *Jerome Kern* (New Haven and London: Yale University Press, 2006), 16ff.

16 Banfield, 153.

17 Miles Krueger, Show Boat: *The Story of a Classic American Musical* (New York: Oxford University Press, 1977), 19, 25–26.

18 "'Show Boat' Proves Fine Musical Show," *New York Times*, December 28, 1928, 26.

19 "'Show Boat' Proves Fine…"

20 "'Show Boat' Proves Fine…"

21 Banfield, 156. For the music of this scene, see: Jerome Kern and Oscar Hammerstein II, *Show Boat* (Greenwich, CT: The Welk Music Group/Cherry Lane Music Co., Inc., 1927), 34–46.

22 Miles Krueger, "Some Words about 'Show Boat," liner notes in *Show Boat*/John McGlinn, EMI CDS 7 49108 2, 1988, p. 18.

23 Kern and Hammerstein, 47–55.

24 Kern and Hammerstein, 58–69.

25 Quoted in: Howard Pollack, *George Gershwin: His Life and Work* (Berkeley: University of California Press, 2006), 513.

26 Anonymous source quoted in: Pollack, 500.

27 Score: George Gershwin, Ira Gershwin, George S. Kaufman, and Morrie Ryskind, *Of Thee I Sing* (New York: New World Music, 1932).

28 Gershwin, etc., 74–103.

29 Gershwin, etc., 74–76.

30 Gershwin, etc., 84.

31 Gershwin, etc., 93.

32 Gershwin, etc., 94.

33 Gershwin, etc., 96.

34 Gershwin, etc., 99.

35 For an excellent account of how they adapted Michener's source material, see: Jim Lovensheimer, South Pacific: *Paradise Rewritten* (Oxford and New York: Oxford University Press, 2010), 35ff.

36 For a fine consideration of the score of *South Pacific*, see Lovensheimer, and Geoffrey Block's *Richard Rodgers* (New Haven and London: Yale University Press, 2003), 121–170.

37 For access to the songs mentioned in this paragraph, see: Richard Rodgers and Oscar Hammerstein II, *A Musical Play: South Pacific* ([New York]: Williamson Music, 1949).

RECOMMENDATIONS FOR ADDITIONAL RESOURCES

Decker, Todd R. *Show Boat: Performing Race in an American Musical.* New York: Oxford University Press, 2013.

This is an overview of the show's creation with an emphasis on both the music and the libretto, important productions and film versions of the show through the 1990s, and a fascinating consideration of the various roles of race in a landmark property involving that crucial lens in American life and history.

Eben, David and Meinhard Saremba. *The Cambridge Companion to Gilbert and Sullivan.* Cambridge: Cambridge University Press, 2009.

This is a one-volume introduction to the topic with essays by numerous experts in the field providing considerations of the background to the operettas, focuses on the works in context and their librettos and music, and their reception in both professional and amateur productions.

Lovensheimer, Jim. *South Pacific: Paradise Rewritten.* Oxford and New York: Oxford University Press, 2010.

This is a consideration of the show's adaptation from Michener's collection of short stories; the creation of the score; the property's relation to and use of race, gender, and Western colonialism; the reception of the original production; and the show's performance history in subsequent versions.

Pollack, Howard. *George Gershwin: His Life and Work.* Berkeley: University of California Press, 2006.

This is a voluminous, chronological consideration of Gershwin's life and work with the material on the creation, reception of each of his works, commentary on the music of each, and performance histories. There is an entire chapter on *Of Thee I Sing.*

CHAPTER 3

"An Ally in the Fight": The civic engagement of activist musicals

Virginia Anderson

As musical theatre evolved from the spectacle-driven shows with minimal plots that previously dominated the form, the shift to story-driven productions laid the foundation for activist musicals to emerge. Starting in the 1930s, after the pioneering *Show Boat* appeared, musical theatre artists began to be taken seriously as citizens participating in and rehearsing for democracy, both on stage, and in highly public actions taken off-stage. Marc Blitzstein, the composer of *The Cradle Will Rock*, observed growing social unrest for the working class in 1936; he wrote that the "public is storming the gates," and insisted music had an important role to play in both instructing and supporting its struggle: "No activity ... can be divorced from it; music becomes an ally in the fight as well as an ideal aim."[1] This chapter explores some of the ways in which musical theatre has embraced and assisted activist causes. Spanning case studies that demonstrate the varied ways in which activism has been embraced by musical theatre, it begins by cataloging representative depictions of labor struggles as a means of inspiring change through such Broadway musicals as *Pins and Needles* (1937), *The Cradle Will Rock* (1937), and *The Pajama Game* (1954). This chapter also highlights the activism of theatre artists that occurred off-stage, including the efforts of the company of *La Cage Aux Folles* (1983), who became leading HIV/AIDS activists during the earliest years of the epidemic. It then addresses how events within a musical's social context can create implied activism that demands social change, as in *Falsettos* (1991). Finally, it explores *Hamilton* (2015) and *Suffs* (2022), more recent works of activist musical theatre.

DOI: 10.4324/9781003256458-4

A musical, as concisely defined by Stacy Wolf, is "an intensely collaborative performance form that communicates meaning and feeling through song and dance, speech and bodies on stage."[2] Musical theatre scholars like Raymond Knapp have documented how musicals are often conservative at their core, reinforcing the status quo even as they appear to promote progressive thinking on such issues as race, gender, and class.[3] Donatella Galella expands on this idea, arguing that many such musicals promote assimilation to white western values, "upholding the imperialist pillars of white supremacy rather than dismantling them."[4] She concludes, "As Americans participate in a democracy and in an academy structured by and in white supremacy, we should listen for the dissonance, ambivalence, and pluralities of minoritized voices."[5] Nevertheless, there is a long, often overlooked history of musicals modeling activism for an audience, often implicitly and explicitly enjoining its participation in political or social change. Stacy Wolf, for example, argues for the ways in which musicals have resisted passive tropes of femininity over decades, arguing instead that:

> The very action of singing and dancing—the foundation of performance in musicals—requires an athleticism that demonstrates women's physical and vocal strength. The female principal in most musicals is visually and aurally dominant. She stands center stage, the story is built around her, and the songs are written for her as solo presentations … And even when the character sings a song of being in love (with a man) … the female performer 'owns' the song; the performance itself is all about her (in a) feminine yet active cultural form that does not locate a woman as a passive to-be-looked-at object but allows her to take up the position of self-spectacle. Women in musicals look back.[6]

In her book *American Cinderellas on the Broadway Stage*, Maya Cantu builds upon Wolf's observations, situating them within broader feminist movements by arguing "for the existence of a canon of musicals by prominent female lyricists and librettists that openly advanced progressive ideas of women's rights within a form that … has not traditionally been considered compatible with feminist ideologies."[7] Cantu's ideological contextualization and Wolf's emphasis on live performance illustrate the interpersonal gathering necessary for activism to take hold: the socially conditioned experience of each audience member meets the embodiment of power. This is communitas at its most potent.

While definitions of activism vary, at their collective roots are a strong conviction, a desire to change from the status quo, and most importantly, direct and intentional steps taken to make such changes happen. Sometimes overt but often subtle, activist musicals require a foundation of civic engagement. "Civic engagement," Thomas Ehrlich writes, "means working to make a difference in the civic life of our communities and developing the combination of knowledge, skills, values and motivation to make that difference. It means promoting the quality of life in a community, through both political and non-political processes."[8] Spanning decades and as discussed through the examples that follow, musical theatre has provided a vital platform for social change through both representation and action.

A CATALOG OF PROTEST: UNION ACTIVISM THROUGH STAGE DEPICTIONS

The 1930s were a tumultuous period of social and economic unrest in the United States and protests found persuasive embodiment on stage with shifts in musical theatre and plays alike. John Wexley's play *Steel* (1931) castigated the way the steel industry forced humans to become like machines; his *They Shall Not Die* (1934) condemned racism and injustice; Clifford Odets' *Waiting for Lefty* (1935) confronts inequitable labor conditions; and the Living Newspapers commonly associated with the Federal Theatre Project (1935–1939) directly addressed social and political issues.[9] Musical theatre modeled protest through its content, and even its form, educating workers and broader audiences alike with *Pins and Needles* (1937) and *The Cradle Will Rock* (1937). Music director Jerome Moross wrote in 1935:

> I envision a new revue in America, a swift and vital form rising above flippancies, the music being more than the banalities of Tin Pan Alley, the lyrics achieving the worth of a Gilbert or a Brecht, the sketches using the blackout technic [sic] not for bathroom humor, but for terse dramatic punches. [...] It is

one of the most important types of native culture yet to be developed and it should be restored to the working class, from whose vaudeville and minstrel show entertainment it came.[10]

Moross's vision would come to fruition with *Pins and Needles* (1937), a Broadway show created and produced by the Labor Stage.

Pins and Needles (1937)

Pins and Needles, a light-hearted revue, mocked the rich and powerful and addressed such topics as unemployment, housing, minimum wage, and the rights of immigrants, always from a pro-union standpoint. Influenced by educational protest theatre developed by such organizations as the Workers' Drama League, the German-language Prolet Buehne, the Yiddish theatre Artef, and the Workers' Laboratory Theatre, the Labor Stage departed from its predecessors in its pursuit of humor. *Pins and Needles* "managed to deal with poignant, even painful matters in a vein of good-natured foolery that was always witty and often hilarious."[11]

With concerns for labor reform at its center, it's fitting that *Pins and Needles* was an extraordinarily collaborative venture written for and performed by members of the International Ladies Garment Workers Union, which documented the thoughts and struggles of its cast. As scholar Harry M. Goldman observed:

> A left-wing revue was unique. Most left-wing drama was socialistic propaganda dished out in heavy, slow pondering productions, designed to arouse thought if not protest. Most revues were mindless entertainments. And all the theatre on Broadway was, of course, professional. Thus to stage a left-wing revue with a garment-worker cast was original, striking and innovatory. It had *never* been done before. It has never been done so successfully since.[12]

Directed by Charles Friedman, the show was largely developed by creator Harold Rome (music and lyrics) with contributions from numerous artists including Arthur Arent, Marc Blitzstein, Emanuel Eisenberg, Charles Friedman, and others. It became the longest running show of its time with over 1,100 performances on

Broadway from 1937 to 1941. Sketches and songs were swapped in and out of the pro-labor revue for several reasons: to keep it topically relevant over the course of its run, to address police demands in specific cities, and to appeal to a wider audience through "safer" stances on controversial issues.[13] The producer further sought audience dividends with casting changes over time. Performer Nina Harary recalled, "Schaffer wanted to make the show more palatable. He put in new, sweeter material, good-looking girls, and talented non-union people. One time he even asked me to get a nose job!"[14] Performer Al Levy remembered, "Originally the cast was all union people. But eventually [Producer Louis] Schaffer weeded out those people with thick, ethnic accents. People who looked Jewish were also weeded out. Replacements came in."[15] Over time, the embodied activism of authentic labor union performers was replaced with the commercial—and lucrative— appeal of more conventional casting. Nevertheless, its pro-union content and legendary creation influenced audience reception, and the musical's enthusiastic published endorsement by Eleanor Roosevelt, followed by a command performance for the president at the White House, pictured in Figure 3.1, fueled a successful run.[16] *Pins and Needles* played at Labor Stage from November 27, 1937, until June 26, 1939, when it transferred to Broadway's Windsor Theatre for a year long run, and then two national tours.

The Cradle Will Rock (1937)

The same year that *Pins and Needles* premiered, Blitzstein's *The Cradle Will Rock* similarly encouraged labor organizing while exposing pervasive societal corruption. Unlike *Pins and Needles*, *Cradle* was famously short-lived. Marc Blitzstein is described by historian John Hunter as "an artist with a social message" who came into his own during the country's Great Depression.[17] Through his work on *Cradle*, Blitzstein learned valuable lessons regarding how to create musical theatre in service of social change. Blitzstein recalled:

> It became clear to me that the theatre is so elusive an animal that each situation demands its own solution. And so in a particularly dramatic spot, I found the musical simply had to stop. I also found that certain pieces of ordinary plot-exposition

Figure 3.1: President Franklin D. Roosevelt and International Ladies Garment Workers Union (ILGWU) president David Dubinsky with cast members of the ILGWU revue *Pins and Needles*. Left to right: Ruth Rubenstein, Rose Newmark, Lynn Jaffe, Millie Weitz, Ann Brown, and Nettie Harari at the White House, March 3, 1938. Courtesy of the Katherine Joseph Papers, Archives Center, National Museum of American History, Smithsonian Institution

could be handled very well by music. ... I also noticed you could say in a song what would ordinarily take pages of dialogue and that you could expand and deepen, too, by means of music. In short, music in the theatre is a powerful, almost immorally potent weapon.[18]

The Cradle Will Rock proved to be just such a potent weapon. Set in the fictional Steeltown, USA in the present (of 1937), the musical interrogates the cause and effect of corporate greed and the necessity of unionization. The allegorical musical begins as Moll, arrested for soliciting, is taken to the local night court along with members of the anti-union Liberty Committee, who had been arrested by mistake and included such figures as a doctor, a journalist, a preacher, and artists. Harry Druggist, also held in jail but for vagrancy, shares the ways in which each of them has sold out. Despite Mr. Mister's attempts at bribery, Larry Foreman leads the formation of a sweeping union that suggests an end to the pervasive corruption.

The circumstances surrounding the production can augment the powerful activist messages in shows like *The Cradle Will Rock*. Labor strikes were happening all over the country and *Cradle's* pro-union message could not have been more clear or more timely. Sponsored by the Federal Theatre Project (FTP), the musical was to launch its preview performances on Broadway at Maxine Elliott's Theatre on June 16, 1937.[19] However, the production was shut down four days before it was scheduled to open allegedly due to budget cuts (though the FTP had been enduring heavy criticism for sponsoring radical productions and the move has been accepted, in retrospect, as an act of censorship). The actors and creative team nevertheless persisted and remained determined to perform the piece for an audience. With the theatre locked and under guard, the company had no access to their props and set pieces. In addition, the actor's union insisted that the actors could not appear on any stage not sanctioned by the FTP. Furthermore, the musicians' union essentially prohibited a move to another theatre, explaining that without the FTP's financial and regulatory support, Producer John Houseman, director Orson Welles, and composer Blitzstein would be responsible for hiring and paying additional musicians to comply with standard Broadway contracts.

A solution was found, however, that has since become the stuff of legend. After a crowd followed the cast and crew on a twenty-one-block march to the rented Venice Theatre, the show, advertised as a concert by Blitzstein, went on, and featured the original actors, who followed the lead of Olive Stanton, who played Moll, and bought tickets, and performed their roles from various places in the house, rather than onstage (thereby maintaining the integrity of their union contracts). Blitzstein, who was not a member of the musicians' union, accompanied them from the stage. The pro-union message of the show was amplified by the very restrictions in place; the spare production modeled unity and perseverance by taking action to oppose oppressive power. *Cradle* ran for nineteen performances at the Venice Theatre before reopening at the Windsor Theatre the following January. The immediate legacy of the 1937 production was palpable, however, as the new production was still performed without props and with Blitzstein at the piano. Even with the disbanding of the Federal Theatre Project in 1939, the premiere haunts every production of the musical that has followed, and it serves as a model of determined activism on both sides of the footlights.[20]

While musicals appeared poised to catalyze social change at the advent of the next decade, the second World War led to a different emphasis on storytelling within commercial musical theatre. This is not to say that activist theatre quelled within this turbulent context; in *Stage for Action: U.S. Social Activist Theatre in the 1940s*, Chrystyna Dail refutes common notions that "social activist performance for working-class audiences vaporized in the aftermath of the atomic bomb,"[21] instead arguing through her titular case study that "the late 1940s did not suffer from any absence of activism; rather, activists' voices were often drowned out by the stentorian shouts of Dixiecrats and red-baiters."[22]

The Pajama Game (1954)

Like *Pins and Needles* and *Cradle* before it, the resonance of union activity within *The Pajama Game* (1954) was heightened for audiences by the circumstances; according to a report for the Congressional Research Service, union membership as a percentage of wage and salary employment and as a percentage of total employment, peaked in 1954 (the same year as *The Pajama Game* premiered) at 34.8% and 28.3%, respectively.[23]

The Pajama Game, based on the novel *7½ Cents* by Richard Bissell, was directed by George Abbott and Jerome Robbins, choreographed by Bob Fosse, with music and lyrics by Richard Adler and Jerry Ross, and a book by Abbott and Bissell. Mark Robinson describes the labor dispute at the heart of the romantic musical comedy as:

> the story of labor at a Midwestern pajama factory on the verge of a union strike (in an effort to get a 7½ cent raise) [that] spoke to the average working American. Complicating matters, of course, is a romance that breaks out between the factory's new superintendent and the head of union grievance committee. In the end, everyone gets what they want.[24]

The manner in which this is accomplished, however, clearly presents the righteousness of union organization.

The musical opens with executive Vernon Hines boasting of how much he loves his job at a pajama factory and the speed with which the company produces garments. The musical abruptly shifts to reveal the intensity of labor at the factory, both through activity on stage and the increased tempo of the musical number, "Racing with the Clock." Even before introducing the attractive new factory superintendent who serves as the musical's romantic lead, the workers establish the elusive raise driving the action of the plot, repeatedly complaining of the physical toll of factory work through the song's refrain and lamenting their inability to buy a secondhand car on their current salaries. Injustice belies the bright up-tempo scene. While the romance between Sid Sorokin, the superintendent, and Babe Williams, the leader of the Union Grievance Committee provides a familiar point of entry for musical comedy, the anti-union and pro-union stances of each, respectively, nevertheless represent very real tension of the time; for all the ways in which the romance plays out off-site, a return to the factory and its relentless clock reminds the audience of what is at stake and captures the lack of individualism and humanity driving capitalist forces following the Second World War.

In fact, despite its romantic resolution, the musical's conclusion nevertheless suggests uncomfortable and unresolved conflict; as Rebecca Burditt emphasizes in her article about the musical's film adaptation:

> a spectator might identify with the union's plight, but it is the management that benefits most from the [musical's] final resolution, which grants workers the seven-and-a-half-cent raise as long as they do not seek retroactive pay. ... *The Pajama Game*'s triumphant ending therefore upholds capitalist individualism under the guise of collective gain.[25]

The factory owner, who has been embezzling and hiding a wage increase prior to what appears to be a climactic union win, remains in power and goes unpunished, his crime kept secret by the romantic hero. While explicitly depicting and even championing union causes, the musical predicts the slowdown in union activity to come, suggesting that unions may not be powerful as they purported to be (at least at the time *The Pajama Game* was written). The Labor Management Relations Act of 1947, the Taft-Hartley Act, had been passed by Congress less than a decade earlier, restricting the activities and power of labor unions and creating fertile ground for conflict like that depicted within the musical. Nevertheless, *The Pajama Game* embodies and normalizes civic engagement through romantic comedy, emphasizing its cultural significance through representation. It was far from the last musical with romance and buoyant energy to offer such commentary.

Activism beyond the stage: *La Cage aux Folles* (1983)

La Cage aux Folles centers on drag club owner George and his partner and star performer Albin. Not only was it the first Broadway musical with openly gay characters in major roles, but the defiant ebullience of the music within Harvey Fierstein and Jerry Herman's musical *La Cage aux Folles* (1983) contrasted sharply with the fear and stigma in the earliest years of the AIDS epidemic in the United States. In the musical, through a mixture of farce and pathos, George and Albin navigate the challenging waters that come with the engagement of George's son, Jean-Michel, to Anne, the daughter of a well-known homophobic and conservative politician. Albeit under the threat of blackmail, the musical ends optimistically as the two families come together; the truth is revealed and there's an implied change of heart within the celebratory ending featuring George's soon-to-be in-laws performing with the chorus of "Cagelles" followed by declarations of love between George and Albin, affirming both the club itself and the relationship between the two men.

When *La Cage* opened, rumors of a "gay plague" were rampant and a disease with the acronym GRID, or Gay Related Immune Deficiency, had been replaced by a new name: AIDS. Still, in the post-Stonewall years, there were many reasons for New York's gay community to celebrate improved political and social recognition, as though the best of times truly were "now." With time, however, Herman's lyrics acquired an eerie prescience. The "tomorrow" that lurked around the corner would prove devastating for the gay community, the American theatre, and ultimately for people

55

around the world. Jerry Herman recounts the atmosphere encompassing the run of the show: "Slowly we were told that so and so was ill and out of the show and then the next time I came in I was told that he had passed away. We were starting to lose our own people, our own beloved cast members. At the same time, we were out there, tapping away, and *thank god for the tap dance*."[26] The music, and the dance, became a mechanism for coping, and for *living*, as death took its mounting toll behind the scenes of the Broadway theatre.

La Cage aux Folles served in an activist capacity off-stage, demanding compassion, acceptance, and community responsibility for care at a time in which the opposite dominated popular opinion. In their 1988 analysis of intersections of blame and public health, Dorothy Nelkin and Sander Gilman historicize and critique the role of the press in exacerbating the stigma and spread of HIV:

> In the twentieth century concepts of morality are frequently translated into questions of lifestyle. Looking to lifestyle as the cause of AIDS, the popular press emphasizes that persons with AIDS are afflicted as a direct result of their chosen lifestyle—their sexual practices or their use of drugs. Blame for the disease is placed not on a retrovirus, but on its victims, on those who maintain a self-indulgent pattern of behavior that places them at risk. While AIDS is clearly spread through sexual transmission and intravenous drugs, the rhetoric of blame discounts the fact that behavior may not be entirely voluntary. Furthermore, blaming the individual for illness limits the responsibility of the larger society.[27]

The activism of *La Cage* worked directly against such condemnation and isolation, going far beyond the musical's plot and representation. The company sponsored the first "Broadway Easter Bonnet Parade and Competition," coordinated by performer Suzanne Ishee, to raise money to support those affected by AIDS. Artists from twelve Broadway shows constructed imaginative bonnets that were displayed at the Palace Theatre. Over the course of a week, company members donated money in support of their favorite. On April 18, 1987, more than four years into its successful run, as recorded by the union newsletter, Equity News, "approximately 600 Broadway performers and their friends were in attendance at the Palace for the parade and judging. *La Cage*, with $5,215.92 [contributed toward a bonnet designed by Howard Crabtree] was the winner."[28] The event raised $20,000 for the National AIDS Network. The following year, the Easter Bonnet parade was developed as a fundraiser for the fledgling Broadway Cares for the first time.

The Easter Bonnet philanthroproduction, a professionally produced and fully mounted performance event that raises money for nonprofit organizations, continues to bring in millions of dollars for Broadway Cares/Equity Fights AIDS (BC/EFA), an organization resulting from the merger of the two groups in 1992. For two six-week periods each year, actors address the audience following performances, explaining the work of BC/EFA and appealing for funds to support social services and other efforts. With these "Red Bucket" appeals (so named for the containers used to collect donations) often comes a call for compassion from the performers to the audience. This effort began on Broadway in 1991 with *The Will Rogers Follies,* naturally led by its star Keith Carradine, who had "spent the majority of the show addressing the audience" in the title role.[29] BC/EFA Executive Director Tom Viola recalled, "It raised a boatload of money. As other shows began to hear about that, they began to ask theatre owners and their own producers and management if they could do the same thing."[30] Now an established tradition, these appeals from the stage have overlapping financial and social goals. Priorities for the organization now include the promotion and encouragement of public support for programs pertaining to HIV and "other critical health issues or respond to an emergency" and "to support efforts by the entertainment industry in other charitable or educational endeavors."[31] The community-focused, collaborative, and creative nature of Broadway musical theatre translated directly to the organized grass-roots efforts at the core of BC/EFA's fundraising and activist work, and both depended on audiences with expendable income.[32]

Activism on the stage: *Falsettos* (1992)

By embodying concern and the prioritization of certain issues, Broadway performers model participation in activist causes. Onstage activism in the wake of the AIDS crisis occurred through the stories depicted in musicals as well, particularly as emotional content met politically charged context. As the first Broadway musical to directly address the issue of AIDS within its story, *Falsettos* (1992) holds a special place in the history of musical theatre and activism.

William Finn and James Lapine's musical, the audience is told, is "about growing up, getting older, living on a lover's shoulder, learning love is not a crime." The year is 1979 and Marvin has left his wife, Trina, and their son, Jason, for his charismatic and athletic male lover, Whizzer. Over the course of the first act (first presented ten years earlier as the standalone musical *March of the Falsettos*), Trina marries Marvin's psychiatrist Mendel, Whizzer leaves Marvin, and Marvin, now alone, reconnects with his son. The second act takes place two years later in 1981; Marvin and Whizzer reunite as Jason's bar mitzvah is planned. Marvin's neighbors and Jason's godparents, Dr. Charlotte and her partner Cordelia take on the role of extended family, supporting everyone, including Whizzer, who falls ill with a mysterious and nameless disease, which audiences in the early 1990s would immediately recognize as AIDS.

The musical served an activist function for the audience in Broadway's John Golden Theatre, merging members of the gay community with the "all-American family" as depicted by the mainstream press.[33] First produced ten years after the time period it depicts, *Falsettoland*, the second act of *Falsettos,* uses this fictional story to capture a moment in history. In the case of Finn's musical, the year is 1981, when doctors noticed "something bad" (as Dr. Charlotte sings) that was killing young men. *Falsettoland* does not contain the word "AIDS" in its libretto, yet the presence of the disease was understood without question, especially for an audience for which AIDS had dominated the media; stories of Rock Hudson, Ryan White, the Ray family, and Magic Johnson had captured the public's attention leading up to the musical's Broadway premiere. The popular press was more than just tolerant of the subject of AIDS—by 1992, they were deeply engaged with it. *Falsettos* brought to Broadway, the most commercial and arguably most mainstream of theatrical institutions, a compassionate portrayal of the group that the popular media had, up until then, often been depicted as deserving of HIV infection.

The musical premiered on Broadway just as there was heavy media coverage of Kimberly Bergalis, a young woman from Florida who claimed to have contracted HIV from her dentist.[34] Bergalis, who was white, blonde and Christian, portrayed herself as an alleged virgin who had neither used IV drugs nor received a blood transfusion, and infuriated gay AIDS activists by insisting on her "innocence" during her public appearances. In a highly publicized hearing before Congress, she implied that gay men deserved the devastating illness, a position supported by much of the accompanying media coverage. This was where *Falsettos* made its intervention. Over the course of its Broadway run from April 29, 1992 to June 27, 1993, like *La Cage* before it, *Falsettos* enacted augmented activism via the emotional connections audiences form with each character in the show, but particularly with Whizzer.

The compassionate and ultimately devastating presentation of Whizzer as a person with AIDS undermines the guilt/innocence binary as defined by Bergalis and the media. Nevertheless, in some ways *Falsettos* reinforced then-popular stereotypes of gay men, working both toward and against a public shift in compassion toward people living with AIDS. In the first act, Whizzer is presented in stereotypical terms often used by the contemporary media to describe gay men in the 1990s: promiscuous, self-absorbed, and superficial; Whizzer introduces himself to the audience in terms of his materialistic attention to clothing and his commitment to sex.[35] He summarizes, "Nothing is everything to me. Nothing is everything… except sex."[36] However, Finn and Lapine subvert any notion of a "deserved" suffering in *Falsettos,* particularly through Whizzer's connection to Jason. The audience's first glimpse of this relationship comes when Jason, begged by his parents to see a psychiatrist, insists that he first wants Whizzer's opinion. The love and trust between the two is understood at several points in the musical, evidenced in the way in which Whizzer admits his own uncertainty about therapy to Jason, by Whizzer's extraordinary baseball coaching skills and, finally, by Jason's proposed bargain with God to keep his bar mitzvah scheduled only if Whizzer will live. It is Jason's decision to hold his bar mitzvah in the then dying Whizzer's hospital room surrounded by the people who love him most: Marvin, Trina, Mendel, Charlotte, Cordelia, and Whizzer—in other words, his family. Such a compassionate and respectful portrayal in this heightened period of stigma and discrimination played a critical role in public perception of AIDS. Later musicals like *Rent* engaged similar strategies to great effect, eliciting audience sympathy and birthing beloved HIV-positive characters who are professors and artists, but also drug addicts and strippers.[37] Musical theatre, as Oskar Eustis describes, is "a moral enterprise. The narratives we tell ourselves as a society deeply inform our values, our sense of who we are and what we believe in."[38] *Falsettos*, and the later *Rent*, opted to use their onstage activism to create a new narrative for AIDS patients, one which contributed to reshaping public opinion about the disease, in spite of negative news portrayals.

LOOKING BACK, LOOKING AHEAD: THE CHALLENGING POLITICS OF THE TWENTY-FIRST CENTURY

Depictions in musicals of activist causes continue to resonate through the social and political circumstances when they are produced. As demonstrated previously by the Broadway Cares/Equity Fights AIDS successful fundraising for AIDS-related causes from the stage, direct address from the actors to the audience establishes a potent connection between the speaker and audience. On November 11, 2016, the production team of *Hamilton* was counting on just that. Notified that conservative Mike Pence, who had just been elected as Republican President Donald Trump's Vice President, would be in attendance at that evening's performance, *Hamilton* creator and star Lin-Manuel Miranda, director Thomas Kail, producer Jeffrey Seller, and actor Brandon Victor Dixon drafted a statement to be read from the stage "with input from members of the company."[39] Dixon, who had just performed the role of Aaron Burr in the musical began by saying, "Vice president-elect Pence, I see you walking out, but I hope you will hear us," from the stage of the Richard Rodgers Theatre. Dixon then turned his attention to the rest of the audience, urging them to record and share what he was about to say "because this message needs to be spread far and wide."[40] He continued:

> We, sir—we—are the diverse America who are alarmed and anxious that your new administration will not protect us, our planet, our children, our parents, or defend us and uphold our inalienable rights. We truly hope that this show has inspired

you to uphold our American values and to work on behalf of all of us."[41]

The speech, which generated a mixed response, still reached a far greater audience than the Vice President-elect then could via social media channels and the popular press. In confronting the new Vice-President, these members of the Broadway community embodied a long tradition of activism on and beyond the stage. Working the press circuit following his on-stage speech, Brandon Victor Dixon insisted, "Art is meant to bring people together. It's meant to raise consciousness."[42]

The *Hamilton* creative team continues to engage in social and political activism, reaching audiences that may never even set foot in the theatre; a subset of cast members and staff use the platform Ham4Progress to "inspire our community, our fans, and ourselves to action" while highlighting social justice issues focused on education, civic engagement, racial justice, and gender equality.[43] In August of 2022, in the wake of the U.S. Supreme Court decision to overturn the 1973 Roe v. Wade decision, the group launched "Ham4Choice," a fundraiser in support of abortion access. They announced:

> We are devastated by the U.S. Supreme Court's ruling elimi-
> nating the right to abortion which has been a right since 1973.
> In response, we are teaming up with organizations providing
> support, access and travel expenses to those seeking these ser-
> vices. ... We're stronger when we work together. We can stand
> up for every person's right to make decisions about their own
> body and their own lives. Join HAMILTON & Friends in the
> fight for reproductive access and reproductive choice today."[44]

While the vehicle for audience connection may have changed, the social efforts of the *Hamilton* company were not new; this sort of community action had happened on Broadway before. Such consciousness (and financial support) raised through activist musical theatre can influence political action. As Marc Blitzstein challenged nearly a century ago, as societies continue to trade in inequality and oppression, musical theatre will be an ally in the fight.

In 2022, Shaina Taub's musical *Suffs* captured the complex story and the compelling people who made up the suffragist movement in the years leading up to the passage of the Nineteenth Amendment in 1920, which allowed women to vote in the United States. The musical had been set to premiere in September of 2020, just before the presidential election that would affect disintegrating rights for women and transgender people. In his program note for The Public Theater, Artistic Director Oskar Eustis places *Suffs* within this context:

> In telling the story of the passage of the 19th Amendment, a milestone in the expansion of democracy, *Suffs* asks us to celebrate the brilliant and courageous women who won that battle, while also seeing their victory in the larger context of the fights that remain to be won. Its vision of our country, flawed and limited and oppressive, yet full of extraordinary promise, is inspiring and true. *Suffs* reminds us of what is good and true about America, reveals how far the struggle for equality has to go, and fills me with humility, hope, and resolution. What more could we ask of our secular church, the theater?[45]

Whether through depictions of protests like the suffragette movement in *Suffs*, the burning of draft cards in *Hair* (1968), Maureen's public performance art against the eviction of the homeless in *Rent* (1996), or the civil rights protest in *Hairspray* (2002) or through augmented and embodied activism, the activist legacy of musical theatre continues on and off the stage.

NOTES

1 Marc Blitzstein, "Coming—The Mass Audience!," *Modern Music*. 13. 4 (May/June 1936), 23–29. 29.

2 Stacy Ellen Wolf, "Keeping Company with Sondheim's Women." *Oxford Handbook of Sondheim Studies*. Ed. Robert Gordon (New York: Oxford University Press, 2014), 365–383. 366.

3 See Raymond Knapp, *The American Musical and the Formation of National Identity* (Princeton: Princeton University Press, 2004).

4 Donatella Galella, "Participating in 'Democracy': *Soft Power*'s Audience and Ambivalence." Song, Stage & Screen XVI. June 29, 2022. Virtual Conference, Keynote Address.

5 Galella, Keynote.

6 Stacy Wolf, "Introduction." *A Problem Like Maria: Gender and Sexuality in the American Musical* (Ann Arbor, MI: University of Michigan Press, 2002), 22–23.

7 Maya Cantu, "Introduction." *American Cinderellas on the Broadway Musical Stage: Imagining the Working Girl from Irene to Gypsy* (New Yok: Palgrave, 2015), 8.

8 Thomas Ehrlich, "Preface." Civic Responsibility and Higher Education (Phoenix, AZ: The American Council on Education/The Oryx Press, 2000), vi.

9 Additional plays depicting labor conditions to consider from this period are Albert Bein's *Let Freedom Ring* (1935), Lillian Hellman's *Days to Come* (1936), Ben Bengal's *Plant in the Sun*, George Brewer's *Tide Rising,* and John Howard Lawson's *Marching Song* from 1937.

10 Jerome Moross, "New Musical Reviews for Old," *New Theatre.* 2.10 (October 1935), 33.

11 Mordecai Gorelik, *New Theatres for Old* (New York: E.P. Dutton & Co., Inc., 1962), p. 406. Cited in Harry M. Goldman, "Workers Theatre to Broadway Hit: The Evolution of an American Radical Revue," *Oral History,* 10.1 (Spring 1982), 56–66; 56.

12 Goldman, 56.

13 Goldman, 62.

14 Goldman, 62.

15 Goldman, 63.

16 Harry Merton Goldman, *"Pins and Needles*: A White House Command Performance." *Educational Theatre Journal. 30.1 (March 1978),* 90–101.

17 John O. Hunter, "Marc Blitzstein's *The Cradle will Rock* as a Document of America, 1937," *American Quarterly,* 18.2 (Summer 1966), 227–233; 227.

18 Marc Blitstein, quoted in *Modern Music,* XV, 85. Cited by Hunter.

19 See John O'Connor's *The Federal Theatre Project Free, Adult, Uncensored* (Methuen, 1986), Barry Witham's *The Federal Theatre Project: A Case Study* (Cambridge: Cambridge University Press, 2003) and Beth Osborne's *Staging the People: Community and Identity in the Federal Theatre Project* (New York: Palgrave Macmillan, 2011) for introductions to the federally supported jobs program for unemployed theatre professionals during the Great Depression.

20 See Marvin Carlson, *The Haunted Stage.* Ann Arbor, MI: University of Michigan Press, 2003.

21 Chrystyna Dail, *Stage for Action: U.S. Social Activist Theatre in the 1940s* (Carbondale: Southern Illinois University Press, 2016), 5.

22 Dail, 7.

23 Gerald Mayer, "Union Membership Trends in the United States." *CRS Report for Congress.* Washington DC: Congressional Research Service, the Library of Congress, 31 August 2004.

24 Mark Robinson, "Broadway Musical Time Machine: Looking back at The Pajama Game." *Mark Robinson Writes.* http://www.markrobinsonwrites.com/the-music-that-makes-me-dance/2016/10/27/broadway-musical-time-machine-looking-back-at-the-pajama-game

25 Rebecca Burditt, "Unruly Excess: Labor, Race, and *The Pajama Game. JCMS: Journal of Cinema and Media Studies* 61.5 (2021–2022), 113–136; 114.

26 *Words and Music*, DVD, directed by Amber Edwards (New York: Public Broadcasting System, 2008).

27 Dorothy Nelkin and Sander L. Gilman, "Placing Blame for Devastating Disease." *Social Research*. 55.3 (Autumn 1988), 361–378; 370–371.

28 "Easter Contest Nets $20,000 for AIDS: 'La Cage' Company Sponsors Holiday Fund-Raiser." *Equity News*. June 1987. The Glines Records. Group No. 1920, Box No. 1. Folder no. 12. Yale Manuscripts and Archives.

29 Mark Peikert, "How Broadway Cares/Equity Fights AID' Red Buckets First Began," *Playbill*. October 26, 2019. https://playbill.com/article/how-broadway-cares-equity-fights-aids-red-buckets-first-began.

30 Peikert, "How Broadway Cares…"

31 See BC/EFA's mission statement at https://broadwaycares.org/mission-statement.

32 See Virginia Anderson, "Choreographing a Cause: Broadway Bares as Philanthroproduction and Embodied Index to Changing Attitudes Toward HIV/AIDS." *The Oxford Handbook of Dance and Theater*. Edited by Nadine George-Graves (Cambridge: Oxford University Press, 2015), 922–942.

33 See Frank Rich, "Discovering Family Values at 'Falsettos,'" *New York Times*, July 12, 1992, Section 2, Page 1.

34 See Walter Goodman, "The Story TV Can't Resist," *New York Times*, November 17, 1991. Bergalis had appeared on *The Maury Povich Show*, *The Oprah Winfrey Show*, and *The Today Show* among many others.

35 William Finn and James Lapine, *Falsettos* (New York: Plume, 1993), 25.

36 *Falsettos*, 157.

37 See Helen Deborah Lewis, "Renting a Queer Space: The Commodification of Queerness in Jonathan Larson's *Rent*." MA Thesis (Tufts University, 2007).

38 Oskar Eustis, "A Note from Oskar Eustis," *The Public Theater Presents: Suffs* (digital program). (New York: Playbill Vault, 2022), 3. https://publictheater.org/contentassets/f7ee9323b9e74f-f699df87f96290522f/programs/508_suffs-in-cycle-3.21.22.pdf

39 Amy B Wang, "'Hamilton' Actor on the Cast's Speech for Pence: 'There's Nothing to Apologize For," *The Washington Post*. November 21, 2016. https://www.washingtonpost.com/news/arts-and-entertainment/wp/2016/11/21/hamilton-actor-on-the-casts-speech-for-pence-theres-nothing-to-apologize-for/

40 Wang, "'Hamilton' Actor on the Cast's Speech…"

41 Christopher Mele and Patrick Healy, "*Hamilton* had some unscripted lines for Pence. Trump Wasn't Happy." *New York Times*. November 19, 2016. "https://www.nytimes.com/2016/11/19/us/mike-pence-hamilton.html.

42 Wang, "'Hamilton' Actor on the Cast's Speech…"

43 "Ham4Progress," *Hamilton Official Site*.

44 "Ham4Choice: A Note from *Hamilton* and Friends." *Prizeo*. https://www.prizeo.com/campaigns/l/lin-manuel-miranda/ham4choice-presented-by-hamilton-friends

45 Oskar Eustis, *Suffs* (digital program). https://publictheater.org/
contentassets/f7ee9323b9e74ff699df87f96290522f/programs/508_
suffs-in-cycle-3.21.22.pdf

RECOMMENDATIONS FOR ADDITIONAL RESOURCES

Anderson, Virginia. "'Something Bad [Was] Happening': *Falsettos as an
Historical Record of the AIDS Epidemic.*" *Studies in Musical Theatre* 13,
no. 3 (2019): 221–234.

This essay argues for the importance of an often-overlooked aspect
of *Falsettos*: the role of Dr. Charlotte, a character whose name is never
spoken in performance. Her identities as a woman, a lesbian and a
doctor—and the signification of each—unlock largely unspoken
histories, reflecting and transforming broader histories of the AIDS
epidemic.

Goldman, Harry Merton. "*Pins and Needles*: A White House Command
Performance." *Educational Theatre Journal* 30, no. 1 (Mar., 1978):
90–101.

With great detail, Goldman reconstructs the performance of *Pins
and Needles* for President Roosevelt at the White House on March 3,
1938, offering insight into its development, staging, and reception.

Hunter, John. "Marc Blitzstein's *The Cradle will Rock* as a Document of
America, 1937." *American Quarterly* 18, no. 2, Part 1 (summer, 1966):
227–233.

Hunter's essay provides excellent contextualization for *The Cradle
Will Rock*, offering insights into the cultural moment of the 1937 production as well as Blitzstein's craft and influences.

Rich, Frank. "Discovering Family Values at *Falsettos*," *The New York
Times*. July 12, 1992. https://www.nytimes.com/1992/07/12/theater/
theater-discovering-family-values-at-falsettos.html

Rich's essay about taking his children to see *Falsettos* offers another
way in which the show serves as an activist musical. Rich contextualizes the show within vehement statements made by Dan Quayle concerning "family values" in which the then–Vice President denounced
anything but a heteronormative nuclear family.

Rosenzweig, Josh director. *Heart of Broadway: The Ensemble behind
Broadway Cares/Equity Fights AIDS* (film). Here Media, 2011.

This documentary provides a comprehensive overview
of the organization, its history, its creators, and three regular
philanthroproductions.

CHAPTER 4

The ascension of the director of the Broadway musical

Mary Jo Lodge

Much of the early story of the musical was shaped by its writers. At the start of the so-called Golden Age in the early 1940s, when now classic musicals like *Oklahoma!* appeared on Broadway, composers and lyricists like Rodgers and Hammerstein dominated the creative teams of new musicals. Certainly, important theatre directors like George Abbott had been instrumental in the success of early musicals, but in the 1950s, a change occurred that moved directors and particularly director/choreographers (after dance gained increased importance in the musical) to the forefront. Nowhere was this shift more dramatic than in Jerome Robbins' ascension to director/choreographer on the musical *West Side Story* in 1957. Certainly, early director/choreographers like ballet master George Balanchine and Agnes de Mille provided a foundation for Robbins and his successors like Fosse, Bennett, Champion, and later Tommy Tune, Graciela Daniele, and Susan Stroman, to chart a new path for musical theatre development. Dance-driven shows were not the only innovation in this period, however; groundbreaking directors who were not choreographers, like Hal Prince, also drove another alteration in musical theatre structure with the advent of the concept musical, starting in the late 1960s with *Cabaret*, but coming to fruition in the 1970s. The concept musical, championed in particular by Prince and legendary composer Stephen Sondheim, marked another paradigm shift for the musical, which had during the Golden Age been driven primarily by plot, most often via literary adaptations. In the 1970s, musicals like *Company* and *A Chorus Line*, perhaps because their directors (Prince and Bennett, respectively) were such a strong force in their creation, were organized around a central idea or concept, rather than an event-driven central plotline. This chapter explores how the director (and director/choreographer) rose to prominence in the

DOI: 10.4324/9781003256458-5

musical due to changes in its structure as it developed, and how this ascension led to a milestone in the history of the musical: a Golden Age of the musical theatre director, which stretched from the late 1950s through the 1980s.

THE ORIGINS OF THE THEATRE DIRECTOR

To understand the meteoric rise of the director of the musical during this period, it is helpful to look back at the history of the position, since the director is a relatively recent addition to the practice of theatre. While historically, someone (typically the actor, or else, in Shakespeare's day, an actor-manager) has always handled the responsibilities now delegated to the director, the position didn't take shape until the late 1800s, and is typically first attributed to Georg II, the Duke of Saxe-Meiningen, whose meticulously created, historically accurate court productions were so successful that they toured starting in the 1870s. The duke's most significant innovation was centralizing control over all aspects of production, and his detail-oriented vision suddenly made the hitherto unheard-of director indispensable. Not long after, master acting teacher and theorist Konstantin Slanislavski demonstrated similar control and a strong preference for **verisimilitude** in his direction of productions for the Moscow Art Theatre, which rose to prominence in the very late 1800 and early 1900s. Stanislavski's work became an important foundation for training actors in the United States in the 1940s and 1950s, around the same time as the director rose to prominence in the musical.

Still, the director was hardly central to the creation of early musicals. Musicals had developed, in part, from operas, which were typically the domain of composers, who often conducted their own opera compositions, and were regarded as their chief creative visionaries. Composer Arthur Sullivan was famously knighted in 1883, twenty-five years before his chief collaborator W.S. Gilbert, a very public endorsement by Queen Victoria of the importance of the composer versus the lyricist/librettist, even though Gilbert also typically filled the role of the director. Of course, impresario Richard D'Oyly Carte, who had brought the team together, likely filled some of the more public facing jobs that a modern director handles, but neither one earned the accolades that Sullivan did, at least not until long after Sullivan did.

All-around showman George M. Cohan is also credited today as a pioneering director of early musicals, but Cohan was a one-man theatre operation: he composed, acted, sang, dance, choreographed, produced, and directed the often-patriotic productions in which he starred in the early decades of the 1900s, but he was not typically crafting shows for artists other than himself. He was, instead, expanding on how vaudeville acts were created by the performers (he had grown up in a family act with his sister and parents) by creating full-length productions in the same way. Historian Denny Martin Flinn opines that, like the duke before him, Cohan sought unprecedented control over his work:

> On the road with his family, he made loud demands of management for better lighting, better placement on the bill, and more rehearsal time. His arrogance probably marks the beginning of a trait in the personality of the American theatre director-choreographer that survives to this day.[1]

While Flinn's supposition that director/choreographers are necessarily arrogant is debatable, he is not wrong that the gradually increasing demands for creative control by those in the position of director drove a shift in how musicals were created, particularly in the first half of the 1900s.

Many early musicals were directed by their librettists, as in the case of Gilbert and Sullivan and then Cohan, and if not, were staged by their dance director, the equivalent of the modern choreographer. This typically worked well since most of the shows that predate 1930 were either constructed around flimsy plots with very brief book scenes or were built on the revue structure favored by the impresario Florenz Ziegfeld in his yearly *Follies* productions. Many of these shows dispensed with a libretto entirely and were simply a collection of songs; no cohesion of plot or concept was expected, so there was little need for a central figure to guide the storytelling, though someone did still need to create and teach the dance steps. Eventually, however, as the plot became more central to the musical, and more tightly constructed shows like the Princess musicals, which played at the small Princess Theatre in Manhattan, gained a following, the structurally integrated musical showed signs of emerging. The Princess musicals featured compositions by Jerome Kern, who would become one of the lauded composers of the American musical, and were directed by the notable directors of the day, including Edward Royce, who staged several of the *Follies* for Ziegfeld as well, though he last directed in 1929 and is little discussed today.

The next major musical composer Kern created was *Show Boat*, a landmark collaboration with Oscar Hammerstein II (later the writing partner of Richard Rodgers), which was one of the first adaptations of a book into a stage musical (the sweeping novel of the same name by Edna Ferber had enjoyed great success in 1926, shortly before its adaptation). Hammerstein, like many of his predecessors, created most of the lyrics and the libretto for *Show Boat*, and served as its director, a co-credit alongside Zeke Colvan, a director and stage manager whose obituary claims he "directed the dialogue for the original 'Show Boat' for Florenz Ziegfeld," which implies that Hammerstein staged the musical numbers not staged by choreographer Sammy Lee.[2] With *Show Boat*, an important musical in its own right, a new era began on Broadway when the story, especially ones adapted from other sources, began to drive musicals. With the shift away from the primacy of the composer, the power of the librettist (and often lyricist) grew, at least for a time. Nowhere was this change more evident than in the awarding of the first Pulitzer Prize for Drama for the 1931 satirical political piece *Of Thee I Sing*, which was famously only bestowed on George S. Kaufman and Morrie Ryskind, who wrote the libretto (Kaufman, as was common then, also directed) and Ira Gershwin, who created the lyrics, rather than on legendary composer (and brother to Ira) George Gershwin (see Paul Laird's discussion in Chapter 2). Such was a stark turnaround from the days of recognition only for Sullivan in the Gilbert and Sullivan partnership.

IMMEDIATE PRECURSORS TO THE DIRECTOR/ CHOREOGRAPHER

In the decades following *Of Thee I Sing*'s Pulitzer win, the construction of the libretto grew in importance for the musical. George Abbott, who got his start on Broadway as a performer in 1913, emerged during this time as a director for Broadway shows, and was also credited as a writer starting in 1925. He continued directing on Broadway through 1987 when he was one hundred years old. Due to both his success and his longevity in the business, he became one of the most influential directors on Broadway. He would eventually mentor several directors who would become critical forces in the directing Golden Age from the late 1950s through the 1980s.

By the 1940s, with the advent of the important creative partnership of Richard Rodgers (who had parted ways with his previous lyricist, the increasingly erratic Lorenz Hart, who then died in 1942) and Oscar Hammerstein II (who had sought a new collaborator after Kern moved to Hollywood to work on movie musicals), the integrated musical, which featured cohesive stories with songs and even dances that advanced the plot, became the norm for their productions and eventually for most Broadway musicals. Nearly all of their shows, from their initial masterwork *Oklahoma!* (based on the 1930 play *Green Grow the Lilacs* by Lynn Riggs), to their Pulitzer winning *South Pacific* (based on Michener's *Tales of the South Pacific*) to the later *The King and* I (based on earlier autobiographical works by Anna Leonowens which were then turned into the novel *Anna and the King of Siam* in 1944) and *The Sound of Music* (based on Maria Von Trapp's autobiography), used literary sources which strengthened their librettos, and the once haphazardly constructed books of musicals were suddenly a thing of the past. Historian Scott Miller notes that with *Oklahoma!*, "For the first time in a popular musical, neither the stars nor the songwriters were the stars of the show; this time the real star of the show was the *plot*."[3] While *Show Boat* had set the stage for librettos to be adapted from pre-existing sources, in *Oklahoma!* and its successors, that process entered its maturity.

The librettist as adapter, however, and the more complex construction of musicals by Rodgers and Hammerstein seemed to usher in a need for a director to lead the storytelling who was not the book writer (though certainly some book writers continued to direct) and not the composer, but someone who understood the contributions of the book and the music to the dramatic thrust of the musical, and could visualize stage movement and design, as well. Rodgers and Hammerstein understood this, and thus *Oklahoma!* was also a significant moment for the musical theatre director, as director Rouben Mamoulian was, "the first director to be given, contractually, entire control over the production in all its details."[4] Yet Mamoulian was not the only creative force beyond Rodgers and Hammerstein that contributed to the unprecedented success of *Oklahoma!*—choreographer Agnes de Mille, who would a few years later become the first female director/choreographer to work on Broadway, created the dream ballet that would assert dance as a storytelling device equal to a song or scene. Historian Lawrence Thelen notes that Mamoulian, as director, then, did something unprecedented when he "turned over sections of the storytelling to choreographer Agnes de Mille (with the help of Rodgers and Hammerstein)" noting that, with that decision, over which he had complete creative control as established by his contract, Mamoulian "was redirecting the direction of art form itself."[5] Mamoulian did not object when, for instance, Hammerstein's libretto dictated that the chorus girls that typically started a Broadway show did not appear until "forty five minutes into the first act".[6] "Laurey Makes Up Her Mind," de Mille's dream ballet which concluded the first act of *Oklahoma!*, "changed Broadway history,"[7] as it made "dance a fully formed narrative language, just like the words and music, instead of merely as a plot device."[8] Mamoulian directed Rodgers and Hammerstein's next hit *Carousel* (based on Molnár's *Liliom*), which de Mille also choreographed, though that was the last collaboration between the director and choreographer, who had a notoriously rocky relationship. Agnes de Mille went on to direct and choreograph the flop *Allegro* for Rodgers and Hammerstein, one of their only creations not based on a pre-existing source, though during the tempestuous rehearsal process, Hammerstein took over the direction, but she retained the credit, and continued to choreograph.[9]

JEROME ROBBINS AND *WEST SIDE STORY*

After *Oklahoma!* and its successors, many of which now contained ballets in a nod to de Mille's influence, dance became increasingly important for the musical, which set the stage for the director/choreographer to rise in prominence. It was on *West Side Story*, the 1957 musical with music by Leonard Bernstein, lyrics by Stephen Sondheim, a book by Arthur Laurents, and direction and choreography by Jerome Robbins that both the influence of the director was cemented, and the creative power of the director/choreographer was truly unleashed. Prior to his work as a director, Robbins first found fame as a ballet choreographer, and in 1949, he joined the New York City Ballet as the Associate Artistic Director, a position he held with his mentor, legendary ballet choreographer George Balanchine (who had also directed and choreographed previously on Broadway). *West Side Story* was not the first production Jerome Robbins had choreographed on Broadway (*On the Town*, in 1944, holds that distinction), nor was it the first show he directed on Broadway (his *Look Ma, I'm Dancin'!* in 1948 was the first show he was billed as both director and choreographer on, alongside another mentor, George Abbott, who held the same credits). In fact, it was not even the first show he claimed credit for conceiving (*On the Town* was billed as "based on an idea by" by Robbins, while the aforementioned *Look Ma, I'm Dancin'!* credits the show as solely "conceived by Jerome Robbins"). However, a milestone was achieved when Robbins directed, choreographed and conceived *West Side Story* on Broadway in 1957. Paul R. Laird notes that "*West Side Story* (1957) marks the full integration of dance into the Broadway musical and the true arrival of the choreographer-director."[10] Historian John Kenrick says of Robbins that he "reached a creative peak with *West Side Story*" a musical retelling of Shakespeare's *Romeo and Juliet,* which "placed a Polish American Romeo and a Puerto Rican Juliet in the middle of a New York City street gang war."[11] Robbins died in 1998, and in his obituary, *The LA Times* called *West Side Story,* the "best-known of his legacies," and noted that it is "considered by many to be Robbins' masterpiece."[12] Kenrick goes on to posit that after *West Side Story,* "all serious Broadway choreography was compared to what Robbins accomplished in this landmark show."[13]

West Side Story was the first musical to integrate singing, dancing, and acting not only in the story but also in the bodies of the performers. It had been customary, prior to *West Side Story,* to employ separate singing and dancing choruses. Indeed, the *Oklahoma!* dream ballet, until more recent revivals, was performed entirely by the dancing chorus, rather than, as is typical today, by the kinds of **triple-threat** performers, capable of singing, dancing, and acting any role, that were first used in the company of *West Side Story* by Robbins. Thelen points out that Robbins' dances "in *West Side Story,* for example, do more than further the plot, they also help define and develop the characters," and he goes on to quote Robbins, whom he interviewed, as saying this occurred "because some of the action went on *into* the dance."[14]

With *West Side Story*, Robbins, who developed a reputation for bullying behavior in his rehearsals, insisted on being in charge of every aspect of the production (though he did share choreography credit with Peter Gennaro, possibly because of the added demands of directing, which limited his ability to be in two places at once). Long calls Robbins, "a harsh taskmaster for whom control was all important."[15] He was involved in *West Side Story* from its earliest stages, and Thelen reports that Robbins felt that "having the director on board from the start... makes the show stronger and more unified."[16] Robbins did insist that everyone on all of his projects, including *West Side Story*, "should be working toward the same end, toward the same goals," and that "it was the director that set the goals for the creative team, not the writer, the composer or the producer," adding that if the director and producer disagreed, the producer, "shouldn't have that director."[17] Robbins was explicit in his belief that the director was the chief creative visionary for a musical, and that all of the other artists involved— including the composer and librettist—must work in service of the director's vision. Thelen reports that, "Robbins would personally take on the task of being the final editor of the script, score and design elements of the shows he directed," and quotes Robbins as saying, explicitly, "I think the director should have the final say (in those matters)."[18]

On *West Side Story*, though, not only did Robbins wield creative control, but he also insisted on being credited with conceiving the show. While it was his idea to use Shakespeare's *Romeo and Juliet* as a source, the idea initially fizzled, and Long reports that, "only later, in the discussion of Laurents and Bernstein did it begin to come together."[19] Librettist Laurents, who was willing to allow Bernstein and Robbins to recreate passages from his libretto "in musical or dance terms," collaborated extensively with them both, but requested that Robbins relinquish his conception credit since Laurents felt the idea of the "juvenile delinquents and the gangs" was his.[20] Robbins refused, and Long notes that, "To this day, Laurents remained galled by Robbins's retention of the credit."[21] Robbins' assumption of credit for the concept for *West Side Story* is significant, for it says a great deal about how Robbins viewed himself as director/choreographer. Curiously, for the production of *Peter Pan* he directed and choreographed on Broadway just before *West Side Story*, he originally held no credit for conception, but the revival, directed and choreographed on Broadway in 1979 by Rob Iscove, was billed as "Original Production Conceived, Directed, and Choreographed by Jerome Robbins," perhaps indicating, as in the conflict with Laurents, the value Robbins later placed on his conception of a musical's central idea. Robbins, as director/choreographer, was in charge of bringing all of the disparate elements of the production into a unified whole. As a conceiver, he was the creative visionary or the auteur. In filmmaking, "Auteur Theory is a way of looking at films that state that the director is the 'author' of a film."[22] On stage, then, as conceiver and auteur, Robbins found a way to claim such full and complete artistic control over a property, that he, in effect, became its author, even if he did not write it. Of course, regardless of his crediting, not everyone viewed his contributions that way; in the original review of *West Side Story* for *The New York Times*, Brooks Atkinson credits Laurents with most of the musical's success, saying, "Mr. Laurents has provided the raw material of a tragedy that occurs because none of the young people involved understands what is happening to them. And his contribution is the essential one."[23] While Atkinson is complementary of Robbins' and Bernstein's work, it is celebrated for its ability to bring Laurents' vision to life. Atkinson says, "Using music and movement they have given Mr. Laurents' story passion and depth and some glimpses of unattainable glory. They have pitched into it with personal conviction as well as the skill of accomplished craftsmen."[24] Robbins garnered no acknowledgment at all as director in *The New York Daily News* review of the original *West Side Story* either, with praise primarily heaped on Laurents' book and Bernstein's music, and Robbins' work rating only one line: "Robbins and his superb young dancers carry the plot as much as the spoken words and lyrics do."[25] After *West Side Story*, Robbins directed and choreographed three major new shows—*Gypsy* (1959), *Funny Girl* (1964), and *Fiddler on the Roof* (1964)—before turning his attention almost entirely to the New York City Ballet, and occasional revivals of his previous Broadway works. Still, Robbins' legacy is that he enhanced the role of the director/choreographer in the musical theatre, and he ushered in the start of a Golden Age for directors of the Broadway musical.

THE DOMINANCE OF THE DIRECTOR/
CHOREOGRAPHER

The years after Robbins' last new work in 1964 (with the exception of *Jerome Robbins' Broadway*, the retrospective of his work that he created in 1989) were an especially notable period for his director and director/choreographer successors, among them Bob Fosse and Michael Bennett. In his review of Fosse's original 1975 production of *Chicago* for *Time* magazine, T.E. Kalam said, of the period:

> Future chroniclers of the New York theater will point to this period as the age of the choreographer-director sun gods. The Apollonian names will be Jerome Robbins, Gower Champion, Michael Bennett and Bob Fosse.[26]

While sun-god status may be a bit hyperbolic, certainly Fosse and Bennett, as well as Champion, who had had a successful career in film musicals before directing and choreographing several massive Broadway hits from 1960 to 1980, including the original productions of *Bye Bye Birdie* (1960), *Hello Dolly* (1964), and *42ⁿᵈ Street* (1980), stand as the innovative directors of the musical at that time.

Bob Fosse got his start dancing in nightclubs and in vaudeville acts but owed his career as a choreographer to both Abbott and particularly Robbins. Robbins served as co-director with Abbott on the 1954 Adler and Ross musical *The Pajama Game* (see Virginia Anderson's Chapter 3 for a more extensive discussion of the show), but he had championed Fosse to take on the job of choreographing in his stead after seeing his work in the film version of *Kiss Me Kate* in 1953 and he "persuaded Abbott to hire Fosse by 'guaranteeing" him—that is, agreeing to do the choreography himself if for any reason Fosse did not work out."[27] Long notes that as a result, Fosse "came to be known as Robbins's protégé."[28] Fosse, whose uniquely stylized movement was first glimpsed in the now iconic dance number "Steam Heat" from *Pajama Game* was in many ways the opposite of Robbins, who created a distinctive style of movement for each show, rather than giving each recognizable signature moves like Fosse did, though Robbins supported Fosse's work because the two shared "similar ideas about dance as a form of dramatic expression."[29] Fosse, like Robbins, had a reputation for being controlling on stage, and Gottfried described his choreography as "precise down to the curling of a pinky."[30] Fosse directed and choreographed a number of hits on Broadway including *Sweet Charity* (1966), *Pippin* (1972), and *Dancin'* (1978), and directed several award-winning films. Fosse had a singular creative vision that was widely praised, though reviews of his later shows, which pulsed with sexual energy amidst a dark, often seedy landscape (sometimes tempered with humor) tended to be negative, as in Walter Kerr's review of the 1975 production of *Chicago*, where he opines:

> Mr. Fosse, of course, is a man without peer when it comes to making navels undulate, hips quiver, toes stutter, white spats and white gloves create succulent pattens against the night sky. But this undue insistence on the tawdriness of it all crowds all wit to the wall...[31]

Still, his work on the film *Cabaret* in 1972 forever changed the way that dance was captured on film, and his choreographic legacy is readily seen in its influence on iconic pop music videos by such artists as Michael Jackson and Beyoncé.

Michael Bennett, who was sixteen years younger than Fosse, reportedly idolized Robbins and Fosse when he was young— Long reports that Bennett's childhood bedroom was adorned with photos of Robbins and Fosse, among other musical theatre stars.[32] After performing in several Broadway productions, Bennett choreographed *A Joyful Noise* (1967), and then found success with *Promises, Promises (1968)* before teaming with director Hal Prince to choreograph the concept musical *Company* (1970). *Company* featured the music and lyrics of Stephen Sondheim, who had written the lyrics for *West Side Story* back in 1957, and who would go on to become one of the great composer/lyricists of the modern musical theatre era. Prince's singular vision, united with Bennett's inventive choreography which required strong technique but prioritized dancers as actors and individuals first, made *Company*, often billed as the first true concept musical, one "united by a thematic idea, rather than a conventional plot," both "strikingly innovative" and a game changer.[33] Bennett and Prince collaborated again on Sondheim's next show, *Follies* (1971), but this time Bennett also co-directed, and he then went on to rescue the floundering Cy Coleman musical *Seesaw* (1973) by assuming complete control as the solo director and choreographer. It was *A Chorus Line*, however, which Bennett conceived, co-wrote, directed, and choreographed, that was his masterwork. *New York Times* reviewer Clive Barnes called it "one of the greatest musicals ever to hit Broadway, and quite possibly the simplest and most imaginative."[34] Both the concept-driven production, set at a Broadway audition and pictured below in rehearsal in Figure 4.1,

Figure 4.1: Director/choreographer Michael Bennett working with the cast during a rehearsal for the Broadway musical *A Chorus Line*. Photo by Martha Swope

as well as the dance it contained, were lauded; Kenrick called the show's finale "spectacular" and noted that in it, "Bennett utilized every eye-popping trick in the Broadway ensemble dance repertory."[35] After *A Chorus Line*, Bennett directed and choreographed two additional shows, the moderately successful *Ballroom* (1978) and the bona fide hit *Dreamgirls* (1981), which caused Frank Rich of *The New York Times* to posit that, "Mr. Bennett has long been Mr. Robbins's heir apparent… But last night the torch was passed, firmly, unquestionably, once and for all."[36]

While not a director/choreographer, the aforementioned Hal Prince also cemented his reputation as a director during this directing Golden Age period. Prince was a year younger than Fosse but got his start in the business a bit sooner, when shortly after his college graduation he landed an interview with George Abbott in the late 1940s, and offered to work for him for nothing just to learn the business.[37] Abbott hired him (and then paid him shortly thereafter), and Prince started work as a theatrical jack-of-all-trades, starting as a writer, and then stage manager, then producer, and finally as director.[38] Prince first directed Sondheim's *A Funny Thing Happened on the Way to the Forum*, a show Robbins was brought in to help with when Prince struggled with it. Long reports that, "Through his collaborations with Robbins, Prince learned how to construct a musical around a concept having a dominant visual image in its staging."[39] He directed the successful stage version of *Cabaret* prior to turning fully to the concept musical with *Company*. He continued to collaborate with Sondheim throughout the 1970s, though they parted ways after Sondheim disagreed with Prince's oppressive factory setting for the dark *Sweeney Todd* (1979). Prince continued directing through 2017, two years before his death, with his last major show being *The Prince of Broadway*, a *Jerome Robbins' Broadway*-style retrospective of his long career that he co-helmed with director/choreographer Susan Stroman.

AFTER THE GOLDEN AGE: THE MODERN MUSICAL THEATRE DIRECTOR

The Golden Age of the Broadway director came to an end in the 1980s for several reasons. First, the "sun gods" Kalem praised in *Time* Magazine in 1975 had stopped creating work on Broadway by the mid-1980s.[40] Champion famously died of cancer on the morning of the opening night of his smash hit *42nd Street* in 1980, while Bennett passed away from complications related to AIDS in 1987, and Fosse died of a heart attack just months later, also in 1987. While Robbins was back on Broadway with his production *Jerome Robbins' Broadway* in 1989, he had not created new work on Broadway for over twenty years at that point (though the Tony Awards did award him the Best Director statuette for the retrospective production). Hal Prince had a wildly successful run as a director through the 1970s and won particular accolades for his production of composer Andrew Lloyd Webber's *The Phantom of the Opera* in 1989, including the Tony Award for Best Director (a year before Robbins' win noted above). *Phantom* has for years held the record for longest running Broadway show (though it has set a closing date in 2023), but Prince's later works, with the exception of the *Show Boat* revival he directed in 1994, never achieved the same level of success as his earlier ones.

In general, however, in the 1980s, the director of the musical became less of a driving force in its development because the musical itself changed. Concept musicals driven by the director's vision were no longer in vogue; the musical instead was dominated by the megamusical, a new form of British import that relied chiefly on spectacle, incorporated mostly sung-through, pop-influenced scores, and included shows like Andrew Lloyd Webber's 1982 hit *Cats* and Boublil and Schönberg's 1987 juggernaut *Les Misérables* (see Knapp and Replogle-Wong in Chapter 6 for more on megamusicals). Notably, almost no women or people of color directed on Broadway until the 1990s; they made inroads in the field only after the position of director was effectively made less important by changes in musical theatre tastes and structures. Also, the AIDS epidemic was taking an exceptional toll on Broadway in this period, as well, and many young gay men who aspired to be Broadway directors and choreographers like Fosse and Bennett died from the illness before their careers had truly started.

The directors who were first to emerge after the directing Golden Age on Broadway were mentored by the famed directors and director/choreographers of the previous generation. Tommy Tune, who had a string of successful shows as a director/choreographer starting in the late 1970s including the critically praised *Nine* (1982) and *Grand Hotel* (1989), was first cast as a performer by

Hal Prince in *Baker Street* (1965), and then Bennett in *A Joyful Noise* (1966). Graciela Daniele, the first female director/choreographer to work on Broadway since Agnes de Mille (on *Once on this Island* in 1990), was cast by Bennett to dance in several shows, which brought her to the attention of Hal Prince, who directed her in *Follies* in 1971 (Bennett choreographed), and she then appeared as Hunyak in the original Broadway company of *Chicago* (1975) for Fosse. She went on to direct and choreograph a number of modest Broadway hits, including a well-received revival of *Annie Get Yor Gun* in 1999. Susan Stroman, another of the small number of women to find success on Broadway as a director, had only limited choreography credits on Broadway (but had earned a Tony Award for *Crazy for Youu*, her choreographic debut in 1992) when Prince selected her to stage the dances in his high-profile *Show Boat* revival (1994), an opportunity that eventually led to her second Tony award for choreography and later to an extensive career as a director/choreographer. Stroman was the first woman to win both the Best Direction and Best Choreography Awards in the same year for a single show for her work on the smash hit *The Producers* in 2001. Certainly, though Tune, Daniele, and Stroman are not the only modern directors or director/choreographers of note, but the era of their success coincided with a fall in the prestige and power of the position. While, for instance, Fosse was very well known at the height of his career (he famously won the first directing "triple crown" in 1972—an Emmy for *Liza with a Z* on television, an Oscar for *Cabaret* on film, and a Tony for *Pippin* on Broadway), today few fans beyond true theatre aficionados recognize the names of Broadway directors. While innovative musical theatre directors like George C. Wolfe, Thomas Kail, Diane Paulus, and Camille Brown continue to direct exciting productions, the era of the dominance of the director on Broadway has ended, at least for now. The time when the director and director/choreographer reigned supreme, however, was a significant milestone in the development of the form.

NOTES

1 Denny Martin Flinn, *Musical!: A Grand Tour* (New York: Schirmer Books, 1997), 121.
2 "ZEKE COLVAN DIES; MUSICAL DIRECTOR; Ex-Associate of Ziegfeld and Shuberts Was 65–Long Active in Civic Opera," *The New York Times*, October 10, 1945, p. 36.

3 Scott Miller, *Strike up the Band: A New History of Musical Theatre* (Portsmouth, NH: Heinemann, 2007), 48.
4 Miller, 48.
5 Lawrence Thelen, *The Show Makers: Great Directors of the American Musical Theatre* (New York, NY: Routledge, 2002), x.
6 Miller, 50.
7 Paul R. Laird, "Choreographers, Directors and the Fully Integrated Musical," in *Cambridge Companion to the Musical*, 3rd ed. (Cambridge, UK: Cambridge University Press, 2017), pp. 264–280, 269.
8 Miller, 49.
9 Carol Easton, *No Intermissions: The Life of Agnes De Mille* (New York, NY: Da Capo Press, 2000), 269.
10 Laird, 266.
11 John Kenrick, *Musical Theatre: A History*, 2nd ed. (London, UK: Bloomsbury Publishing, 2017), 239.
12 "Jerome Robbins, 'Peter Pan' of Dance, Dies," *The LA Times*, July 30, 1998, https://www.latimes.com/archives/la-xpm-1998-jul-30-mn-8528-story.html.
13 Kenrick, 239.
14 Thelen, 197.
15 Robert Emmet Long, *Broadway, the Golden Years: Jerome Robbins and the Great Choreographer-Directors: 1940 to the Present* (London, UK: Continuum, 2006), 100.
16 Thelen, 195.
17 Thelen, 195.
18 Thelen, 195.
19 Long, 104.
20 Long, 103, 104.
21 Long, 104.
22 "What Is Auteur Theory and Why Is It Important?," *Indie Film Hustle*, May 21, 2022, https://indiefilmhustle.com/auteur-theroy/.
23 Atkinson, Brooks, "Theatre: 'West Side Story,' The Jungles of the City." *The New York Times*, September 27, 1957. https://archive.nytimes.com/www.nytimes.com/books/98/07/19/specials/sondheim-westsidestory.html.
24 Atkinson, Brooks. "Theatre: 'West Side Story...'"
25 John Chapman, "West Side Story," *The New York Daily News*, (September 27, 1957), https://www.nydailynews.com/entertainment/theater-arts/west-side-story-recounts-romeo-juliet-1957-article-1.2368364.
26 Kalam, T.E. "CHICAGO: Fossephorescence." Review of *Chicago*, *Time*, (June 16, 1975). https://content.time.com/time/subscriber/article/0,33009,917547,00.html.
27 Long, 149.
28 Long, 149.
29 Kenrick, 238
30 Martin Gottfried, *All His Jazz: The Life & Death of Bob Fosse* (New York, NY: Da Capo Press, 1998), 182.

31 Walter Kerr, "Chicago," *The New York Times*, (June 8, 1975): 109–113, pp.109–113,https://timesmachine.nytimes.com/timesmachine/1975/06/08/105334368.html?pageNumber=109.

32 Long, 222.

33 Long, 232.

34 Clive Barnes, "A Chorus Line," *The New York Times* (October 20, 1977): 44, p. 44.

35 Kenrick, 273.

36 Frank Rich, "Dreamgirls," *The New York Times* (December 21, 1981): C11, p. C11, https://timesmachine.nytimes.com/timesmachine/1981/12/21/issue.html.

37 Prince, Harold. *Sense of Occasion*. Milwaukee, WI: Applause Theatre & Cinema Books, an imprint of Hal Leonard LLC, 2017, 2.

38 Prince, 3

39 Long, 232.

40 Kalam, CHICAGO.

RECOMMENDATIONS FOR ADDITIONAL RESOURCES

Cramer, Lyn. *Creating Musical Theatre Conversations with Broadway Directors and Choreographers*. London, UK: Bloomsbury Publishing, Bloomsbury Methuen Drama, 2013.

In this book, Cramer interviews many of the leading directors and choreographers of the Broadway musical about their process, and it serves as a sort of sequel to Lawrence Thelen's book and picks up with interviews where Thelen left off. It includes profiles of Jerry Mitchell, Kathleen Marshall, and Andy Blakenbuehler, among others.

Long, Robert Emmet. *Broadway, the Golden Years: Jerome Robbins and the Great Choreographer-Directors: 1940 to the Present*. London, UK: Continuum, 2006.

This book tracks the work of notable artists including Agnes de Mille, Robbins, Fosse, Champion, Bennett and Tune.

Thelen, Lawrence. *The Show Makers: Great Directors of the American Musical Theatre*. New York, NY: Routledge, 2002.

This text features interviews about with many Broadway directors about their directorial processes, and includes the last interview given by Jerome Robbins before he died.

CHAPTER 5

"To being an us for once, instead of a them": Musical theatre aesthetics and youth-oriented musicals[1]

Barrie Gelles

Young musical theatre enthusiasts might like a particular Golden Age musical or admire a more contemporary show, but the intensity of their fandom for youth-oriented musicals is often unmatched. Their favorite version of this subgenre might be a popular musical such as *Wicked*, a cult favorite such as *Be More Chill*, a musical with two iterations such as *In the Heights* and its subsequent film adaptation, or a show that makes them feel seen, such as *The Prom*. Their devotion to these youth-oriented musicals (and others like them) stems from the pleasure of feeling represented on stage and the aesthetic delights that are integral to these shows. This chapter focuses on *Hair* (1968), *Rent* (1996), and *Spring Awakening* (2006), using these three popular examples to articulate what youth-oriented musicals have in common in terms of form and content. The chapter also compiles a collective and comparative history of how these shows reached their intended audience through marketing and media. Next, the chapter provides a brief overview of how these shows make meaning through unconventional aesthetics that deviate from typical musical theatre forms. Finally, the chapter articulates a new taxonomy of song conventions, referencing specific musical numbers from *Hair*, *Rent*, and *Spring Awakening*.

Youth-oriented musicals are defined first and foremost by a central group of characters who are on the precipice of adulthood but who are in conflict with the adults and systems of authority that surround them. The musical *Hair* has "the tribe," a gathering of

DOI: 10.4324/9781003256458-6

teens and young adults who share ideologies, politics, drugs, and beds as they protest the unthinkable war that is destroying their generation. *Rent* features a community of young adults, most of whom are queer artists, and some of whom are dealing with drug addiction, while others are living with AIDS. To varying degrees and with a range of consequences, these "bohemians" are outcasts from society and its institutions; they are estranged from their parents but have created a chosen family with each other. *Spring Awakening* has the self-proclaimed "guilty ones," a loose knit set of teenage peers thrown together via their school and community who look to each other for answers when the adults in their lives deprive them of truth, love, and safety. In all three musicals, the young people who have been abandoned on the fringe of society come together and take center stage.

To tell the stories of these young outcasts, youth-oriented musicals had to move outside of the mainstream as well. Musical theatre, even with all its variations and innovations, has a common format that stems from Golden Age musicals. Even now, eighty years after the premiere of *Oklahoma!*, every musical that eschews a white, cis, heteronormative love story, or has a score that veers away from a typical Broadway sound is something of an outlier. Despite the fact that musicals have thrived in their diversity of style and content, musicals still tend to be compared to the Golden Age formula and assessed by the degree to which they replicate or deconstruct the template. As youth-oriented musicals emerged in the late 1950s, their form and content reflected their subjects, rebelling against the status quo. They defied musical theatre conventions by incorporating rock and pop music, destabilizing typical love stories, and embracing new aesthetics onstage.[2] Musicals that tell the stories of teens and young adults do not merely depart from the typical formula for a musical, they create a specific set of aesthetics and a new form that eventually comes to define youth-oriented musicals.

"WE'VE ALL GOT OUR JUNK, AND MY JUNK IS YOU": CONTENT, THEMES, AND INTENDED AUDIENCE[3]

Despite being created decades apart, *Hair*, *Rent*, and *Spring Awakening* have a great deal in common. The musicals share themes such as the challenges and euphoria of adolescence, a penchant for anti-establishment activism, a dedication to the counterculture, a belief in chosen community, and a clear dividing line between the young characters and the adult authority figures. However, because musicals are always of their time, there are differences in the specifics of each of these themes. *Hair* is a musical of the 1960s and carries with it the tensions and subject matter of a nation fraught with change. Much of *Hair*'s anti-establishment content is in opposition to the Vietnam War and the military draft that threatened the lives of the young men in their "tribe." In addition, *Hair* revels in the ideology of the 1960s counterculture brought forth by the Civil Rights Movement, the sexual revolution, and drug culture. *Rent* was originally produced off-Broadway in 1996 but takes place in the late 1980s and the AIDS epidemic is central to the story and defines the lives of many of the characters. *Spring Awakening* is an anomaly in the sense that it is set in "a provincial German town in the 1890s" but is created to be purposefully anachronistic in its style so that the seemingly historically bound content becomes unnervingly universal. It is also worth noting that each of the musicals' cast of characters is situated on a slightly different part of the spectrum of adolescent to young adult. The youthful characters in *Hair* are mostly high school age or just past the age of eighteen (such as Sheila, who attends NYU); the young adults in *Rent* seem to range from nineteen to mid-twenties; the adolescents in *Spring Awakening* are between the ages of thirteen and sixteen.

The three musicals were created for general audiences, not specifically for teens and young adults but, because of the content and themes, the shows were especially appealing for younger audience members. Capitalizing on this potential interest, there were marketing elements in place that helped to grab the attention of young spectators; these came in the form of media releases, the Tony performances, and ticketing initiatives.

MARKETING THROUGH MEDIA

All three shows benefited from releasing media to increase interest in their productions; offering potential audiences a sampling of what made each of the musicals unique. *Hair* wasn't only thriving on word of mouth and reviews—potential audience members could hear the new rock musical for themselves. The off-Broadway cast album of *Hair* was released in 1967 with the original songs from the run at the Public Theatre in advance of the Broadway run. Shortly after *Hair* opened on Broadway, the musical would get a new recording with the Broadway cast and the updated song list. The Broadway album would be listed at "no. 1" on *Billboard 200* for thirteen weeks in 1969, with many of the individual songs becoming Top 40 hits.[4] Similarly, in 1996, *Rent* was relatively quick to release a very successful two-CD album four months after opening on Broadway that gave eager would-be fans a chance to engage with the rock-opera that captured almost the entire story of the musical in the original Broadway recording.[5] It also had the advantage of a very quick succession of accolades: the show opened on April 29, 1996, was awarded the Pulitzer Prize in Drama on May 20, 1996, and won the Tony Awards for Best Musical, Best Book of a Musical, and Best Score on June 2, 1996.[6] When *Spring Awakening* was attempting to reach its target audience in 2006, the production team had the advantage of the internet to reach out to its potential fan base. Like its predecessors, *Spring Awakening*'s original Broadway cast album was released early in its run (December 12, 2006, two days after it opened at the Eugene O'Neill Theatre) in the hopes of creating a buzz. But even before the album's release, the production team shot a music video of "Bitch of Living" on stage at the Atlantic Theatre and released it on YouTube. The crucial decision to capture the performance aesthetics in their entirety and share them with potential audiences would help to define the contemporary vibrancy of the show for young audiences.[7]

PERFORMING REBELLION FOR A NATIONAL AUDIENCE

Though *Hair* and *Rent* didn't have the advantage of YouTube and social media to give potential audience members a sneak peek at their shows, they made use of the annual televised Tony Awards ceremony, which is often considered a commercial for Broadway. The choices made by the production teams of each of the musicals were specific and integral to defining the shows for a national audience. For each of these musicals, the Tony Awards performance was a chance to show their target audience how this musical was different, exciting, and built just for them. Typically, a Broadway musical would choose their most appealing number, something upbeat that promises a pleasurable experience for the spectator. At the 1969 Tony Awards, *Hair* made a radical choice of performing "Three-Five-Zero-Zero," "What A Piece of Work is Man," and "The Flesh Failures (Let the Sunshine In)" in succession creating six and a half minute musical theatre protest against the horrors of the Vietnam War, broadcast on national television.[8] As the ensemble stands on the edge of the stage, singing a rock and roll funeral dirge, their faces filled with anguish, their bodies pulsating with fury and grief, *Hair* is defined as revolutionary in form and content. *Rent*'s performance at the 1996 Tony Awards frames the show as inclusive of both recognizable Broadway traditions and provocative content. The performance began with "Seasons of Love," a ballad that borrows from musical theatre composition styles while focusing on the unmeasurable loss caused by the AIDS epidemic. The second half of the performance is an abbreviated version of "La Vie Boheme" that relies on the audience's love of a big, energetic, musical number while still being radical enough to gleefully sing "to faggots, lezzies, dykes, cross-dressers too" on national television.[9] At the 2006 Tony Awards, the *Spring Awakening* performance began with "Mama Who Bore Me," a soft rock ballad, before launching into the reprise that is decidedly more rock and roll. It is sung by five teenage actresses who stomp with barely suppressed desperation as they sing complex harmonies into handheld microphones. With barely a rest, the stage is taken over by six male actors who sing a truncated version of "Bitch of Living" with the energy of a 1990s alternative rock band as they jump off the stage furniture. Finally, the entire ensemble takes the stage to sing a snippet of "Totally Fucked," having to place a rest beat in place of the expletive (forbidden on television) and covering their mouths every time they do. Suddenly, the Tony Awards stage is flooded with teenagers dancing out their rage, singing about their unfair oppression while having to censor themselves and a new fan base of misunderstood teens was born.

PUTTING FANS FRONT AND CENTER

Prior to the Tony performance, *Spring Awakening* had been struggling with ticket sales and the company regularly played to large swaths of empty seats, but then the show started selling out. Luckily, the production was already designed to be affordable for their target audience with student rush tickets and unique on-stage seats priced at $31.25 that offered an immersive experience.[10] Prioritizing affordable tickets for the most devoted spectators was an essential marketing technique inherited from *Rent* which invented the first Broadway ticket lottery—$20 tickets to first-row seats at the Nederlander Theatre (pictured in Figure 5.1).[11] Both *Rent* and *Spring Awakening* benefited from making their productions financially accessible because their most fervent fans would be integrated into the show's dynamic; *Rent*'s lottery winners were on view as they raved from the first row of house seats and *Spring Awakening*'s devoted fans were on-stage, their excitement on display as part the show. The fandom of these shows evolved to the point that they had names for themselves—Rentheads and Guilty Ones (*Spring Awakening*)—and they found ways to connect as internet communications and social media evolved.

The youth-oriented stories of *Hair*, *Rent*, and *Spring Awakening* got the attention of young spectators, and the marketing and ticketing policies were designed for a new generation of theatregoers. But it was the shows' form and style that assured their target audience that these productions were not typical Broadway musicals. The release of the cast albums and the televised (or digitized) excerpts of the musicals showcased unconventional aesthetics and defined youth-oriented shows as alternative musicals. Each of these musicals—in their own time, in their own way—were contributing to a shift in the form of musical theatre that is more clearly seen with hindsight and by considering these musicals together. The themes of rejecting the status-quo and feeling disconnected from older generations were not just embedded into the content of *Hair*, *Rent*, and *Spring Awakening*—they were instilled in the form of the musicals.

Figure 5.1: The exterior of the Nederlander Theatre in 1999, where the lottery was held, during a performance of the musical *Rent*, which had opened there in 1996

"HATING CONVENTION, HATING PRETENSION...": ALTERNATIVE AESTHETICS IN MUSICALS[12]

Musical theatre aesthetics are part of a larger set of musical theatre conventions that define and redefine the genre every time a musical is produced. In "In Defense of Pleasure: Musical Theatre History in the Liberal Arts," scholar Stacy Wolf explains that "musical theatre has its own set of highly developed, historically specific 'rules'" and that "any musical both relies on and revises the form that precedes it."[13] Wolf asserts that the conventions of musical theatre are tools that can be used to analyze the complexities of the form and that "comparison between any two musicals, especially between a musical by Rodgers and Hammerstein and any other, foregrounds what conventions are present and how the latter show revises the R&H model."[14] A large part of what sets *Hair, Rent,* and *Spring Awakening* apart from typical musicals is the very same thing that groups them together—the use of unconventional aesthetics and new types of songs is in defiance of the typical "form that precedes it." Because of the repeated and constant use of non-traditional, meta-theatrical aesthetics and atypical types of songs, these musicals relish breaking the "rules" of musical theatre.

The three musicals have similar themes and narratives, similar marketing, and similar target audiences, but it is the shared aesthetics that define these musicals as youth-oriented and cool. Teens and young adults are drawn to these musicals because they are quite literally not their parents' musicals. Rather than the distraction of the old razzle dazzle, youth-oriented musicals use expletives and costumes that seem "authentic" to suggest that the musical is grounded in the gritty reality of the story. The unconventional sets don't disguise the theatre space, they proudly flaunt their meta-theatricality by baring the walls of the space. And the rock and roll aesthetic extends to musicians performing on stage and performers using microphones conspicuously. These trappings seem to insist that there is an honesty to the musicals—there is nothing for them to hide.

However, as much as youth-oriented musicals define themselves by moving away from the traditions of Golden Age musicals, they inevitably begin to create a new variation of a musical theatre form that has its own set of repeated and reoccurring elements.

For example, the "tribe" of *Hair*, the chosen family of *Rent*, and the school-aged peer group of *Spring Awakening* all function in a similar way, despite their wildly different contexts. Structurally, these peer groups create an ensemble made up of a wide variety of characters that allows for interaction and identification, providing variations on the themes of youth and rebellion. The convention of a peer group as an ensemble becomes integral to the form of youth-oriented musicals. Similarly, to accompany the rock/pop score, there is a repeated choreographic element in youth-oriented musicals where the movement seems as though it is a spontaneous physical outburst, combining music and movement to convey sound and fury, signifying youth. In this way, eventually, the unconventional aesthetics of youth-oriented musicals become their own sort of conventions.

To further this point, consider that as *Hair*, *Rent*, and *Spring Awakening* substantially shifted away from the traditional forms of musical theatre, the musicals inadvertently create a new set of song conventions, specific to youth-oriented musicals. These new types of songs can coexist with or replace the traditional categories of songs in musicals that are more widely known. Musicologist Paul R. Laird, writing about "Musical Styles and Song Conventions," builds off the work of Lehman Engel to articulate the musical theatre song conventions that are so commonplace that they are sometimes taken for granted.[15] Laird mentions the "I want song" that "takes place early in a show and discloses the character's primary motivation."[16] Engel defined the "charm song" as "a song that embodies generally delicate, optimistic and rhythmic music, and lyrics of light though not necessarily comedic subject matter."[17] Other songs such as the "I am song" or the "hypothetical love song" are well-known conventions in musicals. These categories are based on a typical musical theatre structure and songs that largely adhere to the "Golden Age" or Rodgers and Hammerstein model of musicals. It stands to reason that when musicals such as *Hair*, *Rent*, and *Spring Awakening* depart from the established structure of musicals, the songs would likewise break conventions. Therefore, the categories developed to define the songs featured in typical musicals may not be able to account for the songs created in unconventional musicals. However, because certain types of songs occur consistently in youth-oriented musicals, they deserve their own articulated taxonomy.

"THE NEED TO EXPRESS, TO COMMUNICATE": EXAMPLES OF SONG CONVENTIONS IN YOUTH-ORIENTED MUSICALS[18]

Within *Hair*, *Rent*, *Spring Awakening*, and other youth-oriented musicals, there exist five reoccurring types of songs: the "rebellion song," the "euphoric counterculture song," the "complicated young love song," the "feeling misunderstood song," and the "my body, myself song."

The "Rebellion Song"

A "rebellion song" in a youth-oriented musical is sung about or directly to authority figures. This type of song can range from an expression of dissatisfaction with the status quo to unbridled rage against an unjust world. The "rebellion song" is defined, in part, by its desire for change and the intention of the song is to convey that need to authority figures. Some versions of a "rebellion song" are directed to the audience, ostensibly hoping that the message will impact the adult spectators.

There are multiple examples of the "rebellion song" in *Hair*, but a particularly clear one is "Flesh Failures (Let the Sunshine In)." Contextualized around the Vietnam War, *Hair* examines how the draft impacts the members of "the tribe," most prominently in the plot line about how a main character, Claude, will respond to the draft summons. At the end of the second act, the ensemble gathers for an anti-war protest, singing "do not enter the induction center...what the hell are we fighting for."[19] Claude's friends wonder why he is missing from the protest and the stage directions explain "[Claude] enters, dressed in a military uniform, but they do not see him or hear him."[20] Claude says, "like it or not, they got me" as the song, "Flesh Failures (Let the Sunshine In)" begins.[21] The song is at once a pleading anti-war protest and a mourning wail for the young lives already lost; with rhythmic consistency that recalls the beating of one's breast and vocal styles like rock and roll keening, the song musically conveys "the tribe's" desperation. The song is directed to both the authority figures in the world of the musical and the spectators in their seats, asking them to consider their complacence. Claude looms over "the tribe," remaining unseen and unheard until the end of the song when he is revealed "lying center, on a black cloth."[22] The reality of Claude's fate haunts the audience as the ensemble repeats their fervent cry, "let the sunshine in." Other songs that fit within this category include *Hair*'s "Three-Five-Zero-Zero," "What a Piece of Work is Man," "How Dare They Try (Walking in Space Reprise)," as well as the title song from *Rent* and "All That's Known" from *Spring Awakening*.

The "Euphoric Counterculture Song"

A "euphoric counterculture song" is typically an ensemble number in a youth-oriented musical in which the characters define their collective identities via a list of cultural signifiers. This type of song is a variation of the conventional "list song." David Savran, writing specifically about the works of Cole Porter and Stephen Sondheim, argues that "ballads and love duets may represent characters' affections and intimacies, but with few exceptions, they express rather than generate desire. A list song, on the other hand,…both represents and produces desire by cataloging a wide range of coveted people, places, and things."[23] Savran explains that a list song produces desire in both the characters and the audience and that, in Porter and Sondheim list songs, "the audience members also take great delight in the act of listing, while craving ever flashier and more brilliant rhymes. They are invited to share a private joke and be flattered by the presumption of their sophistication."[24] In a "euphoric counterculture song" the convention of the list is used differently; while it produces desire for the characters, it asks audience members to decide where their desire is situated in relation to the list of culturally bound people, places, and things. This type of song allows the characters to revel in their catalog of counterculture signifiers while the audience must determine if they themselves are already in the know or on the outside looking in. Furthermore, the audience members must locate their desire and consider whether they are content to stay separate from the counterculture or if they are longing to join in.

Perhaps the most evident example of the "euphoric counterculture song" is "La Vie Boheme" in *Rent*.[25] The song is an act of self-affirmation, sung in joyous rebellion, championing counterculture

93

while dancing atop tables, but it also allows the self-proclaimed bohemians to assert that they are being ostracized because of their sexuality, their class status, their belief systems, their politics, and even their HIV status. Musically, the joyful number is fast-paced and high energy, with a beat that pushes audiences to dance with the characters. The attitude of the song is celebratory, flippant, tongue-in-cheek, and defiant. The lyrics list the ways in which the characters define themselves and is, at times, a veritable syllabus of artists and intellectuals that have influenced the characters' counterculture. "La Vie Boheme" proudly talks about sexuality and lovingly chides the characters' own downtown art aesthetics. It claims the need for "revolution, justice screaming for solutions, forcing change, risk, and danger, making pleas," and champions "people...living with not dying from disease."[26] As it defines the characters' East Village, the late 1980s, counterculture lifestyle, it is inclusive rather than exclusive, leaving a trail of references for those who want to experience "la vie boheme." Eager young audience members, fantasizing about moving to New York City to become an artist and/or intellectual, found a way in as they memorized the plentiful lyrics of the song; the repetition in the composition creates a looping pattern that is easily remembered. This "euphoric counterculture song" welcomes the spectators who are longing to belong and sends them home with a cultural map including the works of artists and thinkers that they might not otherwise have encountered in mainstream education: Maya Angelou, Susan Sontag, Stephen Sondheim, Alan Ginsberg, Bob Dylan, Langston Hughes, Pablo Neruda, Gertrude Stein, Akira Kurosawa, and Vaclav Havel among others. Other songs that fit within this category include *Hair*'s title song and "I Got Life" and *Spring Awakening*'s "Bitch of Living" and "The Guilty Ones."

The "Feeling Misunderstood Song"

A "feeling misunderstood song" in a youth oriented-musical is typically directed at parents and/or other authority figures and can either be an expression of frustration or an admission of isolation. This type of song is frequently sung by a character who has been (or is about to be) an outcast from mainstream society because of a perceived difference. The song might have a serious tone if being misunderstood is fraught with anxiety because it jeopardizes the character's safety or disrupts the character's plans for the future. There is another permutation where the tone might be used for a bit of comic levity in which a clueless parent is the root of the problem. Either way, the "feeling misunderstood song" is defined by a pervasive misunderstanding between the younger generation and their elders. It is interesting to note that in many youth-oriented musicals, the adult characters are either doubled (when one actor plays multiple adult characters as in *Spring Awakening*), disembodied voices (as in "Voicemail" in *Rent*), or performed as archetypes layered on top of other characters (when the ensemble plays "Moms 1-3" or "Principals 1-3" in *Hair*). Through these dramaturgical choices, the adult characters are made less prominent that the youthful characters, giving a clear bias to the latter's point of view.

In *Spring Awakening*, Melchior attempts to educate himself and his classmates about the realities of the world that the adults refuse to explain. In particular, at the request of his friend Moritz, Melchior has agreed to write an essay in order to share the sexual education he secretly learned from books. Having discovered Melchoir's writings, his teachers decide that they must rid their school of "the moral corruption of our youth" and summon Melchior for questioning and punishment. It is at that moment that the song "Totally Fucked" begins, an example of a "feeling misunderstood song." The song is not Melchior's explanation of his actions, nor is it an attempt to change the minds of the authority figures. "Totally Fucked" is a commentary on the massive communication gap between youth and authority, filled with frustration and exasperation, expressed through song. The song begins with individual characters singing but escalates into the entire ensemble of young characters unleashing their feelings. Musically, the song is an expletive hurling, foot stomping song of righteous indignation. The characters acknowledge that there is no way out of this misunderstanding: "you're fucked if you just freeze up....but you're fucked if you speak your mind."[27] At the apex of the song, the young characters sing in unison, "blah blah blah blah blah blah blah blah," capturing the way youth and authority become totally incomprehensible to each other. The ensemble finishes the song in an eruption of body-hurling frustration. The "feeling misunderstood" song is not intended to rectify the misunderstanding or to bridge the gap between youth and authority; it is a release akin to screaming into a pillow or slamming a door and cranking the music up. Other songs that fit within this category include *Hair*'s "Ain't Got No" and "Going Down," *Rent*'s "Voicemail" [1-5] and "Will I," and *Spring Awakening*'s "Mama Who Bore Me."

The "Complicated Young Love Song"

Just as the convention of the "hypothetical love song" articulates a particular structure to a musical theatre love song, the "complicated young love song," is another nuanced approach to song analysis that appears in youth-oriented musicals. Borrowing the colloquial phrase "it's complicated" from social media statuses and memes, this type of song denotes that the love (hypothetical or realized) is made complicated by the heightened nature of youthful relationships. The "complicated young love song" is defined by the fact that the obstacles to the relationship are a condition of their youthful circumstances. The complication does not always have to have a negative connotation—it could be something as frivolous as falling in love at first sight (like "Frank Mills"). However, one of the characteristics of a "complicated young love song" is that there is an element of pleasure derived from the complication; the drama of young love is one of its torturous delights.

Examples of this type of song are plentiful in these three musicals (and almost any musical featuring adolescents) and are self-explanatory. In *Rent*, "Light My Candle" is a musical meet-cute for Roger and Mimi made more dramatic by contrasting the literal lack of electricity with the figurative spark between them. However, the song veers away from a typical "hypothetical love song" because the characters focus on avoiding a romance rather than imagining the possibility of one. The characters sing together briefly in "La Vie Boheme" but are annoyed by their awkward interaction and unsure of how to interpret each other's motives. It isn't until "AZT break," that the characters consider pulling down their barriers. And yet, when Roger and Mimi sing their second duet, "I Should Tell You," it still begins with a list of obstacles that would prevent them from falling in love. Though both "Light My Candle" and "I Should Tell You" are musically structured like a typical musical theatre love song, they are defined by the obstacles and limitations of a potential romance and not the imaginings of transcendent love.

Other songs that fit within this category include *Hair*'s "Easy to Be Hard" and "Frank Mills," *Rent*'s "You Okay Honey?," and Spring Awakening's "My Junk."

The "My Body, Myself Song"

The "my body, myself song" in a youth-oriented musical is about sex, drugs, and/or other acts of hedonism and is coupled with an exploration of identity. This type of song can range in intensity from light-hearted exploration to profound discovery and can be comedic or serious. The "my body, myself song" is defined by a moment in which a character or characters has a moment of internal revelation through external exploration. There are physiological reasons why teens and young adults are preoccupied with sex and societal reasons why the frank discussions of it are taboo. Because of this dichotomy, there is an exciting nuance to these songs—they explore desire and identity with an unrepressed expression of hedonistic wonder.

In *Spring Awakening,* "Touch Me" is sung by all of the young characters and though the actors are on stage together, it is understood that each of the characters is exploring this sentiment in isolation, thereby conveying that although the feelings are private, it is a shared adolescent rite of passage. The song is one of longing but not for another person (such as "My Junk"); instead it is a song that longs to know oneself through the experience of physical intimacy (with or without a partner). The "my body, myself song" is rooted in the notion that a physical experience is connected to a profound understanding of self. This can also be seen in "Word of Your Body" where the lyrics attribute language to the body and talk about wounds and bruises as ways of understanding the emotional ramifications of love. Other songs that fit within this category include *Hair*'s "Hashish," "Sodomy," "The Bed," and "Walking in Space" and *Rent*'s "Contact."

CONCLUSION: YOUTH ORIENTED MUSICALS CAN *BE MORE CHILL*

This new song taxonomy, created specifically to discuss youth-oriented musicals, isn't in place of traditional song conventions such as the "I want song" or the "charm song." In fact, as with traditional Golden Age musicals, any given song can be more than one thing at a time (for example, a ballad can be a love song, but it can also be an "I am" song). The new song taxonomy is an exercise in articulating reoccurring tropes that have substantially changed the form of musicals featuring teen and young adult characters.

One might wonder if this level of specificity is useful beyond the three musicals discussed in this chapter. There have been recent musicals about teen characters, such as *Be More Chill* (2019) and *The Lightning Thief: The Percy Jackson Musical* (2019) that have their own fascinating production history, clever marketing techniques, and fervent fan bases.[28] Both of the shows are decidedly more comedic and offer more conventional happy endings than the three musicals in this chapter. Interestingly, the song categories still apply.

One might wonder if this level of specificity is necessary for analyzing and discussing musicals. Stacy Wolf concludes her manifesto, "In Defense of Pleasure," by stating "as educators, I believe that it is our duty to respect and draw out students' preferences and passions and to consider their feelings as being socially contingent, historically grounded, and, in the words of Bourdieu, 'habitus-based.'"[29] Young people are excited by youth-oriented musicals because they recognize themselves as the target audience; they see themselves represented in the content but also revel in the form that breaks away from the "authoritative" template of a musical. For older audience members, musicals like *Hair*, *Rent*, *Spring Awakening*, or even *Be More Chill* can offer an experience of reconnecting to youthful feelings and desires. Through their specific aesthetics, youth-oriented musicals connect audiences to the pleasure of a musical "being [for] us for once, instead of [for] them."

NOTES

1 Jonathan Larson, "La Vie Boheme" recorded 1996, track 23 on *Rent*, Universal City, Calif.: Dreamworks, compact disc.

2 See: Elizabeth Wollman, *The Theater Will Rock: a History of the Rock Musical, from Hair to Hedwig* (Ann Arbor (MI): University of Michigan Press, 2010).

3 Duncan Sheik and Steven Sater, "My Junk" recorded 2006, track 5 on *Spring Awakening: a New Musical*, Decca Broadway, compact disc.

4 The original Broadway cast recording of *Hair* would win a Grammy in 1969 and eventually be selected for the Library of Congress's National Recording Registry in 2019.

5 The original Broadway cast recording of *Rent* debuted on the *Billboard 200* chart at number 19.

6 *Rent* was the seventh musical to win the Pulitzer Prize in Drama. As of 2023, ten musicals have won the Pulitzer.

7 SpringAwakeningBroadway, "Bitch of Living." YouTube video, 2:58. 2006. https://www.youtube.com/watch?v=7JCoA92y24A
See: Laura MacDonald, "Connection in an Isolating Age: Looking Back on Twenty Years of Engaging Audiences and Marketing Musical Theatre Online" in *iBroadway*, ed. Jessica Hillman-McCord (Palgrave MacMillan, 2017), 17–42.

8 "Hot Clip of the Day: *Hair*'s Tony Performance from 1969 Will Give You Life," *Broadway Box* online, December 22, 2015, https://www.broadwaybox.com/daily-scoop/hot-clip-of-the-day-hair-obc-will-give-you-chills/.

9 Them Geier, "18 All-Time Great Tony Awards Performances, From 'Dreamgirls' to 'Hamilton,'" *The Wrap* online, October 15, 2020, https://www.thewrap.com/tony-awards-performances-all-time-best-dreamgirls-neil-patrick-harris-hamilton/.

10 Kenneth Jones, "*Spring Awakening* Will Put Audience in Middle of Action; Student Rush Also Offered," *Playbill* online, October 30, 2006, https://playbill.com/article/spring-awakening-will-put-audience-in-middle-of-action-student-rush-also-offered-com-135945.

11 Suzy Evans, "How 'Rent Reshaped the Theater Industry 25 Years Ago—And Again Today," *Today Tix* online, February 12, 2021, https://www.todaytix.com/insider/nyc/posts/how-rent-reshaped-the-theater-industry-25-years-ago-and-again-today.

12 Jonathan Larson, "La Vie Boheme" recorded 1996, track 23 on *Rent*, Universal City, Calif.: Dreamworks, compact disc.

13 Stacy Ellen Wolf, "In Defense of Pleasure: Musical Theatre History in the Liberal Arts [A Manifesto]," *Theatre Topics* 17, no. 1 (2007): 53–54.

14 Wolf, "In Defense of Pleasure," 53–54.

15 Paul R. Laird, "Musical Styles and Song Conventions," in *The Oxford Handbook of the American Musical*, ed. Raymond Knapp, Mitchell Morris, and Stacy Wolf (New York: Oxford University Press, 2011), 34.

16 Laird, "Musical Styles and Song Conventions," 34.

17 Lehman Engel, *The American Musical Theatre* (New York: Collier Books, 1975), 87–89.

18 Jonathan Larson, "La Vie Boheme" recorded 1996, track 23 on *Rent*, Universal City, Calif.: Dreamworks, compact disc.

19 James Rado and Gerome Ragni, *Hair* (New York: Pocket Books, 1969), 85.

20 Rado and Ragni, *Hair*, 86.

21 Rado and Ragni, *Hair*, 86.

22 Rado and Ragni, *Hair*, 87.

23 David Savran, ""You've got that thing": Cole Porter, Stephen Sondheim, and the Erotics of the List Song," *Theatre Journal* 64, no. 4 (2012): 535.

24 Savran, "'You've got that thing,'"535.

25 Maureen Lee Lenker, "Viva 'La Vie Bohème'!: An oral history of the *Rent* Act 1 finale", *Entertainment Weekly* online, April 29, 2020, https://ew.com/theater/rent-la-vie-boheme-oral-history/.

26 Jonathan Larson, *Rent: The Complete Book and Lyrics of the Broadway Musical* (New York: Applause, 1996), 176–177.

27 Steven Sater and Duncan Sheik, *Spring* Awakening (New York: Theatre Communications Group, 2007).

28 *Be More Chill* had an off-Broadway run at the Signature Theatre in 2018 and a regional production in 2015. *The Lightning Thief: the Percy Jackson Musical* was produced off-Broadway in 2014 and again in 2017 with a revised script. It also had a national tour in 2015 and 2019.

29 Wolf, "In Defense of Pleasure," 55.

RECOMMENDATIONS FOR ADDITIONAL RESOURCES

The librettos for all three musicals discussed above have been published and offer insight into their lyrics and construction.

Cote, David. *'Spring Awakening': In the Flesh*. New York: Melcher Media, 2008.

This book recounts the process through which the musical was created.

Warren, Michael John, dir. *Spring Awakening: Those You've Known*. 2022; New York, NY: Home Box Office, 2022. https://www.hbo.com/movies/spring-awakening-those-youve-known

This documentary follows the original company of *Spring Awakening* as they reunite years later for a concert of the show.

Warren, Michael John, dir. *Rent: Filmed Live on Broadway*. 2008; Culver City, Calif.: Sony Pictures Home Entertainment, 2009. DVD.

Film versions exist of both *Hair* and *Rent*, which differ from their stage productions, as well as this version, which is a video capture of the Broadway performance.

CHAPTER 6

Megahits and megamusicals: Achieving worldwide success with shows that (seem to) run forever

Raymond Knapp and Holley Replogle-Wong

With musicals, art has frequently had to accept second billing to commerce, since there can be no show without money, both upfront and, eventually, from ticket buyers. But advancing money to develop a show is extremely risky, and attracting backers will likely depend on persuading them that the show being developed has strong possibilities for a long run and thus for steady and continuing profits. Mostly, commercial considerations mandate a mix weighted toward conservative imitation of past or still-running successes, but with some accrual of "something new" to entice audiences. Yet the lingering promise that a show will generate extended runs around the globe—the show-business equivalent of winning the lottery—can be a powerful inducement to take greater risks, since megahits have tended to be more innovative in some way, whether artistically, technologically, or in subject matter, though not always so (or at least not by all accounts).

In this chapter, we will survey the milestone megahits and megamusicals that stand as glittery emblems of the commercial potential of musicals, spanning from *The Black Crook* (New York, 1866) and *The Merry Widow* (Vienna, 1905) to *The Phantom of the Opera* (London, 1986), *The Lion King* (New York, 1997), and *Wicked* (New York, 2003), encompassing as well, from recent decades, *Fiddler on the Roof* (New York, 1964), *Man of La Mancha* (New York, 1965), *Hair* (New York, 1967 and 1968), *Grease* (New York, 1972), *A Chorus Line* (New York, 1975), *Les Misérables* (Paris, 1980

DOI: 10.4324/9781003256458-7

and London, 1985), *Cats* (London, 1981), *Rent* (New York, 1996), and *Chicago* (New York revival, 1996).[1] Looking at these shows separately and together allows us to highlight how different they are from each other, at least before the advent of the megamusical, which in many ways has imposed a much decried uniformity regarding both the product itself and its often spectacularized venue, effecting a transformation of Broadway that roughly coincided with the "Disneyfication" of Times Square, which also got underway in the 1980s. In what follows, as we survey this sampling of megahits, we will emphasize how and why they have each created refreshed markets and helped populate those markets, both through long runs in widespread venues and as models for other shows. We will conclude by considering how the megamusical, in its reappropriation of key elements from the pre-history of the much-ballyhooed "integrated" form of the musical, has imposed a kind of historical frame around what has been termed the musical's "Golden Age." But that frame has been only partial, since what it frames—the development of the musical as a distinctive type, spurred periodically by megahits—has continued unchecked, refusing containment.

MEGAHITS BEFORE THE EMERGENCE OF THE MUSICAL PLAY

Before the full "arrival" of the musical as a genre, which some date to *Show Boat* (1927) and others to *Oklahoma!* (1943), there were really only two megahits, if we understand the cross-Atlantic successes and continued popularity of *H.M.S. Pinafore* (1878), *The Pirates of Penzance* (1879), and *The Mikado* (1885) as not quite in line with current understandings of the term. Thus, notwithstanding their early and long-term reportorial success, these three shows tend today to be understood in terms of a different kind of success, as part of the extraordinary tenacity of Gilbert and Sullivan's suite of operettas in cyclical revival, constituting what amounts to a genre unto itself, which has infiltrated the terrain of musicals while also sustaining companies dedicated primarily, sometimes exclusively, to their performance. But before Gilbert and Sullivan, an entirely different amalgamation of European and US American sensibilities appeared in *The Black Crook* (1866), a megahit that either launched or anticipated (depending on who's telling the story) the American musical as a distinct type. And, within a decade of Gilbert and Sullivan's final collaboration, a much different kind of operetta, already established as commercially viable in both Europe and New York, achieved its pinnacle of international success with *The Merry Widow* (*Die lustige Witwe*, Vienna, 1905; Hamburg, Berlin, and Budapest, 1906; London and New York, 1907; Melbourne, 1908; Paris, 1909; Brussels, 1910).[2]

To be sure, achieving a megahit meant something different then, since the lengths of initial runs were not up to today's standards. It matters that *The Black Crook*, as the first "musical" to run for over a year in its initial New York run, set a record with 475 performances, but its full impact derives from its being revived twice in its original venue (1870 and 1871), and its continuing to be revived elsewhere on a fairly regular basis for decades. Similarly, while *The Merry Widow* had impressive initial runs in Vienna (483), London (778), and New York (416), its full success must be reckoned not only in terms of the multiple productions running simultaneously in many cities around the world, along with its frequent revivals (which, taken together, yielded an estimated half a million performances in its first six decades)[3] but also in terms of its lasting innovations—including merchandizing—and its broader legacy. Indeed, a megahit will almost always have some kind of broader legacy, extending well beyond performances of the show itself, simply by virtue of its longevity and geographic spread.

The somewhat improbable success of *The Black Crook* depended on magic-inspired spectacular stage effects and balletic tableaux featuring a then-shocking display of female bodies, with these extravagant elements held together by an earnest (if forgettable and malleable) plot. What makes its success improbable is the mongrel nature of its assorted components, assembled from a reworked English-language version of *Der Freischütz*, long-established as a Christmas staple in German venues before it was performed in 1857 Cincinnati, where it was seen by actor and hack playwright Charles M. Barras; elaborate stage machinery purchased and imported from London; a stranded Parisian ballet troupe set to perform an imported Faerie, *La Biche au bois*, when its New York venue burned down; and a pastiche musical score that could evolve, as needed, over time. Despite these improbable origins, this package proved eminently imitable, establishing new standards of possibility and acceptability regarding both of the spectacularized elements that secured its success. Eventually, these freshly enhanced dimensions, of spectacle and feminine display, not only created new possibilities for book shows, but also supported variety shows such as the *Ziegfeld Follies*—seemingly the main competition for libretto-driven shows until the collapse of vaudeville, but also the wellspring from which landmark shows such as *Show Boat* were born, courtesy of Florence Ziegfeld.

For its part, *The Merry Widow*'s combination of light operatic singing with a romantic story evoking exotic locales filled with political and sexual intrigue not only fed the continued viability of this type of operetta through the subsequent two decades, with follow-up popularity on film and television but also left an indelible imprint on the "musical play" as it largely replaced operetta on New York stages, especially as dramatically "integrated" by Rodgers and Hammerstein. Moreover, *The Merry Widow*'s combination of elaborate singing, romance, and exoticism still attracts audiences over a century later, along the way laying the foundation for the megamusical as a type, which also might be seen as an extension of the spectacular stagings pioneered by *The Black Crook*.

Spectacle, as such, is a compelling form of expression; its primary aim is to elicit excessive reactions from its audience—feelings of awe, excess, pleasure—through lavish, extreme modes of presentation. However, as Baz Kershaw points out, peddling in extremes can result in extreme reactions: "Such potency has ensured that spectacle is customarily splattered with riven responses: it is loved or hated, assiduously embraced or shunned."[4] While "legitimate" theatre turned away from spectacle during its popular boom in the nineteenth century, other theatrical forms such as variety shows and musical theatre (and eventually, film) embraced spectacle. For opera and operetta, spectacle had long been a part of the form. Beyond this on-stage aspect of spectacle, the premiere of *The Merry Widow* in Broadway's New Amsterdam Theatre in 1907 sparked a nationwide fashion and merchandising craze—"Widow Mania"— reproducing the trappings of spectacle across all aspects of culture. After producer Henry Savage sent the show on tour to cities across America, Merry Widow hats, fashioned after the costuming for the production, became the vogue among well-dressed "ladies" of the upper and upper-middle classes. Amateur pianists purchased sheet music and played the "Merry Widow Waltz" in their parlors (along with other *Merry Widow* and Widow-inspired tunes, such as the hastily published "Under My Merry Widow Hat" written by Heath and Benkhart in 1908). Unauthorized merchandise proliferated: companies used *The Merry Widow* to market everything from hats and shoes to cocktails and cigars. As will be seen, this decentralized commodification of *The Merry Widow*, no less than its sense of spectacle, anticipates in many particulars both the spectacle and the comparatively planned and controlled merchandising power of the megamusical.

MEGAHITS BETWEEN THE "GOLDEN AGE" OF THE AMERICAN MUSICAL AND THE MEGAMUSICAL

The "Golden Age" of the musical is a phrase often used by critics, historians, and fans to refer to musicals produced in the period between *Oklahoma!* and *Fiddler on the Roof*, in a way that assumes a shared value and investment in these shows as representative of the American Musical at its best, at the same time strongly implying that a period of decline set in thereafter.[5] Yet the use of *Fiddler on the Roof* as a boundary between the "Golden Age" and what came after is telling with respect to our discussion of megahits, since *Fiddler* itself, set a new record for longest running musical on Broadway (3242 performances), running for nearly eight years and being thereafter frequently revived. If *Fiddler* counts as a "Golden Age" musical, it also counts as that age's biggest hit, succeeding not only on Broadway but also worldwide, with long runs in Tel Aviv (1965), London (1967), Sydney (1967), and Tokyo (1967), among many others—all despite initial concerns that the show would not continue to run long once its star, Zero Mostel, left the show. But tellingly, *Fiddler*'s Broadway record did not stand for long; it was soon broken by *Grease* (1972, with 3388 performances), which had been open for only a few months when *Fiddler* closed, and whose record would soon be eclipsed in turn by *A Chorus Line* (1975, with 6137), which opened early in the third year of *Grease*'s eight-year run.

Arguably, *Fiddler*'s position as the first musical to run for over 3000 performances is as important as its (purportedly) marking the end of an era, since it signals a virtual eruption of megahits over the next few decades. Indeed, this eruption had been simmering even before *Fiddler*, as three earlier "Golden Age" musicals had also broken first-run performance records: *Oklahoma!* (1943, with 2212), *My Fair Lady* (1956, with 2717), and *Hello, Dolly!* (1964, with 2844), the latter opening just nine months before *Fiddler*. But *Fiddler* marks a historical turn in this succession of record-breaking shows quite apart from its breaking the 3000-performance barrier, since it establishes a new, audience-centered profile for megahits regarding innovation, one that will extend to several megamusicals despite the latter's conservative inclinations as a genre. Thus, with some consistency, each megahit from *Fiddler* on both targets a specific audience in a distinctive new way, and then breaks through to a considerably wider audience.

As argued by Andrea Most, while Jewish elements were core to the Broadway musical both before and during its "Golden Age"— especially thematically, regarding the genre's implicit, repeated thematic arguments for assimilating outsiders—by the early 1960s, Jewish experience itself became more frequently the musical's sentimentalized topic, reaching an early culmination in *Fiddler on the Roof*.[6] This aspect of the show makes an unusual connection to another megahit, though a non-musical one, from over half a century earlier. *Abie's Irish Rose* (1922) was the first play to run for over five years on Broadway; though not in line with the cautionary politics of *Fiddler* regarding assimilation, it also deliberately targeted Jewish audiences, along with Irish Catholics. With *Fiddler's* apparent narrowness of focus and seeming dependence on its star, not to mention its Eastern European musical basis, it was relatively slow to discover that its audience base, assumed to be New York Jewry, could be greatly expanded. But by the end of the decade, its success not only in Tel Aviv but also across Europe and even in Tokyo—where it also broke records and was understood as quintessentially Japanese—made it clear that its intergenerational conflicts regarding cultural traditions had wide cultural appeal.[7]

Although *Man of La Mancha* and *Hair* did not come close to *Fiddler's* record-breaking run on Broadway itself, with initial runs of 2328 and 1750 performances, respectively, both enjoyed simultaneous long runs across the world, cementing their status as megahits. Thus, *La Mancha's* book-writer Dale Wasserman estimates that a staggering 10,000 licenses were issued for its production in the twentieth century, for performances in forty-four countries and twenty-nine languages.[8] And *Hair*, despite its being closed or banned in many locations due to its foul language, politics, and nudity, had by the end of the decade played in over twenty countries, often in translation, with over three hundred recordings of its songs, including many popular hits. These two shows, in slightly different ways, combined unusual theatrical experimentation with idealist themes resonant with 1960s politics, and so appealed especially to younger audiences, the former taking place in a Spanish prison during the Inquisition, the second extolling the hippie lifestyle and breaking barriers regarding racial mixing and sexual expression while opposing the Vietnam War. But the first run of *Grease*, opening a few months before *Hair*'s first Broadway run ended, managed to tap more quickly and enduringly into young and middle-aged audience bases alike, with youthful themes and retro music that also managed to seem fresh, while—more conservatively—shying away from the themes of racial tolerance advanced in *Hair*.

As with *Man of La Mancha* and *Hair*, *A Chorus Line*, which broke *Grease*'s record by a large margin, also broke new ground in its presentational mode, for most of its action depending on a stark lineup of auditioning dancers. Also like *Hair*, it focuses on individual profiles culled from a kind of ethnographic research, but importantly dealing more deliberately with homosexuality than did *Hair* (if less so with race). *A Chorus Line*, taking its cue from the backstage musical as a subgenre, engages with the here and now of performance, basing its situation and character types on the realities of the life experiences of actual dancers in the 1970s, through a scenario that plays out as an event in real time, with an excitement approaching that of competitive sports. Its treatment of homosexuality was considered especially daring in its time, even given recent filmic treatments such as *Midnight Cowboy* (1969) or the film version of *Cabaret* (1972). The centerpiece for this dimension of *A Chorus Line* is Paul's monologue detailing his experiences as a gay dancer, which many homosexuals found inspiring and even empowering. Yet, considering the show's daring treatment of other frankly sexual themes (as in "Dance Ten, Looks Three," better known by its hook, "Tits and Ass"), some aspects of Paul's treatment in the show were astonishingly timid. After Zach (the white director) pressures Paul (the son of Puerto Rican immigrants) into telling his story, Paul falls and injures himself, giving him greater dramatic importance but eliminating him from contention. Moreover, this plot device not only conforms to longstanding tropes regarding tragic alterities but also excuses the show from having to clarify how much, if at all, his being a "tortured gay" might have mattered in the selection process. In coercing Paul to "come out" as he is auditioning for a "normal" show after performing in the Jewel Box Revue, which Paul terms "the asshole of show business,"[9] Zach, and the show itself, seem oblivious to Paul's desperate need to deny his own difference, to return to whatever closet might be left for him. To be sure, this callousness is consistent with the show's troubling outcome, in which the selected dancers, whose individuation has provided the primary dramatic arc of the show, perform the ironically titled "One" in such synchrony that audiences can no longer tell them apart. Yet even this does not efface the very important work that *A Chorus Line* performed for many gay men, in giving Paul one of the most moving monologues of the show.

In common to all these shows—aside from their ability to engage audiences in new ways—were relatively low ongoing production costs, which undoubtedly played a key role in their long runs. But even during *A Chorus Line*'s run, this possible route for sustaining a megahit, common as well to off-Broadway shows such as *The Fantasticks* and *Godspell*, was about to disappear with the emergence of the megamusical.

THE MEGAMUSICAL

The phrase "Golden Age," as noted, indicates a subsequent "after," implying that later works are for the most part lesser: less important, less tasteful, less artistic. There are exceptions, of course: the post-1960s work of Stephen Sondheim (much of it subsidized by the nest egg that *Fiddler on the Roof* provided Hal Prince) is often held up by critics and fans as the height of importance, taste, and artistry in the musical. But Sondheim's work is often valorized *contra* the megamusical and musicals that follow in its commercial and aesthetic footsteps—dissonant, intellectual, and challenging, compared to the blockbuster hits the megamusical offers up to the masses.

The arrival of the megamusical on Broadway coincides with the visible gentrification of Times Square, the result of ongoing changes and a series of policies put in place over the preceding decade. Business policies and enforcement of standards of decency in and around Times Square were enacted by New York City Mayor Ed Koch to squeeze out the porn and grindhouse theatres and sex shops that were scaring away moneyed tourists. When Rudolph Giuliani took office in 1994, the so-called "Disneyfication" of Times Square reached its zenith: increased police presence cracked down on street vendors; strip bars were run out of business along with long-standing local bookshops, bars, and diners; and residents in low-rent facilities were pressured to leave so that high-end residences and tourist-friendly attractions could be built. The State of New York took possession of nine historic theatres on 42nd Street for renovation, among them the New Amsterdam Theatre, which The Walt Disney Company acquired on a forty-nine-year lease, completing renovations in time to premiere their visually extravagant musical production of *The Lion King* (1997). As the physical locale of the musical in America was gutted and reformed to capture the tourist audience, the megamusical was at the same time reshaping the musical as a genre to appeal to this broader base. Prior to World War II, the primary ticket buyers for Broadway shows constituted a relatively local audience until the show went on tour. The megamusical, building deliberately on the international success of the megahits discussed above, cast its eye on international audiences from the very beginnings of production, adopting new approaches to spectacle, marketing, and mass media. In these ways, the Broadway musical after 1980 makes its way back into popular culture through the reach of the large conglomerates that provided its principal backing.

Megamusicals are shows that share specific musical, technological, and commercial characteristics, usually combining spectacular visuals with operatic and pop influences and elaborate sound design, and having large, international financial stakes. Quintessential megamusicals of the 1980s and 1990s include Andrew Lloyd Webber's *Cats* (1981) and *Phantom of the Opera* (1986), the Schönberg-Boublil shows *Les Misérables* (1985) and *Miss Saigon* (1989), and Disney's adaptations of their feature films such as *Beauty and the Beast* (1994) and *The Lion King*. Megamusicals are produced by global companies, including Disney, Cameron Mackintosh, and Andrew Lloyd Webber's Really Useful Group, which bring the capital backing to invest in expensive productions, and provide extensive marketing resources and are capable of holding out for a long period of time to recoup their initial financial output. Advertising is one significant way in which the megamusical changes what had been done before on Broadway—carefully crafted logos and filmic taglines such as "No Day But Today" for *Rent* (1996) are emblazoned on t-shirts, posters, and myriad other merchandise. These adoptions of marketing strategies from the megamusical, in particular, become even more significant given that *Rent* in other ways seemed to stand apart from the type, as a "downtown" show that, like *Hair* and *A Chorus Line*, was developed through a kind of ethnographic research and aspired to a kind of gritty realism that large-scale productions tended to forego.[10] Logos, as brands, transfer easily across nations—as Sternfeld and Wollman point out with the logo created for *Cats*, whose golden eyes with dancing human-cat-like figures tell you all you need to know without words—thus making room for international franchising of these big, accessible shows that can be ported anywhere with the same wordless logos.[11]

Broadway's cohort of critics were not entirely welcoming of the megamusical; perhaps they sensed their inevitable obsolescence with regard to the genre, for it was soon shown that the megamusical—like *Abie's Irish Rose*, a full century in the past, as of this writing—did not need rave critical reviews to survive and thrive. Frank Rich wrote a particularly aggressive review of *Phantom of the Opera* in *The New York Times* with a deliberately provocative use of a phrase from the German national anthem that came to have Nazi associations, since it aligned with their belief in cultural and racial superiority: "*The Phantom of the Opera* is as much a victory of dynamic stagecraft over musical kitsch as it is a triumph of merchandising über alles..."[12] Without explicitly stating it, the review points to this international, imported megamusical as a threat to the Broadway stage. With the arrival of the megamusical, for the first time since the early years of American musical theatre, a non-American theatrical style came to dominate the American stage.

Visual and aural spectacle have long been important traits of the musical: as already noted, impressive sets, large casts, dancers in revealing costumes, and great singers are all part of the thrilling effect of a performance. With the megamusical, modern technology is employed to manipulate massive stage machinery: the helicopter landing in *Miss Saigon,* the barricade in *Les Misérables,* ramps and gates and staircases in *Phantom of the Opera,* the ascending tire in *Cats.* Theatres are rebuilt or renovated to accommodate the large set pieces and update the machinery and computers needed to move them. Stage machinery is automated, moving according to computerized cues, and conductors in pit orchestras have timing cues to hit, sometimes needing to wear headphones so they can hear click tracks that keep everything synchronized and running on schedule. These looming set pieces can make the human bodies onstage seem smaller; and while great singers are still a must, the megamusical is less about a single, fantastic person dominating the stage as the show's star (as in Ethel Merman star vehicles) than it is about the performers being part of an assemblage of carefully choreographed parts. As with Golden-Age musicals, performers who originate a role are remembered and celebrated, their voices persisting as a key text of the show, as original cast recordings and special legacy performances are filmed, recorded, or televised. But only the most dedicated fans can keep up with the hundreds of people who have played these roles across the decades in thousands of performances (*The Phantom of the Opera,* pictured in a celebratory performance in Figure 6.1, is the longest running show on Broadway as of April 2023, and had been staged over 13,000 times by 2019, with over twenty-four actors playing the title role at the Majestic Theatre).

Figure 6.1: Gesturing toward the longevity of *The Phantom of the Opera,* four Phantoms joined Christine at the 25th anniversary celebration in 2011 at the Royal Albert Hall to sing the title song; from left to right, John Owen-Jones, Hugo Panaro, Sierra Boggess, Ramin Karimloo, Peter Joback. Screenshot from filmed performance[13]

Hair and *Jesus Christ Superstar* were unique in their time for their use of amplified sound via actors using handheld microphones; the sonic production of the megamusical, now prevalent on Broadway, turns the theatre into a live mixing session. Performers are fitted with body mics that amplify their voices, and sound systems are installed to allow for real-time mixing with the amplified instruments in the pit orchestra, resulting in a sound that is more akin to the sound of a professional recording rather than a live performance.[14] Music in the megamusical is written to take advantage of the mics, allowing pop vocals to be heard over amplified instruments in large spaces. During the title song of *The Phantom of the Opera*, for example, the Phantom and Christine appear in near-darkness on a bridge partway up the proscenium, and then criss-cross their way down dramatically lit and moving bridges until they reach a radio-controlled boat on the stage; much of this spectacle is accomplished with body-doubles and pre-recorded tracks that allow the key performers to safely negotiate their way through complicated set changes.

Megamusicals tend to tell stories that are broadly applicable, without overly detailed intricacies that an audience must understand for the show as a whole to make sense; plot coherence is not necessarily as important as emotional impact. The megamusical also tends to be more conservative with regard to gender roles and sexual identity. In both respects, the megamusical is designed for export, employing a mode of storytelling that lends itself to an ease of translation for international markets. But some early examples required a process of revision to make them viable abroad. *Les Misérables* (1985) started out as a French concept album and partially-staged performance based on Victor Hugo's 1862 novel, for which lyricist Alain Boublil and composer Claude-Michel Schönberg wrote a series of songs to play out *en tableaux*. Since for its initial audience *Les Misérables* was a familiar text widely read in school by many of their generation, the writers eschewed a detailed retelling of the plot in favor of musically highlighting several key emotional moments. When producer Cameron Mackintosh brought *Les Misérables* to London, having just opened *Cats* on Broadway, he adapted it into English, bringing in Trevor Nunn to direct the show and to help reinstate the narrative and musical traditions of English-language musical theatre storytelling, with the characters streamlined from general pop voices into more clearly delimited musical theatre types: Valjean the tenor and noble hero, Javert the brooding baritone, Marius and Cosette the operetta-style romantic couple, and Fantine and Eponine the tragic belters. The topic of the musical centers around general tropes of unrequited love and sacrifice, and historically unspecific themes of rebellion against injustice—all contributing to an ease of translation across national boundaries. The music works to maintain emotional continuity even when the narrative connections are tenuous—familiar melodies are repeated across the show and used for a variety of scenarios, giving listeners a sense of a unified musical tapestry (a device already well-known to audiences through such through-composed scores as *Sweeney Todd* and *Evita*). In Valjean's death scene, he sings a duet with the ghost of Fantine, recalling their duet in the Prologue, "Come to Me," a remnant from the French concept album, where Fantine sang the feature song "L'air de la Misère," itself ultimately adapted in the English production into a second act feature for Eponine, "On My Own." With no apparent narrative justification other than that the melody is "her song" (and also that she is dead), the ghost of Eponine appears to join them. The London production represents both a triumph of spectacle and of marketing: the barricade that constructs and deconstructs itself before the eyes of the audience, and the iconic logo of little Cosette, adapted by Russ Eglin from the nineteenth century engraving by Emile Bayard for Hugo's book. The logo is endlessly adapted with various national signifiers as the show opened in theatres around the world (Cosette in a Viking helmet for Denmark; Maria von Trapp's skirts for Vienna, Statue of Liberty crown and torch for America, and, oddest of all, a beret and Eiffel tower for Paris), and is eventually paired with a matching tagline: "The world's favorite musical." The transnational appeal of *Les Misérables* is reinforced and reflected in the recorded concert performance at Royal Albert Hall in honor of the show's 10th anniversary. After the final bows, a procession of flags and men in tuxedos walk down the center aisle through the applauding audience and join the onstage cast. As an encore, the evening's Valjean (played by Colm Wilkinson, originator of the role in London) kicks off a reprise of "Do You Hear the People Sing." After singing a couple of phrases, he hands the mic off to Phil Cavill, then playing Valjean in the West End, who sings a line before a Valjean from France takes over and sings in

French, followed by Valjeans from Germany, Japan, Hungary, Sweden, Poland, the Netherlands, Canada, Austria, Australia, Norway, the Czech Republic, Denmark, Ireland, Iceland, and the United States, each singing a line in their native language. The performance is simultaneously a demonstration of the international success of the musical and an example of the megamusical being increasingly marked by practices of standardization. Standardization is desired by production companies, since it assures the ongoing currency of a marketable product. Audiences can expect a similar theatergoing experience even if they see the musical in two different cities and recommend it to friends in far-flung places, their purchased merchandise is relevant across the globe.

The success of the megamusical shifts the expectations of audiences and changes how the musical theatre business is done. *Wicked* (2003), written by musical theatre veteran Stephen Schwartz (*Godspell*, 1971; *Pippin*, 1972), is another example of the critic-proof show that the era of the megamusical enabled—although *Wicked* received mixed reviews when it opened, it quickly became a commercial smash hit. By 2006, it was simultaneously playing on Broadway, Chicago, Los Angeles, and London, and with a national touring company. While certain aspects of the megamusical model are clearly adapted for *Wicked*—the marketing, the spectacle and technological wizardry, the pop-influenced songwriting—its popularity and ongoing success was owed in part, as Stacy Wolf points out, to its active fandom of tween and teenage girls who related in a variety of ways to the two leading women, Elphaba and Glinda.[15] This was an audience base the show's creators had targeted from the start, the probable impetus for Stephen Schwartz to ask Winnie Holzman—the creator of a short-lived but beloved TV show about contemporary high school life, *My So-Called Life* (1994–1995)—to write the book. The show made deliberate efforts to be relatable and progressive, dealing more frankly with youth issues in negotiating relationships, bullying, and homophobia than other shows of its time, just as *So-Called* had done relative to television norms. Along these lines, when Schwartz wrote the culminating duet for Glinda and Elphaba, "For Good," he conducted an interview with his pre-teen daughter, asking her what she might say to her best friend if she had to say goodbye forever, or for good.

BREAKING THE FRAME

The megamusical has often been perceived as a threat to the musical, imposing a frame on it and stifling its continued development. As noted near the beginning of this chapter, the megamusical echoes the earlier frame of Gilbert and Sullivan's operettas in "[infiltrating] the terrain of musicals while also sustaining companies dedicated … to their performance." Unlike Gilbert and Sullivan operettas, however, megamusicals occupy important turf on Broadway, sometimes for decades. Yet there is much to indicate that the megamusical's sway is not absolute, nor even, perhaps, absolutist.

For one thing, infiltration cuts both ways; some shows, such as *Rent* and even *Wicked*, in conforming to earlier principles of construction and production, seem more dressed up as megamusicals than *actual* mega musicals. Indeed, it is telling that both these shows, like an earlier generation of megahits, seek and find new audiences. The *Chicago* revival is a latter-day example of a megahit that is too minimalist in its presentation to be considered a megamusical. And shows like *Dear Evan Hansen* (Broadway, 2016–2022) demonstrate the continued viability of seeking out new audiences and new presentational modes, of following an established, innovative line of development without becoming simply nostalgic. Yet, while *Dear Evan Hansen* reflects many of the commercial and aesthetic strategies of the megamusical, it departs in a significant way: the subject matter is not broad and historically unspecific— rather, it hinges on a cultural history of social media that quickly became dated (as the generally panned 2021 film adaptation unintentionally demonstrated).

Even the much-criticized habit of adapting movies to the Broadway stage, which can certainly end up in megamusical territory, can succeed while pointing in more traditional, even intimate directions, as with *Once* (2011), *Groundhog Day* (London, 2016; Broadway 2017), and *The Band's Visit* (2017). Minimalist ensemble casts sustained *A Gentleman's Guide to Love and Murder* (2013) and *Come from Away* (2018), while minimalist reconsiderations of older shows, such as *Chicago* (originally staged in 1975), or John Doyle's Sondheim revivals (especially *Sweeney Todd*, London, 2004 and Broadway, 2005; and *Company*, 2006)—the latter with onstage instrumentations managed by actors—show continued possibilities for success with smaller productions if rarely producing megahits. And the relatively new Broadway composer Dave Malloy, best-known for *Natasha, Pierre & The Great Comet of 1812* (2016), seems to change his presentational spots with each new show with optimism for the future of a still-developing genre that is infectious. But perhaps the best indicator for the continued development of the musical, as such, is Broadway's habit of honoring innovation, whether through reviews or through awards. There is, as yet, no Tony Award for longest running musical.

NOTES

1 Our focus excludes long-running shows in more modest or remote theatrical venues, in particular off-Broadway shows such as *The Threepenny Opera*, *The Fantasticks*, and *Godspell*.

2 Regarding these two types of operetta and their eventual evolution into the "musical play" (better known as the "integrated musical"), see Raymond Knapp, "Camping along the American Operetta Divide (on the Road to the Musical Play)" (*Cambridge Companion to Operetta*, pp. 120–134); see Bordman for a somewhat different typology.

3 Bernard Grun, *Gold and Silver: The Life and Times of Franz Lehar* (New York: David McKay Company, 1970), 129.

4 Baz Kershaw "Curiosity or Contempt: On Spectacle, the Human, and Activism." *Theatre Journal* 55, no. 4, Theater and Activism (Dec. 2003): 592.

5 See Mark N. Grant, *The Rise and Fall of the Broadway Musical* (Boston: Northeastern University Press, 2005) for an extended (and rancorous) argument for this periodization.

6 Andrea Most. *Making Americans: Jews and the Broadway Musical*. Cambridge: Harvard University Press, 2004.

7 Joseph Stein, who wrote the book for *Fiddler*, recounts the producer of the first Tokyo production expressing surprise that the show had done well in New York, since "it's so Japanese." See Stein, "*Fiddler on the Roof* and me," *The Guardian* May 18, 2007 (https://www.theguardian.com/stage/theatreblog/2007/may/18/fiddlerontheroofandme, accessed May 12, 2022).

8 Dale Wasserman. *The Impossible Musical: The "Man of La Mancha" Story* (New York: Applause Books, 2003), pp. 13, 321, 323.

9 In a move that marginalizes gay life and representation in favor of the (white, heterosexual) mainstream, Paul refers here to the Jewel Box Revue in terms inconsistent with its being a much-acclaimed, racially integrated drag show that was itself a megahit of sorts, running for over three decades.

10 David Savran critiques *Rent* for cultivating a veneer of "gritty" urban authenticity while simultaneously being a megahit investing in an expensive, coordinated marketing campaign. David Savran, *A Queer Sort of Materialism: Recontextualizing American Theater*. Ann Arbor: University of Michigan Press, 2003.

11 Jessica Sternfeld and Elizabeth L. Wollman, "After the Golden Age." *Oxford Handbook of the American Musical,* ed. Raymond Knapp, Mitchell Morris, Stacy Wolf. Oxford: Oxford University Press, 2011.

12 Frank Rich, "Theater Review: The Phantom of the Opera," *The New York Times*, Jan 27, 1988. The lyric in question was written in 1841 by August Heinrich Hoffmann von Fallersleben, to a tune by Joseph Haydn written in 1797 to celebrate Kaiser Franz.

13 Figure screenshotted from *The Phantom of the Opera at Royal Albert Hall*, the 25th Anniversary Performance filmed on October 2, 2011. https://www.youtube.com/watch?v=_8cXwAs0SZE (accessed November 1, 2022).

14 Jonathan Burston, "Theater Space as Virtual Place: Audio Technology, the Reconfigured Singing Body, and the Megamusical." *Popular Music* 17, no. 2 (May 1998): 205–218.

15 Stacy Wolf, *Changed for Good: A Feminist History of the Broadway Musical*. New York: Oxford University Press, 2010.

RECOMMENDATIONS FOR ADDITIONAL RESOURCES

Knapp, Raymond. *The American Musical and the Performance of Personal Identity*. Princeton: Princeton University Press, 2006.

This thematic approach to musicals explores how they allow writers, performers, and audiences to explore personal identities, organized by categories and themes including operetta, gender and sexuality, relationships, and idealism.

Replogle-Wong, Holley Dawn. "Crossover and Spectacle in American Operetta and the Megamusical." University of California, Los Angeles PhD dissertation, 2009.

This is a cross-historical analysis of the reception of operetta and the megamusical in America through the lens of American cultural hierarchies, including extended discussions of *The Merry Widow* and *The Phantom of the Opera*.

Stempel, Larry. *Showtime: A History of the Broadway Musical Theater*. New York: W. W. Norton, 2010.

This is a history of the Broadway musical from the nineteenth-century *The Black Crook* through the early twenty-first-century megamusical and "movical" (musicals based on films).

Sternfeld, Jessica. *The Megamusical*. Bloomington and Indianapolis: Indiana University Press, 2006.

This pioneering treatment of megamusicals considers their musical and theatrical qualities alongside commercial concerns to illuminate their success and popularity.

CHAPTER 7

Global musical hits beyond American shores

Olaf Jubin

The Broadway theatre community justly prides itself today on its acceptance of all ethnic minorities, genders, and sexual orientations. That openness, however, does not extend to shows from a diverse background: musicals that originated outside the United States, and became smash hits in their home country and elsewhere. These productions have a decidedly checkered reception history in New York; many global successes did not even make it to the "**Great White Way**."

With the aim of exploring potential reasons for the on-going resistance of the American musical theatre industry to foreign influences, this chapter will present case studies of works from five different countries (Canada, Britain, France, Austria, and Sweden). All of these have achieved outstanding financial success, including listings in the *Guinness Book of Records* for holding various attendance and producing records, while some also have received critical praise, attesting to their artistic success as well. None of these shows has been seen on Broadway stages, apart from *Starlight Express* (1984), which has never been revived. In the order in which they have attempted to gain access to the US market, these are: *Anne of Green Gables* (1965), *Starlight Express* (1987), *Notre-Dame de Paris* (1998), the various hit musicals devised by librettist/lyricist Michael Kunze and *Kristina från Duvemåla* (1995).

ANNE OF GREEN GABLES—TOO GENTEEL FOR BROADWAY

Since its publication 115 years ago, Lucy Maud Montgomery's *Anne of Green Gables* has not only become a classic of children's literature,

 DOI: 10.4324/9781003256458-8

but an international bestseller with sales topping 50 million.[1] Four major TV adaptations (in 1972, 1979, 1985, and 2017–2019) are a testament to the book's continuous popularity, and television is also the starting point for *Anne of Green Gables—the Musical*: a live version of the show with music by Norman Campbell and a libretto by Don Harron and lyrics by Harron, Campbell and his wife Elaine, as well as Mavor Moore, which was aired by the Canadian Broadcasting Corporation (CBC) in 1956.

Eight years later, when Moore was appointed Director-General of the new Confederation Centre of the Arts in Charlottetown, Prince Edward Island, he established the Charlottetown Festival and scheduled the musical for its first year (1965) —after all, Anne's adventures take place on the very same isle. Since then, the musical has been performed at the festival every year, except for 2020 and 2021 because of the pandemic, making it the world's "longest running annual musical theatre production."[2] Although the Charlottetown staging mainly attracts American theatregoers, the show has never been produced on Broadway, not least because its creators felt it was not suited for the "Great White Way."[3] Moore insisted that *Anne* "simply does not have the hard edge that Broadway absolutely required. It's gentle, it's flowing."[4] Don Harron agreed: "We learned long ago it's not that kind of show. *Anne of Green Gables* is not *Annie*."[5]

This impression may have been formed by the reception their work received when it was exported to the West End. The 1969 London production ran for 319 performances without turning a profit, because, according to its producer Bill Freedman, the show "never caught on with adult audiences."[6] While reviews were generally very positive in the British capital, the musical was praised in terms similar to those used by the New York critics when a regional tour of the show played for two weeks at New York's City Centre during Christmas 1971: even the most enthusiastic notices employ benign adjectives like "disarming and likeable"[7] or "warmly charming."[8] Walter Kerr from *The New York Times* attacked *Anne* for its "deliberate simplicity"[9]; this only reinforced the notion that *Anne* has a delicate sensibility that may connect with audiences in Japan, where the book and the musical have an ardent fan base, but which is incompatible with the forceful emotions expected of a typical American show and the hardened disposition of New York theatre professionals as well as theatre-goers.[10] Harron observed this first hand: "I have been at many Broadway openings and seen the brittle sophistication of the first niters [sic] who were much more interested in being seen than seeing anything on that stage..."[11]

STARLIGHT EXPRESS – REJECTED BY BROADWAY; EMBRACED BY GERMANY

In the Anglophone world of musical theatre, Andrew Lloyd Webber's *Starlight Express* is rarely spoken about. Often categorized as the composer's weakest work, the various monographs about the composer give it short shrift. Michael Walsh states categorically, "[t]he score does not warrant close inspection,"[12] while John Snelson, in a more forgiving mood, declares it "musically [...] no more than a stopgap."[13]

The show's failure in New York, where it lost most of its $8 million investment, may be the reason why it is chiefly remembered as "that roller-skating musical." However, in London, the show lasted for 7,406 performances, yet that impressive achievement pales next to the reception it received following its 1988 export to an industrial town in West Germany: when the musical opened in Bochum's custom-built Starlight Halle (pictured in Figure 7.1), nobody expected it to still be racing around the auditorium there 34 years later. With over 17 million tickets sold since 1988, the production is in the *Guinness Book of Records* for "the most visitors to a musical in a single theatre."[14]

What allowed the German *Starlight* to transfer so successfully and to become a fixture in that country's popular culture? One answer may be that in contrast to other long-running musicals, the Bochum production has over the decades repeatedly altered its score, characters, and marketing to reflect changes in musical tastes, gender perceptions, and technology.

When production company Stella AG, co-founded and run by Friedrich Kurz, contemplated presenting *Starlight* in the Ruhrgebiet, the region around the river Ruhr, they could not find a suitable venue. Following World War II, all of Germany's

Figure 7.1: The Starlight Halle, the custom-built theatre in Bochum, Germany

theatres were subsidized and thus owned by the respective city or region. Organized as repertory companies, they were not available for open-ended runs. Kurz negotiated with the city of Bochum to build a brand-new venue for the show at a cost of 25 million Deutschmarks/$13.35 million; the Starlight Halle would be situated near one of the region's main motorways, allowing easy access to visitors from afar.[15]

Thus, while previous productions of the roller-skating spectacle in London and New York were "site-*responsive*" with director Trevor Nunn and designer John Napier adapting the Apollo Victoria and Gershwin Theatres, respectively, to their needs, in Bochum the show actually was "site-*specific*," with a stage measuring 1,200 sqm^2 and two racetracks going directly through the auditorium.

The German *Starlight Express* premiered on 12 June 1988. Overall, the critical response, although not quite as negative as the one in New York, was rather tepid, on a par with the verdict of the London reviewers.[16] The lukewarm notices certainly did not help the Bochum production to attract theatregoers, yet they were not the only reason why the auditorium of the Starlight Halle was half-empty in the first few months: for many tourists, Bochum, in the country's major center for coal mining and steel factories, was simply not an attractive destination. The fate of the German *Starlight* only reversed once its producers changed their marketing strategy a year into the run. Instead of targeting the culturally inclined, it now emphasized the musical's athletic qualities.[17] Around this time the slogan "the fastest show on earth" was born and publicity started to stress that the performers barreled down the racetracks at 60 kmh/37.3 mph. The new figure kickstarted an interest in the production which has lasted to this day. Soon tourism to Bochum picked up and hotel bookings increased by 100%.

Over the years, *Starlight* has added open days with backstage tours, as well as sing-along events and has established a social media presence that includes its own YouTube channel. The show has also been kept in the public eye by three cast albums; the 1989 complete live recording gained Platinum status in 2005 for selling over 400,000 copies. There have also been tie-ins with Europe's biggest manufacturer of toy trains, Märklin, which over the years designed various model trains based on the musical's characters, including a "25th anniversary" special edition in 2013.

Since its première, the Bochum *Starlight Express* has changed ownership several times, a clear indication of how volatile and risky the German-language musical theatre market is for private producers. The first of these producers, the Stella AG, had to declare bankruptcy in 2002. The rights were then acquired by producers Thomas Krauth and Michael Brenner. Their musical and ticketing conglomerate was taken over by Maik Klokow in 2009, who sold it in 2018 to the London-based Ambassador Theatre Group. Throughout these drastic changes behind the scenes, the Bochum *Starlight* has managed to sustain its public profile and maintain its audience. Evidently, the various owners of the intellectual property wisely decided not to interfere with a production that was resilient and had proved profitable.

Walsh asserts that Lloyd Webber "frankly was seeking a hit" when writing the roller-skating extravaganza.[18] Yet none of the show's numbers entered the charts, which helps to explain why its list of songs has been tampered with repeatedly over the last 38 years. In addition, since the score is grounded in popular music, which transforms with each generation, the composer insists that "*Starlight Express* by its nature has to change"[19] because, as Michael Coveney points out, "[t]he targets keep moving."[20] Consequently, there were numerous adjustments to the German *Starlight* in 2003, 2008, 2013, and 2018, usually coinciding with a major anniversary of the production.

Over the years, trains have been cut, added, or renamed; to increase excitement and spectacle, ever since 2003, stunt skaters (who do not sing), have been hired. In reference to the 2016 referendum, the British locomotive "Brexit," the "train that goes nowhere," joined the line-up four years ago.

Most widely publicized was the 2018 decision to change the gender of two characters as a means of strengthening the female roles: Rusty's confidante Poppa became Momma, while French engine Bobo was turned into Coco. In the same spirit, other trains have been reconceived as gender-neutral: Rocky 3, Wrench, Volta, Manga, and Brexit—although primarily meant to be female, female, male, male and male, respectively—may now be played by an actor of a different gender should vacations, injuries, etc. of the original performer warrant it. These changes to the gender of the locomotives and carriages go some way to address the musical's problematic portrayal of the sexes, yet one wonders why the creatives waited 34 years to reconceive it, considering that the show was already accused of sexism when it opened in 1984.

In May 2018, in time for its upcoming 30th anniversary, the Bochum production closed for a month to rehearse new material and to implement some architectural and technological changes. The Starlight Halle received a 4.5 million Euro facelift: it gained a new foyer as well as completely new sound and lighting equipment. The orchestrations were revised towards 1980s rock. Arlene Phillips was promoted to Choreographer-Director and John Napier updated several of his costumes.

Since it is not customary in Germany to declare licensing and weekly running costs or box-office receipts, it is difficult to estimate the profit *Starlight Express* generates. However, since the millennium, the number of visitors has been well above 400,000 per year, which, for a theatre of 1,650 seats and a show with 360–375 annual performances, amounts to an average attendance of around 70% of capacity.[21] Clearly, this constitutes enough interest in the production to keep it in the black.

NOTRE-DAME DE PARIS—TOO DIFFERENT IN FORM

Though a phenomenon not widely known in the United Kingdom or the United States, the French have, since the 1970s, developed their own form of musical theatre which mostly comprises works based on popular novels, plays, or films. These musical productions are usually performed in huge venues like sports "palaces" or rock arenas, a choice dictated by the fact that neither the subsidized French playhouses nor the boulevard theatres present open-ended runs of musicals. In order for the story, acting, staging and choreography to be comprehended by an audience of up to 5,000 people, these musicals have to be big and spectacular, which explains the French term *spectacle musical*.

The most successful of these works is *Notre-Dame de Paris* (1998), an adaptation of Victor Hugo's classic 1831 novel *The Hunchback of Notre-Dame*. The musicalization by Richard Cocciante and Luc Plamondon sold 2.5 million cast albums in France, Belgium and Switzerland, with an additional 450,000 copies in Canada. The first staging in Paris, which attracted 550,000 people, was followed by sold-out tours through French-speaking countries and a highly popular production in South Korea.[22] All in all, the musical has been staged in 20 countries, including Italy, Spain, Japan, China, Poland, and Russia. In an English translation, the Hugo adaptation played for 17 months in London and—in a shortened version—briefly in Las Vegas.

As it is still cheaper to stage a musical in London than it is in New York, the producers of *Notre-Dame de Paris* decided to first present their hit in the West End before even considering a move to Broadway. With union rules being more relaxed, a production in the British capital also allowed them to import three of their original lead actors, Garou, Daniel Lavoie, and Bruno Pelletier.

The very first *spectacle musical*, Alain Boublil and Claude-Michel Schönberg's *La Révolution Française* (1973), was inspired by *Jesus Christ Superstar*, and all of the musical dramas that followed in its wake took their cue for the treatment of dramaturgy from the 1970 British rock opera: not only did they dispense with dialogue, but they relied on the audience to fill in any gaps in the storytelling, which at times was reduced to the absolute minimum. Expecting the audience to share at least a rudimentary acquaintance with the source narrative, the creators of a *spectacle musical* forego a detailed recounting of the plot and any exposition that sets up the characters. Instead, the songwriters musicalize peak moments of the story, key scenes that even people who haven't read the book or seen the movie might recall, so that it is fitting to describe them as "loosely based" on their sources.

In other words, the dramaturgy of a *spectacle musical* doesn't follow that of a traditional American or British musical, with the narrative material carefully shaped as, for instance, an introduction, action intensifying to a climax and resolution. To an Anglophone audience used to these dramaturgical conceits, a French musical seems to have no narrative drive; it may feel static. A similar lack of a dramatic arc can often be observed in the musical numbers themselves, which mainly are "I am" (or "I feel") songs. The opening number of *Notre-Dame de Paris*, "Les Temps de Cathédrales," and the show's big hit song, the trio "Belle," are typical examples: they develop neither musically nor lyrically, instead repeating the same motifs over and over again in the manner of a pop song.

Consequently, a *spectacle musical* has a completely different approach to the narrative than a West End or Broadway show, which is why it is misleading to label it a "musical" for an English-speaking audience. That entrepreneurs have insisted on doing so has been their undoing, since this terminology raised expectations their productions simply could not fulfil. The reactions of London critics when this French "musical" crossed the Channel in the early 2000s are telling: the show got devastating notices, with most critics castigating the creative team for its presumed lack of dramaturgical know-how. In the opinion of the *Independent on Sunday*, "*Notre-Dame de Paris* makes no effort to dramatise the story or waste any time on characters or scenes. [...] There's no pause, no reflection, no dramatic insight."[23] Clearly, instead of being judged in terms of criteria appropriate to French musical theatre, *Notre-Dame de Paris* was evaluated according to standards it didn't even attempt to meet.

THE OEUVRE OF MICHAEL KUNZE: THE HIT-MAKER UNLUCKY WITH HIS COLLABORATORS

In the early 1990s the subsidized Vereinigte Bühnen Wien moved away from importing British blockbuster musicals like *Cats* and *The Phantom of the Opera* to producing home-grown offerings. The Viennese production company soon—and repeatedly—struck gold with works by librettist Michael Kunze. Over the course of fifteen years, the Grammy Award-winner conceived four long-running shows that were later successfully exported to neighboring countries such as Germany, Italy, and Switzerland, while also finding favor with East Asian and Eastern European theatregoers.[24]

With Serbian-Hungarian composer Sylvester Levay, Kunze created the two biographical musicals *Elisabeth* (1992) and *Mozart!* (1999), as well as the Daphne du Maurier adaptation, *Rebecca* (2006). Kunze had another smash in 1997 with the horror comedy *Dance of the Vampires*, based on the 1967 Roman Polanski film with the same title and featuring music by Jim Steinman.[25]

Buoyed by so much global appreciation, it is not surprising that the author may also have hoped to conquer Broadway. However, all of Kunze's works have a European setting (the Austro-Hungarian Empire, Transylvania and England) and are based on intellectual properties which are more popular outside North America, like *Dance of the Vampires* and *Rebecca* which means that the subjects of his musicals do not immediately appeal to producers on the "Great White Way." More importantly, Kunze has been rather unfortunate in the directors and producers he worked or was obliged to work with as they made it either improbable or impossible for his shows to successfully transfer to Broadway.

His two biographical musicals *Elisabeth* and *Mozart!* are steeped in Austrian history, as they cover the lives of Austrian Empress Elisabeth (1837–1898) and Wolfgang Amadeus Mozart (1756–1791), respectively. The former may be an especially tough sell on Broadway, not least because in German-language territories, the musical is closely linked to a pop culture phenomenon that is virtually unheard of in the United States: the *Sissi* film trilogy (1955–1957)[26] became one of the biggest box-office sensations of the decade and was seen by 25 million people in Germany and Austria alone.

For a long time, Michael Kunze, a historian by training, had wanted to write a musical about the fall of the House of Habsburg. When he settled on Empress Elisabeth as the perfect character to illustrate the decline of this dynasty he was determined to correct the powerful, but historically false image of the sweet, nature-loving royal instilled in several generations of audiences by that movie trilogy. Instead, he portrayed the Empress as "a woman fighting for her freedom, far ahead of her time."[27]

When it premiered in 1992, *Elisabeth* failed to attract much attention beyond the German-language media; later, one of the few international reviews decried its "shopworn feminist uplift," further dimming the prospects of a West End or Broadway staging.[28] Still, *Elisabeth* turned into a massive hit. In the Theater an der Wien it ran in repertory for 6 seasons and 1,279 performances, selling 1.25 million tickets.[29] Since then, it has been revived three times (2003, 2012, and 2019) in the Austrian capital. Although never quite equaling that success, the 1999 production of *Mozart!* was another audience favorite, and racked up 419 performances.

While the Austria-centric subjects of these two musicals may give US backers pause, their scenic presentation may be even more alien to Broadway. The Viennese productions by opera luminary Harry Kupfer are prime examples of the kind of European *Regietheater* that to this day is rare—and even more rarely appreciated—in a Broadway musical. They employ striking stage pictures courtesy of set designer Hans Schavernoch, which as is common for opera directors, are framing devices, making intellectual statements without serving to clarify the narrative. Thus, both shows cannot simply be imported with all their design elements intact, as so many British hits have; they would need to be completely re-conceived and re-staged.

Upon its cinematic release in 1967, Roman Polanski's film parody *The Fearless Vampire Killers* was panned by most US critics. Retitled

Dance of the Vampires, the spoof became a cult classic in Continental Europe, not least because it was regularly broadcast on television. Its 1997 musical incarnation with direction by Polanski himself ran for 27 months in Vienna, and then also found an enthusiastic audience abroad. But when the musical was exported to New York in 2002, producer David Sonnenberg decided that the show needed a complete overhaul. This included, of course, replacing the original director, since Polanski's legal troubles meant that he could not travel to the United States for fear of being arrested.

Because *The Producers* had just swept the Tony Awards and become a massive hit, it was decided to transform the through-sung gothic rock opera into a rambunctious, knowingly vulgar musical comedy. Playwright David Ives was brought in to add humor in the style of Mel Brooks.[30] The main draw for audiences was Michael Crawford, in his first Broadway appearance since *The Phantom of the Opera* 14 years earlier. In order to secure the star, the producer granted Crawford creative control over his material. Fearing that the role of vampire Graf von Krolock as originally written was too close to his Phantom, Crawford insisted on drastic changes to make the character less serious, affecting a bizarre accent that mixed Italian and Cockney, designing his own costumes and writing his own punchlines.[31] Moreover, both the show's new director John Rando and choreographer John Carrafa struggled; at a loss regarding how to stage the big dance numbers, the latter simply advised the performers "Just rock on!."[32] Despite an extended preview period of 61 performances, the production was such a fiasco that composer Steinman refused to attend the opening night. Lambasted by the critics, the show closed after 56 performances with a loss of $12 million dollars and remains one of the costliest flops in Broadway history, unlikely ever to be revived in the United States.

Kunze's next shot at making an impact in New York was his 2006 stage version of *Rebecca* (1938), a classic potboiler that has never gone out of print and has sold more than 3 million copies.[33] The English-language rights were bought in 2008 by producers Ben Sprecher and Louise Forlenza. An attempt to bring the musical to London was abandoned after exploratory excavation to see whether the Shaftesbury Theatre could accommodate the elaborate original staging resulted in flooding the theatre's basement. Subsequently, the producers decided to move straight to Broadway and to use a new, less complicated production design. Christopher Hampton was hired to adapt the book and Michael Blakemore was brought in to jointly stage the show with its original director, Francesca Zambello.[34] *Rebecca*, though, never arrived in New York as the production faltered before opening, mired in a bizarre mixture of lies, fraud, whistleblowing, and lawsuits. Sprecher and Forlenza hired Mark Hotton, a Long Island stockbroker, to bring in backers for the pricey musical, but after some questionable business practices related to the production landed Hotton in jail for wire fraud, the production was canceled.

At the time the New York transfer of *Rebecca* was announced, Broadway insiders openly derided shows originating abroad as "Eurotrash," a term which reveals the condescension and suspicion with which the Broadway community regards foreign artists and the musicals they create.[35] In a cultural climate like this, Kunze would have—and will always—face an uphill struggle.

KRISTINA FRÅN DUVEMÅLA—TOO DIFFERENT IN CONTENT

Between 1949 and 1959, Vilhelm Moberg published a quartet of novels *(The Emigrants, Unto a Good Land, The Settlers, The Last Letter Home)*, which were inspired by the historical fact that in the mid-19th century, more than one million Swedes left their home country to emigrate to the United States. Their musical adaptation *Kristina från Duvemåla* with music by Benny Andersson and lyrics by Björn Ulvaeus, the men behind ABBA and the jukebox musical *Mamma Mia!*, premiered in Malmö in 1995. It follows the journey undertaken by the eponymous character, her husband Karl-Oskar, and several of their friends and relatives from Scandinavia to Minnesota. Since its opening, the show has been staged six times around Sweden and has been seen by more than one million people—which equals 10% of the country's population. To put these numbers in perspective, *Hamilton* would have to play at its current Broadway home, the Richard Rodgers Theatre, for 29,204 performances (or ca. 70 years) to attract the same percentage of US citizens.

From the beginning, Andersson and Ulvaeus planned that the musical would be performed in the United States: "[W]e always saw it as an American story just as much as a Swedish one."[36] As a first step, in October 1996, they brought the whole cast over to Minnesota for a concert presentation in Swedish; after all, many people in that state are descended from Swedish immigrants. Yet even though the work on an English translation began early and involved Herbert Kretzmer, who had provided a similar service for *Les Misérables*, a simple transfer of the material seemed out of the question. First of all, there was the running time of the original—roughly four hours. The musical has 39 songs, which is why its original cast album covers three CDs. No Broadway show can be longer than three hours, because that would push the final curtain beyond 11 pm and would necessitate overtime pay. Accordingly, it was clear to Andersson and Ulvaeus that they would have to cut the material by at least 25%—making this an example, not of Stephen Sondheim's famous dictum "content dictates form," but rather of "money dictates form and thus content."

In May 2006, the Broadway Theatre was announced as the New York venue for *Kristina*, but in the end, Andersson and Ulvaeus chose another way to introduce their work to US audiences and potential backers. On September 23 and 24, 2009, there was a concert presentation in Carnegie Hall, an event that would be repeated a few months later, on April 14, 2010, in the Royal Albert Hall, London. Reviews of the concert version, however, were decidedly mixed on both sides of the Atlantic. As a result of this unexpectedly muted reception, which questioned the musical's score and narrative, no further plans for an English-language staging have been announced.

Part of the problem seems to be the issue of categorizing the work. In interviews, the creators were adamant that *Kristina* isn't *Mamma Mia! Part 2*, as its score rarely sounds like the pop hits ABBA regularly released in the 1970s and 1980s. Ulvaeus himself declared: "The music is very different,"[37] while Andersson underlined: "[The show] is very Swedish, it leans on a Swedish tradition [...]. It's much more serious and it's very symphonic."[38] Described by its composer as an "opera,"[39] occasionally even as a "modern opera,"[40] *Kristina* was variously labeled an "operetta"[41] or a "pop opera."[42] *New York Times* critic Stephen Holden saw *Kristina* as another example of "the moribund music-theatre genre facetiously nicknamed poperetta" and berated Andersson's music for being "virtually devoid of syncopation," which presumably is meant to suggest that it doesn't sound American.[43] Unsurprisingly, the most obvious influence on the score, Swedish folk music, went undetected by the English-language critics.

In addition, New York critics were quick to dismiss the predicament of the title character, denigrated by *The Stage* as an "overly-fertile woman."[44] Her dilemma as to whether—after eight children and a miscarriage—she must no longer lie with her husband to avoid another, potentially fatal pregnancy, was declared irrelevant for American audiences. The story of Kristina and her fellow emigrants might resonate in Sweden, reviewers claimed but held a distinct "lack of interest" for the United States.[45] Yet why shouldn't a show which highlights the plight faced by people forced to leave their homeland have global significance at a time when the world sees record numbers of refugees?

The New York workshop the musical received in March 2006 revealed another major potential pitfall: its "downbeat subject" matter. It never crossed Andersson and Ulvaeus' mind that Moberg's tale might not be commercial; in Sweden neither the show's epic scale nor its exploration of the hardships of rural life and emigration had been a hindrance to finding an audience. Prospective US backers at the showcase, however, proved wary of investing in a musical that depicts poverty, religious persecution, the death of a child, a massacre among settlers, and the demise of the title character. Following the workshop, Benny and Björn were told in no uncertain terms that "sad doesn't sell."[46] In this context, many reviewers resented the show's serious tone, complaining that the plot was "a little intense" and that "the relentless portentousness can grate";[47] even the most favorable notices opined that the show may be "too dour."[48]

But this may only be part of the problem. Much like *Les Misérables*, a musical to which it has often been rather glibly compared, *Kristina* features many tragic incidents, but the difference is that the hardships here involve characters who are stoic and passive. This is not a melodramatic musical where the protagonists take charge and then valiantly suffer the consequences. In *Kristina*, "[e]ndurance is heroism" as Richard Corliss put it.[49] Finally, it may be the only musical that highlights the anguish of emigration without ending in triumph and thus without affirmation of the "coming to the New World" experience. Here, trying to find a new life in the United States is just as likely to lead to happiness and prosperity as it is to end in incurable homesickness, despair, and an unmarked grave. As one of my American students once remarked: "A woman who comes to the US, doesn't like it there and then dies? I can't see it on Broadway."

CONCLUSION: FOREIGNERS WELCOME?

The main reason why the musicals above have not yet arrived or been revived on New York stages is that they refuse to meet Broadway on its own terms—they are too different in form, content, physical requirements, and dramaturgical structure to fit into what is rather narrowly defined as "musical theatre" by both US practitioners and critics.

There is a German saying, "Was der Bauer nicht kennt, das frisst er nicht," which means "What the peasant doesn't know, he won't eat" and that assumption reigns supreme when it comes to producing shows on Broadway. Yet always dining out on the same local dishes can prove unhealthy in the long run and might ruin your taste buds—and the same is true for the arts. In this case, the rejection of all that is "foreign" allows innovation only from within the culture, but not from without, reinforcing the mistaken belief that the only place where musical theatre thrives and develops is the English-speaking world, or—an even more isolationist and elitist view—in New York.

NOTES

1 Willa Paskin, "The Other Side of *Anne of Green Gables*," *The New York Times Magazine*, April 27, 2017, https://www.nytimes.com/2017/04/27/magazine/the-other-side-of-anne-of-green-gables.html (Accessed March 22, 2022).
2 Anon.,"*Anne of Green Gables* Musical Hits World Record," www.cbc.ca, March 8, 2014, www.cbc.ca/news/canada/prince-edward-island/anne-of-green-gables-musical-hits-world-record-1.2565129 (Accessed March 30, 2022).
3 Mel Atkey, *A Million Miles from Broadway. Musical Theatre beyond New York and London*. Defta: Friendlysong Company Ltd., 2012, 98.

4 Quoted in Atkey, 231.
5 Don Harron, *Anne of Green Gables—the Musical. 101 Things You Didn't Know*. Toronto: White Knights Books., 2008, 133.
6 Quoted in Atkey, 112.
7 Richard Watts, "Ceremony of Innocence," *The New York Post*, December 27, 1971, 38.
8 Jack Gaver, "*Anne of Green Gables*: A Warm Change of Pace," *United Press International*, December 27, 1971, unpaginated.
9 Walter Kerr, "Is Pollyanna Just around the Corner?," *The New York Times*, January 2, 1972, Section D, p. 1.
10 Atkey, 111.
11 Quoted in Atkey, 98.
12 Michael Walsh, *Andrew Lloyd Webber. His Life and Works*. London: Viking, 1989, 163.
13 John Snelson, *Andrew Lloyd Webber*. New Haven/London: Yale University Press, 2004, 36.
14 Anon., "Musical der Rekorde," undated, www.bochum-tourismus.de, https://www.bochum-tourismus.de/bochum-entdecken/theater-und-buehnen/starlight-express.html#c6856 (Accessed March 26, 2022).
15 Wolfgang Jansen, *Cats & Co. Geschichte des Musicals im deutschsprachigen Theater*. Berlin: Henschel. 2008, 161.
16 Olaf Jubin, *Entertainment in der Kritik*. Herbolzheim: Centaurus, 2005, 701.
17 Jansen, 161.
18 Walsh, 160.
19 Andrew Lloyd Webber, "Programme Notes," *The New Starlight Express*. Programme. London: Really Useful Group, 1992, unpaginated.
20 Michael Coveney, *Cats on a Chandelier. The Andrew Lloyd Webber Story*. London: Hutchinson. 1999, 113.
21 For instance, in 2010/2011, the production sold 424040 tickets (Arnold Jacobshagen, "Musiktheater," 2012, https://www.academia.edu/20121740/Musiktheater, accessed March 26, 2022.)
22 Anon., "*Notre-Dame de Paris*. The Phenomenal Musical," *Variety*, January 25–31, 1999, pp. 80–81.
23 Quoted in Anon., "*Notre-Dame de Paris*," www.thisistheatre.com, undated, https://www.thisistheatre.com/londonshows/notredamedeparis.html (Accessed March 25, 2022).
24 Under the pseudonym Stephan Prager, Kunze wrote the lyrics to "Fly, Robin, Fly"; that disco song with music by Sylvester Levay won the 1976 Grammy for "Best R & B Instrumental Performance."
25 Kunze claims that these works form the core of a new form of musical theatre which he calls "drama musical." For more about this subgenre and its characteristics, see Olaf Jubin, "The German/Austrian, 'Drama Musical' or 'I Sing Alone,'" in Robert Gordon/Olaf Jubin, *The Oxford Handbook ft he Global Stage Musical*. New York: Oxford University Press [forthcoming].
26 The three costume dramas *Sissi, Sissi—the Young Empress* and *Fateful Years of an Empress* were written as well as directed by Ernst Marischka; they starred Romy Schneider and Karlheinz Böhm.

27 Michael Kunze/Sylvester Levay, *Elisabeth*. Libretto. Grünwald: Edition Butterfly, 1992. 5.

28 Matt Wolf, "A Viennese Waltz," *Variety*, September 3–9, 1997, p. 107.

29 Peter Back-Vega, *Theater an der Wien. 40 Jahre Musical* Vienna: Almathea Signum Verlag. 2008, 141.

30 Michael Riedel, "Hate at 1ˢᵗ Bite: How *Vampires* Got Drained of Its Blood" *New York Post*, December 13, 2002, https://nypost.com/2002/12/13/hate-at-1st-bite-how-vampires-got-drained-of-its-blood/ (Accessed March 25, 2022).

31 Riedel.

32 Quoted in Riedel. Without naming names, Kunze later confirmed many of the details in Riedel's account, see Anon., "Alles Negative kam zusammmen. Michael Kunze zum Misserfolg von *Dance of the Vampires* on Broadway," *Musicals*, 100 (2003) 19–20.

33 David Kamp, "The Road to Manderley," *Vanity Fair*, June 2013, pp. 106–118; here, 108.

34 Kamp, 110.

35 Kamp, 110.

36 Benny Andersson/Björn Ulvaeus, "Björn and Benny with a Lyrical Invite to *Kristina*," www.icethesite, July 7, 2009, https://www.icethesite.com/2009/07/bjorn-and-benny-with-a-lyrical-invite-to-kristina/ (Accessed March 26, 2022).

37 Tim Walker, "ABBA Pair Take a Chance on Another West End Hit," *The Daily Telegraph*, April 8, 2009, https://www.telegraph.co.uk/news/newstopics/mandrake/5120921/ABBA-pair-take-a-chance-on-another-West-End-hit.html (Accessed March 24, 2022).

38 Anon., "Abba Members' New Musical *Kristina* Gets New York Debut," www.CBC.ca, July 8, 2009, https://www.cbc.ca/news/entertainment/abba-members-musical-kristina-gets-new-york-debut-1.856076 (Accessed March 24, 2022).

39 Paul Clements, "Benny and Björn on *Kristina*," *The Daily Telegraph*, March 11, 2010, https://www.telegraph.co.uk/culture/theatre/theatre-features/7415529/Benny-and-Bjorn-on-Kristina.html (Accessed March 23, 2022).

40 Eva Sohlman, "ABBA Duo to Play in US, But No Reunion," www.abcnews.go.com, September 8, 2009, https://abcnews.go.com/Travel/abba-duo-plans-us-concert-mamma-mia-follow/Story?id=8514259&page=1 (Accessed March 24, 2022).

41 Richard Corliss, "That Old Feeling: ABBA, without Apologies." *Time Magazine*, October 23, 2001, http://content.time.com/time/arts/article/0,8599,180848-3,00.html (Accessed March 25, 2022).

42 Brian Scott Lipton, "*Kristina*," www.TheaterMania.com, September 24, 2009, https://www.theatermania.com/new-york-city-theater/reviews/kristina_21453.html (Accessed March 26, 2022).

43 Stephen Holden, "Swedes Coming to America, Grandly," *The New York Times*, September 26, 2009, https://www.nytimes.com/2009/09/26/arts/music/26kristina.html (Accessed March 25, 2022).

44 Mark Shenton, "*Kristina* Review at Royal Albert Hall London," www.thestage.co.uk, April 15, 2010, https://www.thestage.co.uk/

reviews/kristina-review-at-royal-albert-hall-london (Accessed March 14, 2022).
45 Steven Suskin, "*Kristina*. Review," *Variety*, September 24, 2009, https://variety.com/2009/legit/reviews/kristina-1200475888/ (Accessed March 25, 2022)
46 Quoted in Cristina Odone, "OK, Yah? Sadly not, at Today's Prices," *The Guardian*, October 7, 2007, https://www.theguardian.com/commentisfree/2007/oct/07/comment.comment1 (Accessed March 13, 2022).
47 Keiron Quirke, "*Kristina*. Review," *The Evening Standard*, April 15, 2010, https://www.icethesite.com/2010/04/kristina-gets-3-out-of-5-stars-in-london-newspaper-updated/ (Accessed March 24, 2022).
48 Richard Corliss, "*Kristina*: A New Musical from the ABBA Guys," *Time Magazine*, September 24, 2009, https://content.time.com/time/arts/article/0,8599,1925955,00.html (Accessed March 16, 2022).
49 Corliss, 2009.

RECOMMENDATIONS FOR ADDITIONAL RESOURCES

Gordon, Robert/Olaf Jubin (eds.) *The Oxford Handbook of the Global Stage Musical*. New York: Oxford University Press, 2023.

This is an overview of the development of musical theatre as a global phenomenon; includes detailed analyses of the musicals discussed in this chapter as well as of other national and international hit shows.

Anne of Green Gables. 1969 London Cast Recording. CD 53495. London: Sony West End, 1993.

This is the only available recording of the full score.

Elisabeth. Live aus dem Theater an der Wien. Directed by Sven Offen. DVD 6682527. Vienna: Hit Squad Records, 2006.

This is a filmed record of the original 1992 production, re-staged in 2006; it includes English subtitles.

Kristina at Carnegie Hall CD 2734981. New York: Universal Music/Decca Broadway/Mono Music, 2010.

This is a live recording of the abbreviated English version of the musical.

Notre-Dame de Paris. Version Intégrale. Directed by Gilles Amado. DVD 952509. Paris: Pomme Music, 1999.

This is a filmed record of the Paris staging, with the original stars; includes English subtitles.

CHAPTER 8

From the West Side to Washington Heights: Transforming Latinx representation in American musical theatre

Colleen Rua

In 2021, film adaptations of *West Side Story* and *In the Heights* premiered in theatres and across streaming platforms. The eagerly anticipated iterations of two landmark musicals reignited the discussion around what makes a "Latinx musical." Because it features Puerto Rican characters, *West Side Story* is often considered a Latinx musical, despite the fact that the creators of the original stage production as well as of the recent film adaptation are not Latinx. One of the most well-known works of the American musical theatre genre, the 1957 stage production of *West Side Story* and its iconic 1961 film adaptation presented Puerto Rican characters as violent gang members and set a foundation for harmfully stereotypical depictions of Latinx individuals as criminals on stage and on screen. These criminal depictions were added to already popular representations of Latinx individuals as inherently performative. Over eighty years of American musical theatre history, much of which has catered to elite, white, monolingual English speakers, criminal and performative stereotypes of Latinx communities have been reiterated, resisted, and/or transformed in works like *The Capeman* (1998), *In the Heights* (2008), *Hamilton* (2015), and *On Your Feet* (2015).

The earliest commercially successful representations of Latinx characters on Broadway were associated with Franklin D. Roosevelt's

DOI: 10.4324/9781003256458-9

Good Neighbor Policy, which encouraged the recruitment of talent to Broadway in support of a propaganda campaign that would paint Latin America as a land of trustworthy friends. In 1939, Broadway producer Lee Schubert traveled to Rio de Janeiro to scout singer and actress Carmen Miranda, the star who would come to be known as "The Lady in the Tutti-Frutti Hat." Presented as a South American souvenir, the commodified Miranda was exotic yet nonthreatening. From 1939 to 1943, Miranda appeared in two Broadway revues and eight Hollywood films and was the highest paid actress in the United States. Miranda became a symbol of government relations and of an American idea(l) of Latin America: sexy, mysterious, and fun. These traits, along with Miranda's singing and dancing tempered and tantalized American fear of and appetite for things south-of-the-border and firmly established the Latinx stereotype in Anglo-created musicals.

Carmen Miranda, Desi Arnaz (featured in the Rodgers and Hart musical *Too Many Girls*), and their contemporaries started out as "specialty acts"; they were performers playing performers. These characters sang and danced as their occupation and had nicknames like "The Puerto Rican Pepperpot," (Olga San Juan) and "The Cuban Hurricane" (Marie Antoinette-Pons), suggesting sexiness, sassiness, and strength. Rather than rejecting these stereotypes, it became necessary for those who wished to be a part of American entertainment to embrace them, even going so far as to use them as a form of resistance; exaggerating the stereotype to illuminate its ridiculousness.[1] As Latin American icons, Miranda and Arnaz were forced to objectify their own identities, creating characters that would meet Anglo audience expectations.

The 1950s and 1960s were a time of growth for Latinx theatre in New York City. In 1954, the first self-sustaining professional Hispanic Theatre troupe, Nuevo Circulo Dramatico, was founded by Puerto Rican director René Marques and actress Miriam Colón. On Broadway, however, the performative stereotype of the Latinx character persisted and added to it was a "criminal" stereotype presented for majority non-Latinx, majority white audiences. Adler and Ross's *Damn Yankees* (1955), for example, featured Señorita Lolita Banana (Lola), played by Gwen Verdon. A sexy South American dancer and sidekick to the Devil(ish) Applegate, Lola's presence drew a parallel between Latin America and hell.

WEST SIDE STORY

Intentionally or not, Leonard Bernstein, Arthur Laurents, and Stephen Sondheim's 1957 *West Side Story* highlighted immigration, racism, and cultural identity. Unlike the lighthearted musical reviews that preceded it, *West Side Story* was set in New York City, where the population of Latinx identifying residents doubled from 1950 to 1960. Departing from earlier productions, *West Side Story* featured a score and lyrics that emphasized its dramatic story: a gang rivalry punctuated by the ill-fated romance of star-crossed lovers Tony and Maria.

What Carmen Miranda did to stereotype the Latina body as performative, *West Side Story* matched with the tropes of the innocent virgin (Maria) and the sassy spitfire (Anita). In the original Broadway production, Italian American Carol Lawrence was cast as the "pure" Maria, while Chita Rivera, who is half Puerto Rican, was cast as the "fiery" Anita. Each had a prominent musical number whereby these stereotypes were explicitly performed: Maria's innocence was celebrated in "I Feel Pretty," and Anita's defiance showcased in "America." Frances Negrón-Muntaner argues that the 1961 film adaptation of *West Side Story* "perseveres in a long tradition of representing Latinos as inherently musical and performative subjects, ready to wear their sexualized identity for a white audience at the drop of a hat."[2] This performative legacy, inherited from the time of Carmen Miranda, paired with an unidentifiable musical background and rooted in no particular culture influenced perceptions of Latinx communities on and offstage.

Just as the musicals associated with the Good Neighbor Policy had formed an image of Latin America for a collective Anglo consciousness, *West Side Story* would construct a new perception of Latinx youth, represented onstage by The Sharks. The Sharks, on a microcosmic level, are invaders of the Jets' space and, on a grander scale, are representative of Puerto Rican immigrants intruding on the stateside territory and way of life. The rumble that the Sharks and Jets engage in is more than territorial; it is a battle between rich and poor and white and non-white which will decide who belongs and who does not. In attempting to find space, the Sharks are forced to fight for it, quite literally. While both the Sharks and the Jets are gang members who engage in criminal activity (including murder), the focus of wrongdoing is placed heavily on the Sharks, both within the context of the script and in its original staging. When Detective Shrank encounters the two gangs on the street, he orders the Sharks to leave and blames them for degrading the neighborhood. Contrarily, Shrank engages with the Jets, taking an almost fatherly tone of "boys will be boys" and telling them that they simply have to put up with the Sharks. By sending the Sharks away and allowing the Jets to stay, the colonizer's power, represented by Shrank, is reconfirmed and the colonized are kept subjugated. The Sharks are also tagged as serious criminals, whereas the Jets are simply delinquents.

FROM *WEST SIDE STORY* TO *THE CAPEMAN*

Latinx representation in American musical theatre in the 1970s included Broadway's iconic *Evita* (1978) and two Latinx characters in *A Chorus Line* (1975), Diana Morales and Paul San Marco, the latter two sustaining the Latinx-as-performer trope.[3] Luis Valdez's 1979 *Zoot Suit* remains the only Chicano-created and Chicanx-centered musical to have appeared on Broadway. Melding history, fiction, and mythology in a retelling of the events of the Zoot Suit Riots in Los Angeles in 1943, *Zoot Suit* presented the injustices of the US legal system toward Chicanx youth, in particular. Despite the fact that it featured a Latinx creator, a largely Latinx cast, and that it was intended for Latinx audiences, it too, featured Chicanx teenagers engaging in criminal behavior. In addition, its use of bilingualism featured Caló, a slang created by and for Chicanx youth. *Zoot Suit* was not well-received by Broadway audiences and critics, one calling its political arguments "stilted and paper-thin."[4]

The 1990s saw two attempts at Latinx representation in the Broadway musical. Direct reference to any character's ethnicity is never made in *Rent* (1996). However, two characters, Angel Schunard (originated by Wilson Jermaine Heredia) and Mimi Marquez (originated by Daphne Ruben-Vega) carry traces of past performative and criminal Latinx stereotypes into the 1990s. Both are presumed to be of Latinx descent, evidenced by the fact that the roles were originated by Latinx actors and in song lyrics assigned to them, for example, Mimi's "feels too damn much like home, where the Spanish babies cry" ("Out Tonight").[5] Mimi is an exotic dancer and uses illegal drugs, while Angel is a busker and is comically hired to orchestrate the demise of a yappy neighborhood dog. Set among a diverse cast that increased opportunities for actors of color in major roles on Broadway in a production that championed inclusivity, Angel and Mimi were on the lowest rung of the socioeconomic ladder.

THE CAPEMAN

In 1998, popular songwriter Paul Simon and St. Lucian Nobel Prize winner Derek Walcott collaborated to create *The Capeman*, a musical that lasted for just sixty-eight performances at Broadway's Marquis Theatre. Simon, known for his experiments with world music and Walcott for his treatment of the Caribbean subject matter, seemed a promising duo. *The Capeman* is based on the true story of Salvador Agrón, a teenage Puerto Rican member of a New York City gang known as the Vampires. Agrón was accused of murdering two teens in a Hell's Kitchen park in 1959 and came to be known as "the Capeman" when he began donning a black cape. Agrón's dual status as immigrant and criminal is conflated, and so, by wearing a cape to engage in criminal activity, Agrón's on stage performance became symbolic of what it meant to be Latino, even as he concealed his identity under the cape.

The Capeman jumps chronologically, using flashback sequences that move between Puerto Rico and the states, and emphasize the complicated relationship between the two locations. This dual geographic setting, along with Agrón's bifurcated character (originally played by both Marc Anthony and Rubén Blades) mirrors Agrón's status as being not wholly American, yet not Un-American. Simon claimed in one interview, "It doesn't really matter whether the protagonist is Puerto Rican.... it's not essential to the central issue of redemption."[6] Despite Simon's protests, it is unavoidable that Agrón's Puerto Rican identity is an essential part of his story, especially in relation to geography and the US legal system.

The Capeman was widely considered a critical flop. It was, however, applauded for Simon's blend of gospel, doo-wop, and Latin music. It also lent exposure to Latinx actors, the majority of whom were specifically Puerto Rican, as were the characters in the musical. While Simon and Walcott's status drew a traditional Broadway demographic to the theatre, the story likely brought many Latinx individuals to the theatre, too. When they arrived at the Marquis Theatre on January 29, 1998, they were greeted by a red, white, and blue curtain designed to resemble the Puerto Rican flag. Alberto Sandoval-Sánchez, recalling his own attendance at the production, argues that the reproduction of the Puerto Rican flag at the premiere of *The Capeman* "provided a space of/ for identification in such a persuasive manner that attending the musical validated Puerto Rican national identity."[7] For Sandoval-Sánchez, this immediate visual connection to Puerto Rico evoked both pride and nostalgia.[8]

IN THE HEIGHTS

In 2000, Wesleyan University student Lin-Manuel Miranda began an eight-year journey in the making of a new musical; one centered around New York City's Washington Heights barrio, whose residents include three generations of Latinx individuals. Narrator Usnavi, his love interest Vanessa, her co-workers at the beauty salon, the Rosario family, and the neighborhood's Abuela Claudia, among others, navigate gentrification, identity, and the definition of "home" as they both celebrate and critique the quotidian events of their community. Debuting on March 9, 2008, and garnering thirteen Tony Awards nominations and four wins, *In the Heights* was a significant marker of progress on Broadway. Its premiere came just two years after the 2006 National Hispanic Media Coalition and the Free Press public hearings on media diversity held in New York City. The hearings instigated responses from both Latinx and African American New Yorkers, who demanded more diverse programming with representations showing that "we're more than violence, drugs and poverty."[9] Both composer/lyricist Miranda and book writer Quiara Alegría Hudes identify as Puerto Rican and the entire cast of the first commercially successful Broadway musical to take a Latinx community as its focus was composed of Latinx and Black actors playing Latinx and Black characters. Incorporating Latin and Afro-Latin music styles and with lyrics and dialogue in Spanish, English, and Spanglish,

In the Heights, pictured in Figure 8.1, challenged familiar depictions of Latinx lives on stage and in popular film and television. Miranda describes one motivation for writing *In the Heights*, "I wrote *In the Heights* to fix *The Capeman*. Forty years after *West Side Story* and we're still knife-wielding gangsters." By perpetuating such harmful stereotypes, he says, "*The Capeman* broke my heart."[10]

In the Heights transforms earlier depictions of Latinx communities by redefining the very definition of what community means within the context of such representations. While gang membership formed the central community unit within the worlds of *West Side Story* and *The Capeman*, *In the Heights*'s community was constructed around mutually beneficial caretaking without transactional exchange or involvement in life-threatening or illegal activities. *In the Heights* further transforms the criminal stereotype by presenting alternate examples of rebellion. Nina drops out of Stanford. Sonny speaks out against systemic oppression. Graffiti Pete defies expectations by spray painting the bodega grate as a memorial to the community. This gesture finally convinces Usnavi to stay in Washington Heights and declare that it is his "home."

Figure 8.1: Lin-Manuel Miranda (center) and the original Broadway cast of *In the Heights*. Photo by Joan Marcus.

Robin DeJesus, who originated the role of Sonny, expressed with relief, "Finally a role where I do not have to carry a gun, I am not in a gang, I am not selling drugs. I am just a normal human being who happens to be Hispanic and who happens to live in this wonderful place called Washington Heights."[11] Indeed, the only crime committed in *In the Heights* is looting that occurs during a power outage. The vandals are never seen by the audience. This choice holds great significance when considering *In the Heights'* attempt to not only resist harmful stereotypes of individuals but to reconstruct stereotyped notions of geography. The choice to omit these vandals from view performs several functions. First, because they are never seen, the audience is not subjected to images of the barrio as a locus of crime. Second, the audience cannot know the race or ethnicity of the vandals, eschewing reinforcement of such stereotypes. Next, the vandals are outsiders, not a part of the community represented here, so suggestion of inter-community violence is also avoided. Finally, because the perpetrators are never seen, this vandalism is an anomaly, an occurrence that happens during the unique but desperate situation of the blackout. Not only are the characters on stage freed from any culpability, but the audience witnesses a community that is victimized and joins together to recover. The focus is on the recovery and not the crime. The in-the-margin presence of the vandals does reinforce that, in desperate times, external factors can and will threaten the community. *In the Heights* does not deny that such issues exist; instead, vandalism along with gentrification are both presented as outside forces impacting the neighborhood, not ones internal to the community.

Within a framework that seeks to transform previous representations of Latinx people, Miranda often uses *In the Heights* to echo that which came before, and in some instances reiterates iconic moments associated with *West Side Story*, in particular. Like Maria, Nina is "the good daughter." A high-achieving student, Nina finds herself questioning her ability to succeed at Stanford. In the song, "Breathe," Nina expresses the pressure she feels from the entire community to succeed as a chorus of voices from the neighborhood reminds her to "*sigue andado el camino por toda su vida*" ("keep following this path for all of your life").[12] Echoing Maria's relationships with Tony and with her disapproving brother, Bernardo, Nina's father, Kevin, does not approve of her relationship with

Benny. Despite the fact that Benny, who is Black, is Kevin's star employee, Kevin confronts Benny, saying "you will never be part of this family," noting the racial tensions historically present between Black and Latinx communities in New York City.[13] Like Maria and Tony fifty years earlier, Nina and Benny find themselves on a fire escape, a liminal space between the earth and the sky, and that for both couples, despite its public nature, becomes a private and sacred space.

This moment on the fire escape not only represents Maria and Tony's evolution into Nina and Benny, but it also highlights another way in which *In the Heights* is distinct from its predecessors. Intentionally written with lyrics and dialogue in Spanish, Spanglish, English, and rap, *In the Heights* uses feats of linguistic agility and codeswitching to simultaneously speak to a Spanish-speaking audience while educating monolingual English speakers. As Nina and Benny unite on the fire escape, they sing "Sunrise." Constructed as a language lesson, Nina quizzes Benny on his knowledge of Spanish vocabulary. In this metaphorical "morning after" song, the *In the Heights* equivalent of *West Side Story*'s "A Place for Us," the couples' two languages become one. The song is very simply constructed. Nina offers up a word in Spanish, and Benny recites its English equivalent. The manipulation of language in this scene serves a dual purpose. First, it advances both the plot and the relationship between the two characters. Benny needs this skill in order to communicate with the other taxi dispatch drivers, which will advance his position with the company. By teaching him, Nina creates an intimate connection with Benny and lets him into her world. In doing so, she simultaneously allows Benny the opportunity to get close to her father. This scene also functions to educate monolingual English speakers in the audience, who share a role with Benny, learning words and phrases along with him and relying on Nina to guide them through the story.

While *In the Heights* has done much to transform previous Latinx representation, it must be noted that the production has faced criticism for catering to the comfortability of Anglo audiences. This came to particular prominence with the 2021 release of the film adaptation of *In the Heights*, in which the casting of principal roles excluded dark-skinned Afro-Latinx people who accurately reflect the demographic of Washington Heights. Responding to accusations of colorism, Lin-Manuel Miranda offered, "I hear that without sufficient dark-skinned Afro-Latino representation the work feels extractive of the community we wanted so much to represent with pride and joy," he continued. "In trying to paint a mosaic of this community, we fell short. I'm truly sorry."[14]

WEST SIDE STORY 2009

In 2009, *West Side Story* returned to Broadway with a long-anticipated and much-hyped revival. The production retained its performative Anita and Maria, and its criminal stereotypes, but newly featured lyrics and dialogue were translated into Spanish by Lin-Manuel Miranda. Book writer Arthur Laurents's intention in creating a bilingual adaptation was reported to give the production greater authenticity. "The idea was to equalize the gangs," he explained, "by allowing the Sharks ... their own language."[15] In addition, the production would be cast with Latinx actors, including Argentine Josefina Scaglione as Maria and *In the Heights'* Karen Olivo as Anita.

Bilingual interventions in *West Side Story* revival functioned in several ways and led to mixed results. First, Spanish lyrics and dialogue provided a new perspective on character development and motivations. Second, mirroring the use of song in musical theatre, Spanish was used to indicate places where extreme states of emotion are reached. The Spanish-language additions also changed the relationship between characters and audience. Finally, these alterations simultaneously resisted and reinforced the stereotypes of the original musical.

This is most evident in the popular song "I Feel Pretty," performed by Maria with the help of Anita and their friends. Originally composed of English lyrics, this song is both Maria's celebration of newfound love and her friends' lamentation of her foolishness. The Spanish translation calls attention to the fact that Maria is changing in a way that is more pronounced than it is in the original English version. Love has made her less innocent. She refers to herself as *mujer* ("woman") and brings focus to her body, situating this song as her transition into womanhood. With the assistance of the Spanish language, Maria no longer represents the virginal Latina, but takes control of her sexuality and celebrates her body, resisting the long-reinforced virginal stereotype. In doing so, she takes control over a part of her life that has heretofore been dictated by her brother, Bernardo.

In the first two translated verses of "I Feel Pretty," Miranda looks to the sky for metaphor, positioning herself as more stunning than a goddess, and brighter than the brightest star. With the celestial goddesses and stars as her rivals, Maria is raised to an otherworldly level. She is no longer a mere mortal; Tony's love has raised her status and her stakes. With these new lyrics, Maria transcends her status as a hopeful immigrant. She sees the love between her and Tony as something divine, something that can transcend their obstacles. However, through the Spanish language, this divine relationship is poised for greater tragedy, and the lovers have farther to fall. In the Spanish version, they do not see their dreams as futile, yet they are more tragically lost.

This use of Spanish mirrors the function of song in the American musical. When the emotional charge behind characters' circumstances leaves them with no other way to express themselves, they must find release through song, first language, or both. A mix of two languages can indicate either stress and confusion, or a comfort in successfully navigating two worlds. From a linguistic point of view, this codeswitching relieves tension or frustration that has been built up over the time in which a character's second language is spoken. Eduardo Cabrera credits codeswitching with offering the speaker "flexibility of expression" at times of heightened emotion.[16]

The 2009 revival of *West Side Story* played to audiences for a mere five months before another change was deemed necessary. The reasons for this change were enumerated by Laurents in an interview with the *New York Times:* "Audiences were getting the general idea of 'A Boy Like That,' but they weren't getting hammered by it. The sheer power of 'A boy like that who'd kill your brother' has no real equivalent, and for people who don't understand Spanish, the impact was diluted."[17] Audience members were never formally surveyed to gauge their response to the Spanish lyrics, but Laurents's justification indicates a prioritizing of white comfortability.

HAMILTON

The next step in transforming Latinx stereotypes was taken with Lin-Manuel Miranda's landmark musical *Hamilton*. Debuting at the Richard Rodgers Theatre on August 6, 2015, the cast was composed of actors of color playing white historical figures of the American Revolutionary period, including Christopher Jackson as George Washington, Daveed Diggs as Thomas Jefferson, and Lin-Manuel Miranda in the title role of Alexander Hamilton. The production also drew upon Alexander Hamilton's origins on the Caribbean island of St. Nevis to create a foundation for a production that sought to decolonialize the ways in which US history is traditionally framed, shifting perspective to reflect Hamilton's Act I line, "immigrants/we get the job done."[18] Wildly popular and featuring a Latinx creator, *Hamilton* opened space for diverse casting choices and for highlighting actors of color in major roles. *Hamilton*, however, was not without controversy.

Reflections of Maria and Anita continued with *Hamilton*. This time they were presented in the form of sisters Angelica and Eliza Schuyler, played in the original production by Renée Elise Goldsberry and Phillipa Soo, respectively. Eliza, who becomes Hamilton's wife, is described as "trusting" and "kind" ("Satisfied"). She is steadfast and true in her loyalty to Hamilton, despite his multiple indiscretions. She is, however, pushed to her limit, and in the song "Burn," she destroys letters from Hamilton that "might have redeemed" him, "erasing [her]self from the narrative," and leaving future historians to wonder.[19] While *West Side Story's* Maria, who picks up a gun and threatens the men who have destroyed her life, is stopped short of carrying out an act of violence against them or against herself, Eliza follows through, albeit in a manner that is devoid of physical violence. Unlike Maria, the audience witnesses Eliza carrying on and moving forward. It is Eliza, in fact, who takes central focus at the close of each performance, suggesting that she is perhaps the "Hamilton," that this story is meant to highlight. In contrast to Eliza, Angelica is a confident and flirtatious intellectual who matches wits with Alexander. The musical depicts the relationship between Angelica and Alexander as one of a romance that will never be. Echoes of Anita and Vanessa both reverberate here, as all three women are unsatisfied with the status quo. By reshaping tropes associated with Maria and Anita, *Hamilton* works to resist stereotypes of women and color while establishing solidarity between Latinx female representation and that of non-Latinx women of color.

The strongest criticism that *Hamilton* has received is that the musical glorifies enslavers including Thomas Jefferson, Alexander Hamilton, and Eliza Hamilton. In addition, the musical does not explore the experiences of people of color during the American Revolution. While the major characters are understood to be white, the ethnicities of the characters embodied by ensemble members who shift in and out of multiple roles throughout the production is unclear, and the figures that they are sometimes meant to represent are nameless.

In addition to presenting *Hamilton* as an immigrant story, its ties to the Caribbean were strengthened in the aftermath of Hurricanes Irma and Maria, which devastated Puerto Rico in September 2017. Lin-Manuel Miranda and his father Luis Miranda, Jr. mobilized relief efforts in collaboration with non-profit entities, including the Hispanic Federation and through artistic events including the recording of the song "Almost Like Praying" and a tour of *Hamilton* to Puerto Rico in 2019. It was during this tour that the line between for-profit and non-profit was blurred and ethical concerns were highlighted. Miranda's announcement of the tour was met with University of Puerto Rico student protesters holding signs with slogans like "Our lives are not your theatre," and statements pointing to the glorification of enslavers in *Hamilton*.[20] By entering the geographical site of multiple traumas, including hurricane, earthquake, mass migration, austerity measures, and neoliberal privatization, *Hamilton* penetrated an open wound. Onstage, though, Miranda used the curtain call to demonstrate his commitment to the island by waving a full-sized Puerto Rican flag. Daniel Pollack-Pelzner recalls his Air B&B host in San Juan celebrating the moment. "When Lin-Manuel takes out the flag, it's like, *Yes, we exist*."[21] Miranda's flag performance not only celebrates Puerto Rico in defiance of the hurricane, but it affirms his own Puerto Rican identity through co-ownership of the Hurricane Maria period. By claiming witness to the event, he justifies his status as "responder" in the face of criticism, a status that empowers him to validate his Puerto Rican audience.

ON YOUR FEET!

As with *The Capeman, On Your Feet!* focused on a non-fictive subject but rejected a criminal stereotype and transformed a performative one. Based on the autobiographical story of pop music icons Gloria and Emilio Estefan with music, lyrics, and orchestrations by the married couple, and with a book written by Alexander Dinelaris, it debuted at Broadway's Marquis Theatre on November 5, 2015, just three months after *Hamilton*'s debut. Cuban American Ana Villafañe, who is from Miami, originated the role of Gloria, with Josh Segarra as Emilio. A jukebox musical, *On Your Feet* featured Estefan's most popular solo hits as well as those from her time with Miami Sound Machine, including the title song, as well as "Conga," and "Rhythm is Gonna Get You." In his review of the musical for *Theatre Journal*, Horacio Sierra notes that the production "extends the Cuban American tradition of hybridization by amalgamating English-language hits, Cuban-inspired choreography, American immigrant tropes, and a universal love story."[22] While Gloria and Emilio Estefan are both performers, the autobiographical nature of the story validates its authenticity and makes their status as performers essential to exploring life "on the hyphen."[23] As they navigate an "American Dream," the couple is met with obstacles including Gloria's mother's disapproval of Emilio, her father's battle with Multiple Sclerosis, and the 1990 bus accident that left Gloria seriously injured. Largely a story of resilience and triumph, *On Your Feet* depicts the couple overcoming these obstacles and navigating the complexities of what it means to be Cuban American in a positive and celebratory light.

As with *In the Heights* and the 2009 revival of *West Side Story*, the bilingualism employed in *On Your Feet!* makes the musical accessible to multiple audiences. However, in *On Your Feet!*, codeswitching between Spanish and English is directly reflective of the Estefans' experience in navigating bilingualism within a music industry meant to cater to young, white, monolingual English speakers. The string of hits that make up the score of *On Your Feet!* were intended to be "welcoming liminal spaces for non-Hispanic fans."[24] Just as *In the Heights* employed bilingualism as a tool to hold Latinx audiences close and invite non-Latinx audiences in, the Estefan's and their producers shaped their repertoire to be just Latin enough and just American enough through the inclusion of Spanish and English backed by Latin beats. This resulted in wide appeal for audiences during the height of Gloria Estefan's recording career and again with *On Your Feet!*. David Rooney's *Hollywood Reporter* review notes:

> It's impossible to deny the production's generosity of spirit.... the story is packed with heart, above all in its tender depiction of the couple's sustaining love. And there's such genuine joy—plus a refreshing suggestion of modesty—in the telling of this Cuban-American success story. The show's arrival at a historic point in the renewal of diplomatic ties between Cuba and the U.S. makes its timing serendipitous.[25]

Indeed, the relevance of *On Your Feet!* was highlighted by President Barak Obama's 2014 announcement that the United States would shift policy regarding Cuba, in a move toward "United States-Cuba Normalization."[26] The new policy would allow increased travel to Cuba, encourage commerce between the two nations, and allow for a free flow of information to Cuba. This change is significant in relation to the musical, as it recalls Estefan's own relationship to Cuba, as a member of the "1.5 Generation," those who emigrated as young children, with no memories of their time in Cuba. Estefan's father, however, was a political prisoner under the Castro regime, having previously worked for Castro's predecessor, Fulgencio Batista. The Estefans' passionate and complicated ties to Cuba are highlighted in the songs "Mi Tierra," and "Cuando Salí de Cuba." Their "on the hyphen" experience is best expressed in the musical when a record executive deems their bilingual songs as unmarketable. Emilio responds, "You should look very closely at my face, because whether you know it or not ... this is what an American looks like."[27] *On Your Feet!* pushes back against stereotypes by asserting its position as both a Cuban and an American story.

CONCLUSION

On April 24, 2022, *Americano!,* premiered off-Broadway at New World Stages. Based on the true story of Tony Valdovinos, who grew up in Phoenix, Arizona, and was inspired by the events of September 11, 2001 to join the United States Marine Corps, *Americano!* tells the story of Valdovinos's discovery that he is a

"Dreamer," an undocumented immigrant. The production features a nearly all-Latinx cast and a creative team of both Latinx and non-Latinx identifying artists. In Herbert Paine's review of the 2020 Phoenix Theatre production, he notes, "*AMERICANO!* is an effusive and exuberant celebration of idealism and fortitude as well as a fervent call to action."[28] Valdovinos says that the musical is about "continuously moving forward. This is a story of what it means to be an American, and what it also means to be resilient, and to not give up."[29] As Latinx stories told by Latinx creators and performers continue to move forward, they too, demonstrate resilience and perseverance. As they resist and transform harmful stereotypes, they reshape the Broadway canon, paving the way for a diverse and decolonized musical theatre that truly reflects the American experience.

NOTES

1 Michelle Habell-Pallán, Mary Romero, and Alberto Sandoval-Sanchez, "Paul Simon' s *The Capeman*: The Staging of Puerto Rican National Identity as Spectacle and Commodity on Broadway," in *Latino/a Popular Culture* (New York University Press, 2002), 48.

2 Negrón-Muntaner, Frances—Feeling Pretty: *West Side Story* and Puerto Rican Identity Discourses. *Social Text* 18, no. 2 (2000), 83–106.

3 Diana Morales was originally played by Priscilla Lopez, who went on to play Mrs. Rosario in the original Broadway cast of *In the Heights*. For this accomplishment, she received the honor of her portrait displayed in Sardi's restaurant in New York City. Lopez accepted the award "for my people."

4 Eder, Richard. "Theater: Zoot Suit,' Chicano Music-Drama." *The New York Times*, The New York Times, Mar. 26, 1979, https://www.nytimes.com/1979/03/26/archives/theater-zoot-suit-chicano-musicdrama-a-tale-of-los-angeles.html.

5 Larson, Jonathan. *Rent: The Complete Book and Lyrics of the Broadway Musical* (Applause Theatre and Cinema Books, 2008), 42.

6 González, Fernando. "Capeman Album Includes Doo Wop, Country, Mambo," *Miami Herald* 16, (November 1997), 81.

7 Sandoval-Sanchez, 152.

8 See Sandoval-Sanchez's firsthand account of his attendance at *The Capeman* in 1998 in "Paul Simon's *The Capeman*: The Staging of Puerto Rican National Identity as Spectacle and Commodity on Broadway." *Latino/a Popular Culture*. Edited by Michelle Habell-Pallán and Mary Romero (New York: NYU Press, 2002), 147–158.

9 Arlene Dávila, *Latino Spin: Public Image and the Whitewashing of Race* (New York: New York University Press, 2008), 81.

10 Teresa Wiltz, "Onstage and in the Seats, People of Color Are Showing Producers New Ways to See Green." *The Washington Post,* (June 15, 2008), M01

11 *In the Heights: Chasing Broadway Dreams.* Television Broadcast. Directed by Paul Bozymowski. PBS, Aired May 27, 2009. (25:32–25:44).

12 Hudes, Quiara Alegría, et al. *In the Heights: The Complete Book and Lyrics of the Broadway Musical* (Applause Theatre & Cinema Books, 2013), 17.

13 Hudes, 110.

14 Althea Legaspi, "Lin-Manuel Miranda Responds to 'in the Heights' Colorism Criticism," Rolling Stone (Rolling Stone, June 15, 2021), https://www.rollingstone.com/tv-movies/tv-movie-news/lin-manuel-miranda-responds-to-in-the-heights-colorism-criticism-1184394/.

15 Green, Jesse. "Theater Legend Arthur Laurents Comes Back to Broadway with 'West Side Story' Revival – New York Magazine - Nymag." *New York Magazine,* Mar. 13, 2009, https://nymag.com/arts/theater/profiles/55341/.

16 Cabrera, Eduardo, "The Encounter of Two Cultures in the Play Doña Rosita's Jalapeno Kitchen," *The State of Latino Theatre in the United States.* Edited by Luis A. Ramos-García (New York: Routledge, 2002).

17 Patrick Healy, "Some 'West Side' Lyrics Restored to English," *New York Times,* August 26, 2009.

18 Miranda, Lin-Manuel, and Jeremy McCarter. *Hamilton: The Revolution* (Melcher Media, 2016), 121.

19 Miranda, 238.

20 Daniel Pollack-Pelzner, "The Mixed Reception of the 'Hamilton' Premiere in Puerto Rico." *The Atlantic,* Atlantic Media Company, Jan. 18, 2019, www.theatlantic.com/entertainment/archive/2019/01/hamilton-premiere-puerto-rico-stirs-controversy/580657/.

21 Pollack-Pelzner, 2019.

22 Horacio Sierra, "Performance Review of on Your Feet!." *Theatre Journal* 69, no. 1 (2017), 100 01. *Academia.edu,* May 2, 2017, https://www.academia.edu/32778062/Performance_Review_of_On_Your_Feet_Theatre_Journal_69_1_2017_100_01.

23 Gustavo Perez Firmat, *Life on the Hyphen: The Cuban-American Way* (University of Texas Press, 1994).

24 David Rooney, "'On Your Feet!': Theater Review." *The Hollywood Reporter,* The Hollywood Reporter, Dec. 1, 2015, https://www.hollywoodreporter.com/news/general-news/gloria-emilio-estefan-bio-musical-837203/.

25 Rooney, 2015.

26 Barack Obama, Barack, "Presidential Policy Directive – United States-Cuba Normalization." *National Archives and Records Administration,* National Archives and Records Administration, Oct. 14, 2016, https://obamawhitehouse.archives.gov/the-press-office/2016/10/14/presidential-policy-directive-united-states-cuba-normalization.

27 Isherwood, Charles. "Review: 'on Your Feet!' Rides the Rhythm of the Estefans." *The New York Times*, The New York Times, Nov. 6, 2015, https://www.nytimes.com/2015/11/06/theater/review-on-your-feet-rides-the-rhythm-of-the-estefans.html#:~:text=%E2%80%9CYou%20should%20look%20very%20closely%20at%20my%20face%2C%E2%80%9D,hands%2C%20as%20their%20struggles%20bring%20them%20closer%20together.
28 Herbert Paine, "BWW Review: The Phoenix Theatre Company Presents Americano!" *BroadwayWorld.com*, BroadwayWorld.com, Feb. 11, 2020, https://www.broadwayworld.com/phoenix/article/BWW-Review-The-Phoenix-Theatre-Company-Presents-AMERICANO-20200211.
29 Muri Assunção, "'¡Americano!': Powerful Musical about 'Dreamers', Immigration and What It Means to Be an American, Opens in NYC." *New York Daily News*, April 21, 2022, https://www.nydailynews.com/entertainment/broadway/ny-americano-musical-tony-valdoninos-dreamer-sean-ewing-immigration-mexico-daca-20220421-2db7kegecbhwnhp5eutjvby7my-story.html.

RECOMMENDATIONS FOR ADDITIONAL RESOURCES

Bernstein, Leonard, et al. *"West Side Story: The New Broadway Cast Recording."* New York: Sony Masterworks, 2009.

This cast recording includes Spanish-language versions of "I Feel Pretty" ("Me Siento Hermosa") and "A Boy Like That" ("Un Hombre Asi") with translations by Lin-Manuel Miranda.

Herrera, Brian Eugenio. *Latin Numbers: Playing Latino in Twentieth-Century U.S. Popular Performance.* Ann Arbor, MI: Univ. of Michigan Press, 2015.

This text examines the influence of twentieth-century Latino stage and film actors on the American understanding of Latinos as a distinct racial and ethnic group.

Hoffman, Warren. *Great White Way: Race and the Broadway Musical.* New Brunswick, NJ: Rutgers University Press, 2020.

This is a chronological study of how American musicals have reflected changing perceptions of race in America. This second edition includes a discussion of *Hamilton*.

Simon, Paul, et al. "The Capeman: Original Broadway Cast Recording." New York: Decca Broadway, 2006.

This two-disc set features the entire score of the musical and includes performances by Ruben Blades, Marc Anthony, and Ednita Nazario.

CHAPTER 9
My Fair Lady in Japan: The dawn of the East Asian musical theatre boom

Rina Tanaka

On September 1, 1963, the Japanese Tōhō Company celebrated its premiere of Lerner and Loewe's *My Fair Lady* (1956) at the Tokyo Takarazuka Theater, where, at that time, the all-female Takarazuka Revue was not the only resident company, but its sister company Tōhō also produced various productions. The premiere was just after the 1961 film adaptation of *West Side Story* clocked an incredible 511-day run in Japanese theatres, though the American musical in general was much less popular than Japanese and European musical theatre even in the pre-war era. Despite that, Japanese director and playwright Kikuta Kazuo created the first full-scale Japanese-language production of a Broadway musical with an all-Japanese cast. *My Fair Lady* closed a month later in what was considered a successful run.[1]

The success of Tōhō's *My Fair Lady* in Japan pales in comparison to the huge sensation it had already been in London (1958), Australia (1959), Russia (1960), Germany (1961), Iceland (1962), and Vienna (1963). However, Tōhō's *My Fair Lady* was one of the earliest and most important productions in the region given the history of East Asian musical theatres and their interconnection because of the import of the Broadway musical. While Hollywood film musicals had a significant overall impact on East Asian musical theatre in the early Cold War period, Japan was the first among East Asian countries to offer licensed local productions of American musicals. While the first Korean Broadway-style full-scale production of *Porgy and Bess* (1935) appeared in 1966, licensed Broadway musicals didn't appear in South Korea until after the country joined the Universal Copyright Convention in 1987 (Japan joined the convention in 1956).[2]

DOI: 10.4324/9781003256458-10

My Fair Lady is a milestone in both Japanese and global musical theatre history. The success of Tōhō's *My Fair Lady* led to the proliferation and mainstreaming of the "translated musical" as a fully commercialized genre in the Japanese entertainment industry. Japanese private companies vied with each other to secure licenses to run hit musicals, a new trend in the country. In 1964, a year after the Japanese premiere of *My Fair Lady*, three additional Broadway musicals appeared in Japan. Tōhō adapted *No Strings* (1962) at Geijutsu-za. Shinjuku Koma Theater launched its production of *Annie Get Your Gun* (1946). Nissei (the Japan Life Insurance Company) Theatre produced the Japanese premiere of *West Side Story* (1957) at Nissei Theatre, after holding auditions in New York.

In 1962, the two companies, Tōhō Theater and Nissei Theatre, aspired to produce *My Fair Lady* using different approaches. Although both companies recognized the importance of introducing the Broadway musical to Japanese audiences in the early 1960s, Nissei Theatre criticized Tōhō's approach to adapting the Broadway musical with the conventions of Japanese musical theatre. Ishihara Shintaro, the director of Nissei Theatre and later the governor of Tokyo, emphasized that the "orientation to the new genuine musical can break and change the cheap concept of the musical misrepresented to Japan" only by bringing the "complete production by the Broadway cast and staffs."[3] The Japanese productions of musicals produced by the Nissei Theatre strived for authenticity and sought to replicate the performance quality of the original Broadway productions. This guiding principle was later taken over by the Shiki Theatre Company, the Japanese producer of musicals licensed by Andrew Lloyd Webber's Really Useful Group and Disney Theatrical Group. Nevertheless, Tōhō's "misinterpreted" translated musicals have been as popular as Shiki Theatre's licensed megamusicals in Japan. Regarding this situation, a question remains: What is an *authentic* Broadway musical in Japan?

The understanding of the Broadway musical in Japan is related to how the musical was introduced to the country, and how it has been practiced in light of Japan's traditions, on-site requirements, and limitations. These factors strongly affected—and often regulated—the process of creating and promoting a professional Japanese production of Broadway musicals. The Japanese premiere of *My Fair Lady*, which will be examined in this chapter, is a good example because the director Kikuta interpreted this musical as an innovative tool to compete with the conventional Japanese entertainment industry, while not distancing the structure too far from what Japanese audiences expected. This chapter also explores how rich traditions of hybridity in musical theatre and show business have rooted the later megamusicals of the 1980s and beyond that have played with great success in the East Asian market.

THE 1963 PRODUCTION: THE INTRODUCTION OF THE BROADWAY MUSICAL TO JAPAN

On January 1, 1964, director Kikuta Kazuo gave a speech at the award ceremony where Tōhō's 1963 production of *My Fair Lady* was awarded the fifth Mainichi Art Award. He explained how *My Fair Lady* was once considered boring by Japanese theatergoers fluent in the foreign—English or German, or both—language(s), saying:

> [*My Fair Lady*] can become an interesting, refined musical in the classic style, not to let the Japanese musical go on the wrong way. I was confident [I would] direct the Japanese production well. Critics would give it a favorable review. However, there remained concerns about whether we could sell out tickets.[4]

Kikuta's concerns stemmed from the vast difference between the 1950s musicals in Japan and those on Broadway. During the 1950s, many original Japanese musicals were created in theatres and on television in the country. Hata Toyokichi, Tōhō's managing and artistic director of Western-style popular musical theatre in Japan from the 1930s onward, helmed eight original musicals at the Imperial Theatre from 1951 to 1954. Meanwhile, Shōchiku, another large Japanese entertainment company, launched "magemono" musicals set during the Edo period (1603–1868). At each of the bustling theatres in Japan, these musicals appeared and were beloved, but they were similar to traditional Japanese theatre, Western-style operetta and revue, and the hybrids of those styles.

According to Hata, the 1950s musicals in Japan were meant to be "something new and international to master the foreign style, and whereby, digest and re-create the Japanese tradition. [...] The style is nothing but 'musical theatre.'"[5] However, the name of the style was titular. He continued, "I named this musical theatre style 'Teigeki (Imperial Theatre) comic opera,' but because that name had been worn out in Europe, I renamed it American 'musicals [sic].'"[6] Not adhering to the American understanding of the musical, but borrowing its novelty, Hata created Japanese musicals based on the localized styles of European operetta and revue.

However, after Japanese audiences witnessed the film musical *West Side Story* in 1961 and started becoming familiar with Broadway musicals, the 1950s-style Japanese musicals faced criticism as "a travesty of jumbled revues and comedy shows."[7] Against that backdrop, Kikuta attempted "not to let the Japanese musical go on the wrong way," not by producing Rodgers and Hammerstein's *Oklahoma!* or *South Pacific*, whose film versions were released in Japan during the late 1950s but didn't succeed commercially, but by putting on Lerner and Loewe's *My Fair Lady* instead.

In his award speech, Kikuta also explained that Tōhō did not replicate the Broadway production because they "purchased only the performing rights of the book and music" and "did not have any license to replicate [...] the overseas production."[8] While revealing that Tōhō "had no budget to buy the licensed direction or hire the director of the Broadway production," since the competition between Tōhō and Nissei Theatre caused Columbia Broadcasting System (CBS) to raise the price of the *My Fair Lady* license fee by thirty thousand US dollars, Kikuta insisted that Tōhō's production succeeded in Japan since it was "created under instructions of the book."[9] *My Fair Lady* introduced the concept of book-based musicals to Japan, where major Japanese musical theatre previously offered musical comedies that existed entirely as star vehicles.

It is striking that Kikuta developed the concept of "the musical as drama," the same phrase as the title of Scott McMillin's much later book *The Musical as Drama* (2006), to describe *My Fair Lady*.[10] Kikuta placed "the good book translated by Kurahashi Ken above everything else" in his production of *My Fair Lady*.[11] Clearly, Kikuta believed that what McMillin later called "a better book" of *My Fair Lady* could be the savior of the Japanese pseudo-musical in the 1950s that had, until then, failed to switch over from the European-Japanese style to the contemporary American form.[12]

MAKING IT SENTIMENTAL WITH THE
SHITAMACHI DIALECT

Although Kikuta directed *My Fair Lady* with a concept similar to the original Broadway musical, Tōhō's production, based on the translated libretto from English to Japanese, was created "in the Japanese style better for the Japanese audience" with substantial changes to the original text.[13] In Kurahashi's translation, the character Eliza, who in the original production speaks with the cockney accent traditionally used by working-class Londoners, spoke instead in the crisp Shitamachi dialect. This language used to be spoken among commoners in Edo (the former name of Tokyo before 1868) and has been associated with an assertive, cheerful, and chic person born and raised in Tokyo. It was a clear contrast to Professor Higgins, speaking in the standard Japanese language established and spread with Tokyo-centric westernization in the late nineteenth century. Unlike cockney, the Shitamachi dialect is not the lower status mark; on the contrary, it gives Tokyoites their local identity. Therefore, Eliza's Shitamachi utterance brings a nostalgic sound to the times before the outside world increasingly came and settled in Tokyo. Tōhō's *My Fair Lady* reflected the rapidly changing Japanese society in the translation, letting Eliza transform from the Edo woman to the Tokyo lady.

Regarding the cast members, Kikuta initially approached some Japanese performers who could play the characters as the Broadway casts did, but those actors mostly turned down the offers. Instead, Kikuta let the Japanese production go on the road with some locally famous performers. Eri Chiemi, a 26-year-old best-known singer in pop and jazz music, played the role of Eliza (pictured with Takashima Tadao in Figure 9.1). Tadao, a famous 33-year-old film actor with a talent for singing, appeared as Higgins. Happa Mutoshi, the 37-year-old comedian who had appeared in many comedies at the Imperial Theatre, took the role of Alfred P. Doolittle. Takashima and Happa were significantly younger than the original cast of the Broadway production. Casting stars from a younger generation allowed the Broadway musical in Japan not to be embodied by veterans associated too closely with Japanese style musical comedies (and saved the seasoned performers from gambling their careers on a Broadway import).

Figure 9.1: Eri Chiemi as Eliza; Takashima Tadao as Higgins in the 1963 Tōhō production of *My Fair Lady*. ©2022 Tōhō Co., Ltd. Theatrical Department

Despite promoting the show by using famous Japanese stars, ticket sales for Tōhō's *My Fair Lady* moved slowly because the Broadway musical was too unfamiliar to the company's audiences. To improve the situation, Tōhō's manager added the subtitle a "Roar-with-laughter comedy" to *My Fair Lady*, framing the production as something similar to Tōhō's traditional repertoire of musical comedies. Kikuta, who had wanted to run *My Fair Lady* in the style of the Broadway musical, did not oppose this change. He needed to avoid a box office failure that might affect his vision of the future, which involved increasing imports of Broadway musicals. Tōhō used more insurance to draw a full house by selling group tickets, for example, in partnership with Tomin Gekijo (Tokyo Citizens' Theatre), the oldest Japanese membership society. They offered cheaper tickets to its members, which included citizens in Tokyo and its surrounding neighborhoods.

After the success of the premiere, box office sales took off. Before the last day of the performance came—Tōhō had failed to extend the period of borrowing the Tokyo Takarazuka Theater to run *My Fair Lady* longer because the schedule of the theatre was already full of other programs—the company quickly sold out tickets for the next run, slated for the coming January. In the next season,

Tōhō's *My Fair Lady* ran 92 performances with 240,000 people in attendance, recording the largest box office draw since the Tokyo Takarazuka Theater opened in 1934.

THE SECRET OF THE SUCCESS OF TŌHŌ'S *MY FAIR LADY*

What was it that made Tōhō's *My Fair Lady* such a success? First, *My Fair Lady*'s Broadway sound appealed to Japanese audiences, especially as it characterized the rise and fall of the characters' complicated emotions (under the skilled baton of conductor Koseki Yuji, who was well-versed in European classical music and Japanese popular music). The Japanese version of the musical used the essential elements of the Broadway production, but the result was quite different. Asakusa-born Eri's knack for performing as a comedienne in the native Shitamachi accent was well suited for Eliza before her transformation and accentuated the first part of the play, including the last scene of the 1963 production that ingeniously made *My Fair Lady*'s story coherent with Shitamachized Eliza. Kikuta directed the 1963 production's end very sentimentally and therefore familiarly to the Japanese audiences. The show closed with Eliza staring at Higgins and holding back her tears. At the same time, he forlornly said, "Where the devil are my slippers, Eliza?" The critics pointed out that Eliza's return to Higgins even made the audience sob.[14] The sentimentalized drama was borrowed from shimpa, the Japanese early modern theatre genre that featured a hybrid of traditional **kabuki** performance styles and realistic western drama. The critic Watanabe analyzed the similarity of dramatic structure between Tōhō's *My Fair Lady* and Kawaguchi Matsutaro's shimpa play, *Tsuruhachi Tsurujiro* (1934).[15] That bittersweet melodrama dealt with an artist pair in business, who loved each other without knowing, but both ended up lonely. If that play is considered a counterpart to Tōhō's *My Fair Lady*, the Japanese version of Eliza and Higgins would establish a more intimate partnership with mutual trust and hidden love.

Takashima and Eri supported that interpretation in their performances. Takashima's gentle Higgins "lacked the arrogant manner of the Rex Harrison version"[16] and focused more on how "earnestly" he taught Eliza "without understanding the girl's feeling(s)."[17] Takashima eventually presented a pleasantly singing and more personable Higgins, clearly going against Lerner and Loewe's original vision of the character as a non-singing male leading actor who could carry the character's highly demanding speeches.

Eri's performance as Eliza also attenuated the pupil-and-teacher relationship between Eliza and Higgins. Her strong, husky voice singing Eliza's songs precisely and emphatically in the alto range, considerably lower than the original scores, shaped Eliza as a woman standing her ground. And her personality, which Japanese artist Terayama Shuji described as "embodying 'happiness'" oozed through her performance as Eliza and connected with audiences.[18] In the Broadway musical, Eliza was initially designed as "the ultimate Broadway musical heroine [...] [who] embodies the triumph of aspiration [...] with aspects of the American Dream."[19] In Tōhō's production, she turned into the character who symbolized the rapid change in Japanese society, not only in her accent from nostalgic pre-modern Edo to modernized Tokyo, but also in her favorable representation of the petit bourgeois in the post-war economic boom.

In short, Director Kikuta and Translator Kurahashi adjusted the 1963 production to appeal to local tastes. The casting played a very important role in adapting the production so that the audience could immerse themselves in the show. Additionally, Eri and Takashima discovered their new talents through Tōhō's *My Fair Lady* and later became involved in other translated musicals. Tōhō's *My Fair Lady* thus became a turning point from the previous musical-comedy-like musical to the translated musical in Japan.

Additionally, it is notable that the Japanese audiences regarded Tōhō's *My Fair Lady* as an "excellent reproduction of Broadway."[20] This was not surprising since only a small number of Japanese people saw the original production on Broadway, excluding journalists like Emerson Chaplin from *The New York Times*. The playwright Koyama Yushi even wrote in *Mainichi* newspaper that "the biggest cause of the success at both aesthetic and business levels was Lerner's good libretto freely interpreted from Shaw's *Pygmalion* and Loewe's good composition."[21] In other words, the success of

Tōhō's production was initially attributed to the elements from the original Broadway musical, without considering how much it was adapted. Moreover, as the critic Senda Akihiko wrote in 2000, "*My Fair Lady* [...] has been a touchstone of the musicals in Japan," even after the Hollywood film version starring Audrey Hepburn was released in Japan in 1964, and the Broadway production held guest performances for Japanese audiences in 1989.[22]

Indeed, in the years since its Japanese premiere, *My Fair Lady* has become a Japanese "classic" musical. Tōhō has run it in 24 cities more than 1,200 times almost annually for 59 years, presenting a different system for counting long runs than the continuous Broadway counts. Tōhō ran *My Fair Lady* for a couple of months almost every year, sometimes casting the same performers each season. This "Japanese long-run system"—so-called later by Tōhō's chairman, Matsuoka Isao (in office: 1977–2009)—enabled Tōhō to continue offering *My Fair Lady* and other hit musicals with the most popular Japanese stars in each era and to continually revitalize the production with the latest looks.[23]

The rewritten image of the Broadway musical since *My Fair Lady* innovated the Japanese entertainment industry and successfully birthed the Asian musical theatre boom. Tōhō's musicals played in this fashion, though occasionally new works were introduced, like the original musical *Scarlett* (1970), a musicalization of *Gone with the Wind* that was a collaboration of Kikuta with Harold Rome. Although *Scarlett* was the first musical exported from Japan to London and American cities, it failed to reach Broadway. Consequently, Tōhō continued concentrating on the domestic market with two exceptions for the original musicals, *Roman Holiday* (1998) and *Marie Antoinette* (2006).

TAKARAZUKA REVUE: A UNIQUE JAPANESE MUSICAL THEATRE TROUPE

Any discussion of the musical in Japan would be incomplete without a mention of this distinctive and famous all-female company, founded in 1914, who are well known for their performances of Broadway-style musicals. *Takarazuka Chicago*, a faithful reproduction of the Broadway revival, even toured to New York in

2016—historically, they had international tour performances as Japan's artistic ambassador until their first overseas business expansion to Taiwan in 2013. The Tokyo Takarazuka Theater, which was home to the groundbreaking production of *My Fair Lady*, also housed the Takarazuka Revue, which was created as an alternative to the traditional all-male form of kabuki theatre. The Takarazuka Revue had its own music school for teen girls and the company was peopled exclusively by its graduates specializing in playing either *otokoyaku* (male roles) or *musumeyaku* (female roles). Some actresses later moved from the Takarazuka Revue to sister company Tōhō's musicals and several have played Eliza in *My Fair Lady* during Tōhō's long run. Former Takarazuka actresses are desirable for Tōhō because they are carefully trained with voice and acting lessons, as well as with both Broadway style and traditional Japanese dance classes. Their popularity—each Takarazuka star has her own fan club—is also attractive for producers.

THE INTRODUCTION OF THE MEGAMUSICAL THROUGH JAPAN TO EAST ASIA

The success of Tōhō's translated musicals had an impact on the development of Japanese musicals in the local entertainment industry. In 1979, Asari Keita, the producer of rival Nissei Theatre and the co-founder of Shiki Theatre, explained the necessity of adapting the American musical "to match the emotional landscape of Japan," saying "we should dare to transform from *Blondie* to *Sazae-san*, as perfectly done by Morishige in *Fiddler on the Roof*."[24] Indeed, Tōhō's very popular *Fiddler on the Roof* (1967) starred Morishige Hisaya, another famous Japanese actor and comedian in the Showa era, who declined the initial offer of the role of Higgins for Tōhō's *My Fair Lady*. He interpreted Tevye as a nostalgic "stubborn father" and let the production shift from the original Jewish theme to the human-interest comedy centered on Morishige's Tevye. It is notable that producer Asari also praised *My Fair Lady* performer Eri Chiemi by mentioning the Japanese long-running (since 1946) manga *Sazae-san*. Chiemi was known for playing the title role as a typical Japanese post-war housewife in the ten films and the TV drama series when she was appearing as Eliza in Tōhō's *My Fair Lady*. This producer attributed the success in early adaptations of the American musical by Tōhō to the stars' acting, especially the stock characters that they continually represented in various media.

Asari had firsthand knowledge of the Japanese market demand in his engagement for the long series of recital shows at the Nissei Theatre featuring the former star of the Takarazuka Revue, Koshiji Fubuki, with Shiki Theatre's performers in the supporting roles. This experience led him and Shiki Theatre to its unique strategy without stars but with a highly skilled ensemble, all of whom could play any featured role with high quality performances. On that basis, Asari and Shiki Theatre initiated the import of the megamusical to Japan, where they created many Japanese-language replica productions of Andrew Lloyd Webber's and Disney's blockbuster hit musicals and have run them with rotating casts at their own theatres, under the sponsorship of Japan Railways and other companies, for as long as they are able.

Shiki Theatre's style of indigenizing the megamusical for Japan affected China and South Korea, as well, starting in the 1980s. Those countries introduced the company's method to their citizens through touring performances, including Shiki's productions of the West End musical *Hans Christian Andersen* and Lloyd Webber's *Jesus Christ Superstar*, and the original musical *Ri Kōran* (Li Xianglan, 1991). Their visits were initially not welcomed in terms of Japan's invasion and occupation of both countries until the end of World War II, but subsequently, the company built relationships with theatres in each country.[25] Asari and Shiki Theatre offered technical support for China's Central Academy of Drama so it could establish a musical theatre department in 1995 and launch Shiki's *The Cat Who Wished to Be a Man* and *West Side Story* with all-Chinese casts. Meanwhile, Shiki Theatre reached 330 performances of *The Lion King* with their Korean cast (from 2006 to 2007) as a part of the opening of the Charlotte Theater in Seoul, South Korea's first theatre designed exclusively for large-scale musicals. Their activities abroad were less profitable—Shiki's long run in Seoul ended in a deficit of 3.6 billion KRW (2.8 million USD)—but birthed the musical theatre boom across several East Asian countries. Moreover, an intra-East Asian circulation of human resources resulted in the diversification of Shiki Theatre's performers in Japan, 6% of which came from China or South Korea by 2018.

The increasing global significance of Asian musical theatre in the early 1990s supported that Japan was, at least initially, the birthplace of the Asian musical boom. For instance, the Japan Foundation ASEAN Culture Center invited the first Singaporean musical *Beauty World* (1992) and two Filipino musicals, *El filibusterismo* (1993) and *Noli Me Tangere* (1995), to Japan. The Asian boom in Japanese pop music resulted in the collaboration between the director Miyamoto Amon and the Singaporean composer Dick Lee, resulting in the original musical *Hong Kong Rhapsody* (1993). However, these intra-Asian circulations slowed down due to the Asian financial crisis starting in 1997 and the bursting of Japan's bubble economy in 1992, which necessitated structural changes for the Japanese theatre industry from the late 1990s to the early 2000s.

THE UNIQUE MULTI-CAST SYSTEM

Tōhō, however, did not miss out on the megamusical, but their approach to producing them was different from the Shiki Theatre. The Japanese productions of *Les Misérables* (West End 1985; Tōhō 1987) and *Miss Saigon* (West End 1989; Tōhō 1992) expanded Tōhō's practices of producing translated musicals by introducing multiple casts, who were discovered through a full audition process and trained at a fully paid school, and by running performances irregularly, but for longer periods—including 200 performances of *Les Misérables* and 745 performances of *Miss Saigon*. Previously, Tōhō rarely held auditions because Tōhō's production of *Fantastic* (1967), the first Japanese commercial theatre that used large-scale auditions, was not successful. The success of using multiple casts resulted not in a switch to completely skill-based casting but in a hybrid system of casting both stars and skilled, but less famous performers.

Indeed, the nationwide stars on whom Tōhō's musicals had previously relied on were vanishing as audiences' tastes changed. The crash of the Japanese economy also changed the audiences for Japanese theatre. Group visitors, whose tickets were bought by Japanese companies and local governments as part of their customer care and benefits programs, decreased during the recession. This caused a wave of closures of commercial theatres and troupes. Nevertheless, the number of musical theatre audiences increased and reached eight million, 60% of all Japanese theater-goers, in 2005. Musical fans became the target audience group of the Japanese entertainment industry. The large, well-established companies, Tōhō, Shiki Theatre, and the Takarazuka Revue, survived and consequently monopolized approximately 90% of the total musical theatre market sales.

Tōhō developed their ticket sales by offering a variety of choices to see multiple casts by announcing in advance who would appear in each performance and allowing audiences to choose their favorite combination of actors. The increase in touring productions gave rise to the fans' "expeditions," wherein the ardent fans would visit regional theatres to experience their favorite performers interacting with each other during the tour, or simply because they could not get the highly competitive tickets for the performances in large cities. The increased need for performers in multi-cast shows also allowed various performers, who were not necessarily nationally known but were popular in a specific genre, to find success. The double, triple, and quadruple casts became common in Japanese large-scale musical theatres, as parodically described in Takahira Tetsuo's musical comedy *That's Japanese Musical 2000*, "On my own, pretending *two or three are* beside me."

This particular selling-by-multiple-cast system cast was also similar to commercial musical theatre in South Korea from the mid-2000s. With the development of the "Hallyu," or the Korean wave, Korean pop singers expanded their activities from the music industry to musical theatre, bringing their enthusiastic fans, including Japanese ones, to new performances. Based on the similarity between the two countries in the way of industrializing musical theatre, South Korea also succeeded in exporting its musicals to Japan in the 2010s. Tōhō has been one of the active companies in creating Japanese productions of Korean musicals since *Love Is In The Rain* (1995; Tōhō 2008).

The rise of Korean musicals in East Asia during the 2010s looked like it was taking the same path Shiki Theatre trod in the region in the 1990s. Korean productions of licensed Broadway musicals and original Korean works reached Chinese audiences, exemplified by the annual "K-musical road show" in Shanghai for networking with local partners. One of the significant differences between Japan's export of musicals and Korea's is the difference in those countries in what public subsidies are available to the musical theatre industry. In Japan, musicals have been carried out and funded mostly by private companies, marked by the establishment of the New National Theatre (1997) with three departments of opera, dance, and drama, excluding the musical. Although the Tokyo Metropolitan Theatre's project (1999–2008) once encouraged the creation of original musicals by leasing theatres without a rental fee, exporting musicals turned out to be costly. In contrast, the South Korean government has promoted the creation and export of Korean musicals since the mid-2000s, which has in turn enhanced the international presence of Korean musicals starting in the 2010s.

The case study of Tōhō's *My Fair Lady* stresses the importance of local and transnational perspectives to connect incidental findings to global phenomena. While the macro understanding of the Broadway musical illuminates how it established a new common basis to connect East Asian musical theatre practices on a deeper level and was a bridgehead for the intra-Asian permeation of the megamusical, tracing incidental details of the production provides insight into how it really worked and how it directly and indirectly affected the actual progress of the East Asian musical boom. Musical theatre practice as a crossroads of local and global phenomena is best described by combining the micro and macro perspectives.[26] As seen in this chapter, Shiki Theatre's indigenizing method of the Broadway musical developed in contrast to the practices of Tōhō in Japan, but later it fostered the introduction of the megamusical to the rest of East Asia. Tōhō, through which Broadway musicals and later megamusicals had infiltrated the Japanese entertainment industry, ultimately became a good partner for Korean export-oriented musicals. Considering the far-reaching consequences of Tōhō's *My Fair Lady* on the Japanese musical theatre, and by extension, on East Asian musical theatre history, the dynamics of the on-site musical theatre practice remarkably affect its local and trans-local developments, supporting the coexistence of different but interrelated musical theatre practices, which are an important part of global musical theatre history. Accordingly, Tōhō's *My Fair Lady* is a milestone that heralded the dawn of the long-lasting East Asian musical theatre boom.

ACKNOWLEDGMENT

This chapter was supported by Suntory Foundation's Grant for Groundbreaking Young Researchers, 2020.

NOTES

1 In the chapter, the Japanese names are written in their original order, in which the family name is followed by the given name, except for the names of scholars who have had English-language publications with their names spelled in the customary order in English.

2 See also Hyunjung Lee, "Emulating Modern Bodies: The Korean version of Porgy and Bess and American popular culture in the 1960s South Korea," *Cultural Studies*, 26: 5, 2012, 723–39; Ji Hyon (Kayla) Yuh, "Korean Musical Theatre's Past: Yegrin and the Politics of 1960s Musical Theatre," in *The Palgrave Handbook of Musical Theatre Producers*, Laura MacDonald and William Everett eds. (New York: Palgrave Macmillan, 2017), 253–60.

3 Ishihara Shintaro, "Honmono no Tame no Doryoku" (Efforts for the Real Things), *Asahi Shimbun* newspaper, December 27, 1962.

4 Kikuta Kazuo, "Mainichi Geijutsu Shō wo Jushō shite" (Awarded the Mainichi Art Award), *Asahi Shimbun* newspaper, January 9, 1964.

5 Hata Toyokichi, "Myūjikarusu to wa" (What are Musicals?), in *Gekijo Nijū-nen* (Theater 20 Years) (Tokyo: Asahi Shimbun-sha, 1955), 197.

6 Hata, *Gekijo Nijū-nen* (Theater 20 Years), 197.

7 Abe Yasushi, *Shō Bijinesu ni Koishite* (Loving Show Business) (Tokyo: Kadokawa Shoten, 1996), 71.

8 Kikuta, *Asahi Shimbun* newspaper, January 9, 1964.

9 Kikuta, *Asahi Shimbun* newspaper, January 9, 1964.

10 Kikuta Kazuo, "*Mai Fea Redī* Nihon demo Jōen e" (*My Fair Lady* will be performed in Japan), *Yomiuri Shimbun* newspaper, November 26, 1962.

11 Kikuta, *Asahi Shimbun* newspaper, January 9, 1964.

12 Scott McMillin, *The Musical as Drama* (Princeton, NJ: Princeton University Press, 2006), 15.

13 Kikuta, *Asahi Shimbun* newspaper, January 9, 1964.

14 Takano Masao, "Honba wo Migoto ni Saigen: Tōhō no Mai Fea Redī" (Excellent Reproduction of Broadway: Tōhō's *My Fair Lady*), *Asahi Shimbun* newspaper, September 6, 1963; "Honkaku-teki Myūjikaru no Jōen: *Mai Fea Redī*" (The performance of full-scale musical: *My Fair Lady*), *Mainichi Shimbun* newspaper, September 8, 1963.

15 Watanabe, *Weekly Asahigraph*, vol. 3972, 24.

16 Emerson Chaplin, "'Fair Lady' Wins Tokyo Applause," *The New York Times*, September 2, 1963.

17 Takano, *Asahi Shimbun* newspaper, September 6, 1963.

18 Honchi Eiki, "Kaisō no Haiyū to Butai 4: Eri Chiemi no *Anī yo Jū wo Tore*" (Actors and Stages in Reminiscences 4: Eri Chiemi's *Annie Get Your Gun*), *Geinō*, September 1985.

19 Dominic Mchugh, *Loverly: The Life and Times of* My Fair Lady (New York: Oxford University Press, 2012), 201.

20 Takano, *Asahi Shimbun* newspaper, September 6, 1963.

21 Koyama Yushi, "Nihonteki Myujikaru no Syuhen: *Mai Fea Redī* wo Mite" (The Surrounding of Japanese Musicals), *Mainichi Shimbun* newspaper, October 17, 1963.

22 Senda Akihiko, "Mai Fea Redī: Rasuto-sīn wa Happī Endo ka" (*My Fair Lady*: Is the last scene a happy end?), *Myūjikaru no Jidai* (The Era of the Musical) (Tokyo: Kinema Shumpo-sha, 2000), 48.

23 "Matsuoka Isao: Engeki Bumon. *Yaneno ue* Hantoshi-kan Jōen, Nihon-gata Ronguran, Hokano Enmoku nimo" (Matsuoka Isao: Theater Section. *Fiddler* Ran in Six Month, Japanese-styled Long Run for the Other Productions), *Nihon Keizai Shimbun* newspaper, June 26, 2016.

24 Kozuki Akira, Morishige Hisaya, Koshiji Fubuki, and Asari Keita, "Nihon-muki Tenaoshi Seikō. Tanoshiki kana, Myūjikaru. Senkaku-sha Ōini Kataru" (The success of Japanese-oriented Modification. How Wonderful the Musical Is. The Forerunners' Talk), *Yomiuri Shimbun* newspaper, January 3, 1979.

25 Regarding the relation between Shiki and China, see also Rina Tanaka, "De- and Repoliticization of the Second Sino-Japanese War in Japanese Contemporary Musicals: *Ri Kōran* and after," in *Music Theatre and Politics: Hegemonies, Resistances, Utopias*, Marcus Tan and Tereza Havelkova, eds. (Oxford University Press, 2023, forthcoming).

26 See also Tasos Zembylas und Peter Tschmuck, "Einleitung: Kulturbetriebsforschung und ihre Grundlagen," in *Kulturbetriebs-forschung: Ansätze und Perspektiven der Kulturbetriebslehre*, Tasos Zembylas und Peter Tschmuck, hrsg (Wiesbaden: VS-Springer, 2006), 7–14.

RECOMMENDATIONS FOR ADDITIONAL RESOURCES

Chiemi, Eri. *Chiemi Show Time: My Fair Lady/Chiemi At The Coma*. CD. Tokyo: King Records, 2020.
    This remastered CD album, originally released as LP (1964), captures how Eri sang *My Fair Lady*'s songs. It is not the live recording of Tōhō's production due to mechanical rights issues, but her voice and the sound reveal a great deal about how Broadway sound was reproduced for Japanese audiences.

Wetmore Jr., Kevin J., Siyuan Liu, and Erin B. Mee eds. *Modern Asian Theatre and Performance 1900-2000*, London/New York: Bloomsbury, 2014.

This historical overview of modern drama in Asian countries and regions introduces where and how European and American musical theatre was produced in the region.

Yamanashi, Makiko. *A History of the Takarazuka Revue Since 1914: Modernity, Girls' Culture, Japan Pop.* Leiden: Global Oriental, 2012. This English language book is a comprehensive historical survey of The Takarazuka Revue, discussed briefly in this chapter, as it is one of the most important and long-running Japanese musical theatre companies.

Yamanashi, Makiko, Sissi Liu, Gilbert C. F. Fong, Shelby Kar-yan Chan,, Fan-Ting Cheng, Ji hyon (Kalya) Yuh, and Caleb Goh. "Modern Musicals in Asia." In *The Routledge Handbook of Asian Theatre*, edited by Siyuan Liu, 527–551, Abington/New York: Routledge, 2016. This country-by-country survey provides basic and essential knowledge about how the American musical was introduced and has subsequently developed in Japan, China, Hong Kong, Taiwan, Korea, and Southeast Asia.

CHAPTER 10

Women in charge: Female creative teams and *Waitress*

Paige Allen and Stacy Wolf

On April 24, 2016, *Waitress* opened as the first Broadway musical with all major creative roles filled by women: composer/lyricist Sara Bareilles, librettist Jessie Nelson, director Diane Paulus, and choreographer Lorin Latarro. (The musical supervisor/arranger, Nadia DiGiallonardo, and costume designer, Suttirat Larlarb, were also women.) Three years later, *Hadestown* boasted a women-led team of composer, lyricist, and librettist Anaïs Mitchell, director Rachel Chavkin, set designer Rachel Hauck, and lead producer Mara Isaacs. And in 2020, *SIX* featured women's contributions as co-writer, co-director, choreographer, musical director, set designer, and costume designer, plus an all-female cast and four-woman on-stage band.[1] Perhaps the male domination of Broadway is coming to an end.

Though creative teams with at least two women—a production "Bechdel test" and the focus of our examples in this chapter—have been rare in Broadway musical theatre history, many individual women have contributed as lyricists and librettists, composers and orchestrators, directors and choreographers, and designers and producers. In the late nineteenth and early twentieth centuries, their artistry was often erased or disregarded. Pauline Elizabeth Hopkins, for example, wrote *Peculiar Sam* in 1879, "the first musical by a Black person ever," according to Eric Glover.[2] Glover contrasts the obscurity of Hopkins' ballad opera to the fame and canonicity of the (white, male) Gershwins' *Porgy and Bess* (1935).[3] Between 1866 and 1943, Korey R. Rothman observes, "prolific female songwriters," such as Rida Johnson Young, Anne Caldwell, and Dorothy Donnelly, "wrote lyrics for some of the most popular shows and performances" but have been relegated to footnotes in musical theatre history.[4] Rothman and other contributors to the 2008 collection, *Women in American Musical Theatre*, argue that musical theatre historians have ignored the contributions of women by writing a history that focuses on a few white men, offering a corrective in their anthology.[5] Maestra, the nonprofit organization that "provides support, visibility, and community to the women and nonbinary people who make the music in the musical theatre industry," created timelines of female composers, both on and Off Broadway.[6] These efforts make visible the achievements of women artists to tell a more accurate Broadway musical theatre history, even as few women have had opportunities on Broadway.

Given women's historic, if underappreciated, contributions to musical theatre, why is it still unique to see a women-led, let alone women-*only*, creative team? Producing musical theatre is expensive and producers are decidedly risk averse. In 2003, *Wicked* (libretto by Winnie Holzman), for example, cost $14 million, setting a new record, though it made back its capital investment in a record-breaking 14 months. *Frozen* (2018; Kristen Anderson-Lopez co-wrote the music and lyrics; Jennifer Lee wrote the book) cost $25 million and the megaflop *Spider-Man: Turn Off the Dark* (2011; directed by Julie Taymor, who also co-wrote the book) close to $80 million.[7] As a commercial enterprise, Broadway depends on ticket sales to survive and thrive, and only 20% of musicals recoup their capital. Producers invest in what they hope will be surefire hits and unapologetically repeat popular trends, from megamusical spectaculars of the 1980s to jukebox musicals of the 1990s to *Hamilton* imitators in the 2010s.

Broadway producers, like Hollywood movie producers, are reluctant to take a chance on women artists who might not have had the opportunity to collaborate on large-scale projects. Moreover, Broadway hiring—like that of many industries—relies on reputation and connections, and white men have been the beneficiaries of this system. The fewer people you know, the less likely you are to get a job. If you're not getting jobs, you're not making new connections. People of color and women artists are caught in a vicious cycle that excludes them. As Mitchell said, "In terms of people [producers] trusting women and people of color with the money that it takes ... the people who have that money tend to be white men."[8] The glass ceiling common in other industries persists for Broadway musicals, too. In light of these economic forces, the formation and success of an all-female creative team is remarkable.

When women take the reins and compose, write, direct, and/or choreograph musicals, their work is as rich, compelling, entertaining, and varied as the work of men. This chapter provides an overview of women-led musicals throughout Broadway history, leading up to and beyond the history-making production of *Waitress*. In some cases, such as *Fun Home* or *Hadestown*, women artists innovate formally and renovate the genre of musical theatre. Other musicals focus on women's lives, including *SIX* and *Waitress*. While we praise any musical with more than two women on the creative team, we also examine a musical's political and ideological project to assess how it represents women and what story it tells. In other words, we advocate both for the practice of hiring more women and for telling feminist stories.

THE WORK OF WOMEN IN THE 1940s–1960s: BROADWAY'S "GOLDEN AGE"

From the 1940s to the mid-1960s, musicals were part of mainstream US popular culture. Cast albums regularly landed on Billboard charts; sheet music sold thousands of copies; and Broadway stars appeared on *Ed Sullivan* and other tv shows. White men dominated every aspect of musical theatre production, even as most musicals starred great women performers like Ethel Merman, Mary Martin, Lena Horne, Juanita Hall, and Barbara Cook.

A few women artists broke the mold. According to Maestra, only three women composed musicals that landed on Broadway during this 25-year period: Anna Russell, Marian Grudeff, and Mary Rodgers. Only Rodgers, composer of the witty and frequently performed *Once Upon a Mattress* (1959) and daughter of Richard Rodgers, which surely aided in her success, is well-known.[9] Women lyricists and librettists fared better, though seldom equaled composers' notoriety. Dorothy Fields had a long and remarkable career, co-creating feisty women characters from Annie Oakley (in *Annie Get Your Gun* [1946]; music by Irving Berlin) to Charity Hope Valentine (in *Sweet Charity* [1964]; music by Cy Coleman). Betty Comden teamed up with Adolph Green and Leonard

Bernstein to bring her sharp, urban, sassy lyrics to *On the Town* (1944) and *Wonderful Town* (1953), two New York City-set hits.[10]

Starting in the early 1940s, choreographer Agnes de Mille revolutionized musical theatre by using dance to tell the story and "creating dance from a female perspective," as Liza Gennaro writes.[11] De Mille choreographed Rodgers and Hammerstein's *Oklahoma!* (1943), the story of farmgirl Laurey and her two suitors, the charming cowboy Curly and the intimidating farmhand Jud. During Laurey's laudanum-induced sleep at the end of Act One, De Mille staged Laurey's unconsciousness in a 15-minute "dream ballet," revealing Laurey's conflicted fears and desires about Curly and Jud. The "dream ballet," which became a staple of Broadway musicals in the mid-twentieth century, transformed chorus girls into actor-dancers and made women's psychologies visible.[12] Gennaro writes that de Mille created choreography that "express[ed] the complexity of women's emotions, including desire, loss, longing, love, fear, pride, and joy ... [S]he was successful with the help of dancers who could embody character and legibly convey movement ideas."[13] De Mille crossed over to directing with Rodgers and Hammerstein's *Allegro* (1947), which flopped, and for which she wrongly had to bear the brunt of the blame, but she paved the way for future women director-choreographers.[14]

SECOND WAVE FEMINISM's BROADWAY SHOWS: THE 1970s–1990s

From the 1970s to the 1990s, musical theatre continued to be dominated by white men, but the Women's Liberation and Civil Rights Movements brought increased attention to and expanded opportunities for women and artists of color. In 1972, Micki Grant became the first woman (and the first Black woman) to write the music, lyrics, and book of a Broadway musical: *Don't Bother Me, I Can't Cope*. Grant collaborated with director Vinette Carroll, the first Black woman to direct a hit on Broadway,[15] to create a show about Black lives, including "living in tenements, slumlords, ghetto life, student protests, Black power, and feminism,"[16] which references both Archie Bunker and Sojourner Truth.[17] Grant employed a range of musical styles—"gospel, jazz, funk, soul, calypso, and soft rock"—and won a Grammy for Best Broadway

Score.[18] Reflecting on the musical 47 years later when a limited-run revival was in the works, Grant said that "I was just writing about my community, about what I saw on the news and on the streets and in the church,"[19] and that "[t]his musical was written to give recognition of things that are ignored."[20]

Don't Bother Me earned rave reviews, including from *New York Times* reviewer Clive Barnes, who described it as "a mixture of a block party and a revival meeting."[21] The musical took a different approach than the politically charged theatre of the Black Arts Movement. At the end of the show, for example, performers went into the aisles, took audience members' hands, and encouraged everyone to hold hands. Grant said, "I wanted to come at it with a soft fist. I wanted to open eyes but not turn eyes away."[22] She and Carroll wanted audiences to "see that we are more alike than we are unalike as human beings."[23]

In 1978, two musicals by white women achieved visibility. Elizabeth Swados wrote, composed, directed, and choreographed *Runaways*, a hit which garnered several Tony nominations. Meanwhile, Gretchen Cryer and Nancy Ford's overtly feminist *I'm Getting My Act Together and Taking It on the Road* was panned by critics but found an enthusiastic audience of women and enjoyed a three-year Broadway run.[24]

In the 1980s, fewer women writers broke into musical theatre. Megamusicals like *Les Misérables* (1987) and *The Phantom of the Opera* (1988) dominated Broadway, and US culture experienced what journalist and author Susan Faludi identified as an "anti-feminist backlash,"[25] a conservative cultural reaction to the political movements of the previous two decades that portrayed women as either childlike ingenues or evil shrews. Barbara Damashek and Molly Newman's *Quilters* (1985) was a notable exception to this male-dominated decade, though perhaps its short run of 24 performances and five previews was also evidence of the backlash.

By the 1990s, third-wave feminism, which included both the "Girl Power" movement and increased attention to intersectionality, grew more visibly mainstream, and more women composers and lyricists found a foothold on Broadway.[26] In 1991, *The Secret Garden*, based on the beloved 1911 novel by Frances Hodgson Burnett (whose well-known title mitigated risk), became the first

Broadway musical created by an all-female team: music by Lucy Simon, book and lyrics by Marsha Norman and Lucy Simon, direction by Susan H. Schulman, scenic design by Heidi Ettinger (then Landesman), costume design by Theloni V. Aldredge, and lighting design by Theron Musser.

The all-women creative team was unintentional but ultimately essential to the show.[27] As Schulman said, "People ask me all the time, 'Did being a woman affect the way you directed this?' Well, of course! Being a woman affects how I do everything! I'm a woman!" In 2016, Norman equivocated, "We began to feel at the time, though, that it was distracting people from the show itself. That it's this, 'Oh it's odd. These girls.'" Still, she said, "We believed that we were opening the door," and they hoped "that all the other musicals written by women would come storming in—but no...."[28]

The musical's feminism—telling the story from a girl's point of view—was central to the artists. As Schulman said, Mary Lennox, the young protagonist sent from India to England to live with her uncle after her parents' death, "is stripped of any sense of power in that time and under those particular circumstances.... It was important that she regain her stamina, regain her sense of grit, regain her agency ..., that we see her able to rescue herself, and she does it through rescuing others."[29]

Reviews—almost all written by white male critics—were decidedly mixed. *New York Times* reviewer Frank Rich wondered if the production was "a compelling dramatic adaptation of its source or merely a beautiful, stately shrine to it" and concluded, "I, for one, often had trouble locating its pulse."[30] David Richards whined of feeling "claustrophobic" and accused the show of being only interested in the story's high-minded moral: "For fear of succumbing to mawkishness, the creators have made *The Secret Garden* nearly emotion-free."[31] Schulman, who'd previously directed an acclaimed revival of *Sweeney Todd* (1989) and went on to direct revivals of *The Sound of Music* (1998), *Little Women* (2005), and many more musicals, attributed negative reviews to the production's non-linear storytelling and a level of abstraction.[32] We suggest that male critics were also biased against the all-female team. Still, *The Secret Garden* won three Tony Awards, and countless spectators connected with the musical; it is regularly produced in regional theatres, community theatres, and high schools, and as of this writing in 2023, is slated for a Broadway revival.

In 1996, Disney Theatricals hired Julie Taymor to direct their second animated-movie-turned-Broadway show, *The Lion King*. Taymor was known as an avant-garde director with a strong visual sensibility. She said she was "keen to increase the presence and potency of the female roles" from the movie and to cast nonwhite performers in the show.[33] Taymor was the first woman to win a Tony Award for Direction of a Musical, and *The Lion King* (as of June 2022) continues to sell out.

Several important women directors and choreographers broke into the industry in the later 1980s and 1990s, including Susan Stroman, who won four Tony Awards for Choreography (*Crazy for You* [1992], *Show Boat* [1995], *Contact* [2000], *The Producers* [2001]), and one for Direction (also for *The Producers*). Gennaro observes that the tragic deaths of gay men during the AIDS epidemic decimated the Broadway community and created a creative void that women directors and choreographers filled.[34] Several of these successful director-choreographers like Stroman, Graciela Daniele, and Patricia Birch, Mary Jo Lodge notes, all followed similar career trajectories, starting as a performer, relying on a male mentor, and holding other positions on Broadway musicals to prove their worth before directing a show on their own.[35] In addition, except for Daniele, all are white women.[36]

WOMEN-LED BROADWAY MUSICALS IN THE TWENTY-FIRST CENTURY

By the twenty-first century, feminism was a part of mainstream US culture, even as feminists were divided in their politics and values. Third and fourth wave feminist activists articulated intersectional analyses of identities and power, urging feminism to address all forms of oppression women face (racism, classism, homophobia, ableism, etc.). In contrast, the early 2010s were also marked by "neoliberal feminism": high-profile women like Sheryl Sandberg urged women to "lean in," assert themselves, and aspire to the same middle-class goals as their male corporate counterparts. As Catherine Rottenberg explains, neoliberal feminism pursues individualist feminist ideals without threatening normative structures of power, making feminism "more easily mainstreamed and popularized since it has been defanged of most if not all of its oppositional force."[37] On Broadway, gender equity and racial diversity were increasingly valued in assembling production teams, even as white men continued to dominate and control the industry.

During this time, musicals with at least two women on the creative team became slightly more common and included a revival of *Ragtime* (2009) and new shows *Violet* (2014) and *Jagged Little Pill* (2019). These musicals focus on women's lives and/or race and power in society. Though all are tuneful and entertaining, none are the frothy, escapist musicals associated with the genre.

In 2015, *Fun Home* broke ground as the first Broadway show written by two women to win the Tony for Best Musical. Composer Jeanine Tesori wrote the music for an extraordinary range of shows and had a string of commercial successes under her belt in an eclectic range of musical styles, including big, bright mainstream musicals like *Thoroughly Modern Millie* (2002) and *Shrek* (2008), and the quieter, more serious and cult-gathering *Caroline, or Change* (2004) and *Violet* (2014). Lyricist and librettist Lisa Kron was a downtown playwright and performer, known for her work with the performance ensemble the Five Lesbian Brothers and her witty, sharply observed plays. Critics praised their collaboration, as Ben Brantley wrote in his *New York Times* review, "The music is woven so intricately into Ms. Kron's time-juggling script that you'll find yourself hard pressed to recall what exactly was said and what was sung."[38]

Fun Home, a "musical about a family that's nothing like yours—and exactly like yours," as one 30-second tv ad intoned, is adapted from Alison Bechdel's 2006 graphic novel of the same title. The lighthearted title, which refers to the Bechdel family business—they own and operate a funeral home—and universalizing blurb belie the musical's actual story, which is unusual—or rather, radical—for a Broadway musical: a lesbian graphic artist remembers her family, her sexual awakening, and her closeted gay father's suicide.

A year after winning the Tony, the show embarked on a national tour, and in 2017, Samuel French released the title for licensing by regional and community theatres and schools, with 126 productions performed across the United States in the first two years.[39] The musical's commercial success surprised theatre critics since *Fun Home* puts queer lives front and center, values feminism, and presumes the audience—any audience—will be engaged in and moved by its story.

Waitress

When *Waitress*, pictured in Figure 10.1, opened at the Brooks Atkinson Theatre in 2016, for the first time in Broadway musical history every lead creative position on a production (book, music, lyrics, direction, and choreography—this last role differentiating *Waitress* from the history-making team of *The Secret Garden* 25 years earlier) was held by a woman.[40] Adapted from the 2007 film written by Adrienne Shelly, *Waitress* follows Jenna, a waitress and baker at a diner in the American South. When Jenna discovers she is pregnant, she faces decisions about her future, complicated by her abusive husband, Earl, and an attraction-turned-affair with her married gynecologist, Dr. Pomatter. Jenna plans to enter a pie-baking competition to win money so that she can leave her husband. Her friends and fellow waitresses, Becky and Dawn, provide support, comic relief, and romantic subplots of their own. After Jenna gives birth, she divorces her husband and ends the affair with Dr. Pomatter. Though Earl has taken the money Jenna saved to enter the contest, the owner of the diner passes away and leaves the restaurant to her. An epilogue depicts Jenna running the diner with her daughter by her side.

Waitress assembled a team with a proven track record and ticket-selling appeal. The musical had name recognition from its source film starring Keri Russell. Lead producers Barry and Fran Weissler were an established powerhouse producing couple. Paulus was known as the artistic director of A.R.T. who directed Tony award-winning revivals of *The Gershwins' Porgy and Bess* (2012) and *Pippin* (2013). However, Bareilles was the biggest influence on the musical's potential and eventual success: a celebrity musician and Grammy-award winner, Bareilles promised a built-in fan base. Within 10 months on Broadway, *Waitress* recouped its investment, aided in no small part by Bareilles herself stepping in to

Figure 10.1: From left, Keala Settle as Becky, Jessie Mueller as Jenna, and Kimiko Glenn as Dawn in Broadway's Waitress. Photo by Joan Marcus.

play Jenna. (The show's overall highest grossing weeks occurred in January 2018 when Bareilles starred as Jenna opposite two-time Grammy-award-winner Jason Mraz as Dr. Pomatter.)[41]

When speaking to the press, the women behind *Waitress* walked a fine line between celebrating their achievement and downplaying the importance of gender. Paulus said, "It's kind of hard to believe it [an all-women creative team] hasn't happened, but my attitude is rather than dwell on what hasn't happened, we're here to say, 'It's the twenty-first century. So come on, everyone!'"[42] As with *The Secret Garden*, the gender make-up of the *Waitress* team was unintentional, and its significance was recognized only after they began working together.[43] Paulus told *Time*, "[W]hat's important to me is that every woman is in the position on this team because they're the best person for the job," emphasizing that the artists received no special treatment on account of their gender.[44] Latarro acknowledged that "there might be something I might see in telling a woman's story that someone else might not see, like when we choreographed a ballet around having contractions," and admitted, "It's just nice to be around women sometimes."[45] Still, she concluded that "the work didn't feel that different without the men around."[46] Bareilles more fully embraced the significance of the all-female team and her power to create opportunities for women: "This experience has really educated me in terms of reflecting on my own hiring practices, remembering to look for and seek out women to fill roles that are sometimes traditionally filled by men."[47] Still, she hoped for a gender-neutral future: "I think ideally we get to a place where the gender isn't even a part of the conversation."[48] This desire to move beyond gender—expressed, too, in Paulus' assurance that gender played no part in hiring—is typical of the neoliberal moment in which *Waitress* debuted, which believed women's liberation could be achieved if only they were treated just like men.

The musical's opening predated two important national conversations about identity-based social justice. In October 2017, major film and theatre producer Harvey Weinstein was accused of sexual abuse, sparking the social media-driven #MeToo Movement. Posts containing #MeToo (indicating that one had experienced sexual harassment or abuse) proliferated, and other terminations of prominent men followed. In the summer of 2020, the American theatre faced a reckoning with how racism is embedded in its structures, exposed comprehensively in a letter and list of demands crafted and disseminated by artists, "We See You, White American Theater."[49] Had *Waitress* premiered a few years later, the team may have been more comfortable asserting that their gender identities and experiences—in addition to their artistic skills—made them well-qualified to tell this story. They also might have noted that the creative team was mostly white. (Latarro is Latina and costume designer Larlarb's parents are Thai.)

Despite the landmark of *Waitress*' all-woman creative team, an interrogation of the womanhood celebrated in *Waitress* reveals that the musical itself is no wholesale feminist victory. Bareilles praised the "sisterhood amongst friends" at the heart of *Waitress* and said, "The story deals with traditional value systems, but we're challenging them within the world of the musical."[50] Bareilles' optimism notwithstanding, *Waitress* is undeniably safe, straight, and—with the scent of the fresh-baked pies for sale wafting through the theatre—entirely palatable.

Each of the women in *Waitress* is bound by her relationship with a man. Book writer Nelson cited these "adventures" with men as key to the story's feminism: "I thought it was such a unique part of the script that [Shelly] wasn't heading towards like, 'Oh, we hope they get married to whoever they're sleeping with.'"[51] Perhaps *Waitress* empowers its women to explore relationships without the inevitability of marriage, but they are still motivated and contextualized by those relationships. The popular feminism of the 2010s appears again here: the musical rejects the marriage finale typical of Golden Age musicals, but simply removes the wedding scene rather than altering the patriarchal and heteronormative structures that define each woman in relationship to men. Moreover, while the musical condemns the obvious abuse of Jenna's husband, it rewards unhealthy behavior from Dawn's stalkerish suitor Ogie, who sings, "I love you means you're never, ever, ever gettin' rid of me" in a disconcerting anthem to not taking no for an answer. Even Jenna's ultimate freedom is funded by Joe, the demanding owner of the diner. Finally, as much as Jenna values her friends, the musical privileges heterosexual romance over female friendship. If *Waitress* is considered a "liberated" depiction of women, we still have a long way to go.

New York Times critics Laura Collins-Hughes and Alexis Soloski agreed that *Waitress* came up short as a feminist musical. Collins-Hughes noted that one of the most compelling parts of Jenna's character is her reaction to her pregnancy: she does not want the child. However, the hard questions raised by Jenna's difficult situation and dread of motherhood are avoided: abortion is never mentioned as an option, and "the moment she gives birth, she is utterly transformed as a human being," a character change Collins-Hughes found "creepy and reactionary."[52] Two other women-centered musicals in the 2015–2016 Broadway season, *Bright Star* and *The Color Purple*, also ended with reunions with children, implying for Soloski that "[n]o matter how much women achieve...they will never be complete without their children."[53] While classic musicals end with marriage, these musicals of the 2010s glorify a reunion with children; neither formulation prioritizes a happy ending for the single, unattached woman.

Both Collins-Hughes and Soloski worried that *Waitress* repeats the limited pattern of "female-driven" stories "allowed" to be produced on Broadway, which requires women to suffer as victims to triumph as heroes. "[M]en get to struggle with politics and power and art and conflicts deep within the self," Soloski said, but "women's struggles are about overcoming or confronting abusive men."[54] She added, "Next season, I'd like to see women suffer a little less and run the world a little more."[55]

Waitress also navigated an ambivalent relationship to race. The creative team was mostly white, another reason why they likely were "trusted" to lead a Broadway production. Some casts of *Waitress* slipped into racial stereotyping: Jenna, the white leading lady; Dawn, the demure Asian sidekick; and Becky, the sassy Black belter. However, understudies, swings, and replacements frequently played the three leads and their love interests. On September 17, 2019, for the first time, *Waitress'* three leads were all played by Black actors: Jordin Sparks as Jenna, NaTasha Yvette Williams as Becky, and Jessie Hooker-Bailey as Dawn. This casting provided an additional layer to the solidarity among the working-class women featured in *Waitress*. It also resisted Broadway's tendency to default to white actors when stories are not explicitly about race and only foreground actors of color, especially Black actors, through stories of racial struggle.

The original Broadway production of *Waitress* closed on January 5, 2020, after 1,544 performances.[56] Two months later, the COVID-19 pandemic shuttered Broadway.[57] Despite the difficulties faced by the theatre community and the country at large during the pandemic, the halt in production allowed activists to organize and be heard as national attention focused on systemic racial injustice after the murder of George Floyd in May 2020. In response, many theatre makers and productions examined how they were contributing to racism.

On September 2, 2021, Broadway reopened, and *Waitress* did, too, with Bareilles once again in its starring role.[58] On September 3, 2021, the production grossed $197,878 in ticket sales and broke the single-performance house record at the Ethel Barrymore Theatre.[59] During its four-month limited return, *Waitress* featured many actors of color in leading roles, which may point to the effect of industry-wide conversations regarding racist practices. However, more cynically, one could argue that producers cast more actors of color only after *Waitress* had proven successful, grossing $168,426,425 in its original run.

After *Waitress*

Waitress paved the way for more female-driven productions to make it to Broadway stages, and it drew attention to women-centered stories, even if its politics were feminist-lite. Moreover, *Waitress* set the stage for feminist critics to assess both the number of women working on a musical and the message of the show.

In 2019, *Hadestown* opened with a female-led creative team and won the Tony for Best Musical—the first written by a solo woman to do so—and Best Direction, making Chavkin only the fourth woman to receive the honor (the third was Paulus for *Pippin*).[60] The creators of *Hadestown* owned the importance of their achievements. Mitchell said, "[W]hen I showed that sign [with her and Chavkin's names] to my kid, I felt proud ... to be able to show her a Broadway marquee with two women's names on it. And that will be normal for her."[61] Moreover, the musical—a contemporary riff on the Orpheus and Eurydice myth concerned with climate change, labor exploitation, and migration—represents gender complexly and self-reflexively. *Hadestown* foregrounds toxic masculinity through the character of Hades, who possesses Persephone and viciously rules over his underground workers. Orpheus, the musician who dooms his lover by turning around to see her, is feminized, awkward in his masculinity and his role as "hero."

Several other shows that opened (or re-opened) on Broadway starting in the fall of 2021 were helmed by women in leading creative positions and told women-centered stories. The bio-musical *Tina: The Tina Turner Musical*, which opened in 2019 and resumed performances in October 2021, features the music of Tina Turner with a book by Katori Hall and direction by Phyllida Lloyd.

SIX, which opened in October 2021 after the pandemic forced the last-minute cancellation of its scheduled opening in March 2020, has women and non-binary artists in lead creative roles: book, lyrics, and music are written by Lucy Moss along with Toby Marlow (they won a Tony for Best Original Score); Moss co-directed the production with Jamie Armitage; and Carrie-Anne Ingrouille choreographed. *SIX* explicitly addresses the difficulty of telling women's stories when they've long been confined to the narratives of men. The one-act pop musical rewrites the six wives of Henry VIII with an overt and playful feminist flair.

Marianne Elliot's 2021 Tony Award-winning, gender-bent revival of Stephen Sondheim's *Company* (West End, 2018), with set and costume design by Bunny Christie (who also won a Tony for her *Company* work), recenters George Furth and Sondheim's musical around a leading woman. As Elliot said in her Tony acceptance speech, "Thank you first and foremost to Stephen Sondheim for trusting me to tell his story in a different way and putting a woman front and center."[62] Though casting Bobbie as a woman highlights societal pressures on single women in their mid-30s to marry, the musical still ends with Bobbie longing for a relationship with a man. Some spectators were disappointed that, even with the gender bending, Bobbie was portrayed as unremittingly straight. Moreover, Bobbie's future is not only linked to marriage but explicitly to motherhood. A consciousness of Bobbie's ticking "biological clock" is present throughout the musical; like the pressures of marriage, it is simultaneously critiqued and accepted as an inevitable desire by the production. In addition, by changing many of the women's roles to men's, the score is no longer dominated by great songs sung by women; musically, the production features men.

All the productions we've examined demonstrate the complex dynamics of gender in Broadway musicals. As feminist scholars, we'll continue to (and hope that readers will) pay attention to creators' identities, to characters and their stories, and to the ideological messages of shows—past, present, and future, new and revived. We'll continue to enjoy many shows that frustrate or disappoint us and to celebrate those that manage to fulfill our feminist expectations and succeed on Broadway, too.

NOTES

1 https://sixonbroadway.com/team.php Accessed May 16, 2022.
2 Eric Glover, et al, "What Do We Do with the Musical Theatre Canon, edited by Stacy Wolf," in *Troubling Traditions: Canonicity Theatre, and Performance in the US*, ed. Lindsey Mantoan, Matthew Moore, Angela Farr Schiller, NY: Routledge, 2022, 211.
3 Also see https://www.broadwayworld.com/article/On-Her-Shoulders-presents-PAULINE-HOPKINS-315-20180219 Accessed May 16, 2022.

4 Korey R. Rothman, "'Will You Remember': Female Lyricists of Operetta and Musical Comedy," *Women in American Musical Theatre*, ed. Bud Coleman and Judith Sebesta, Jefferson, NC: McFarland & Co, 2008, 9.

5 See Coleman and Sebesta. On Rittman, also see Jim Lovensheimer. *South Pacific: Paradise Rewritten*, NY: Oxford UP, 2010, 130. In this chapter we focus on composers, lyricists, and librettists, and directors and choreographers. We regret not attending to the valuable work of designers, stage managers, technicians, producers, and more.

6 https://maestramusic.org/resources/timelines/female-composers-on-broadway/ https://maestramusic.org/resources/timelines/time-line-of-female-composers-off-broadway/ Accessed May 16, 2022.

7 https://amp.theguardian.com/stage/2018/feb/23/frozen-movie-disney-musical-broadway Accessed May 16, 2022.

8 Qtd in Leah Marilla Thomas, "How Anais Mitchell's Musical 'Hadestown' Is Making Broadway History for Women," *Bustle*, May 6, 2019. https://www.bustle.com/p/anais-mitchells-hadestown-is-making-broadway-history-for-women-but-she-wants-it-to-be-normal-for-the-next-generation-17130069 Accessed May 16, 2022.

9 Georgia Stitt, et al., "What Do We Do with the Musical Theatre Canon?, edited by Stacy Wolf" in *Troubling Traditions: Canonicity, Theatre, and Performance in the US*, eds. Lindsey Mantoan, Matthew Robert Moore, and Angela Farr Schiller (New York: Routledge, 2022), 213.

10 See Gary Konas, "Working with the Boys: Women Who Wrote Musicals in the Golden Age," in *Women in American Musical Theatre: Essays on Composers, Lyricists, Librettists, Arrangers, Choreographers, Designers, Directors, Producers and Performance Artists*, eds. Bud Coleman and Judith Sebesta (Jefferson, NC: McFarland, 2008), 92–129.

11 Liza Gennaro, *Making Broadway Dance*, NY: Oxford UP, 2021, 53.

12 Gennaro, 74.

13 Gennaro, 74.

14 Gennaro, 110.

15 Anne Fliotsos and Wendy Vierow, "Carroll, Vinette," *American Women Stage Directors of the Twentieth Century*, Urbana: University of Illinois Press, 2008, 110.

16 Linda Armstrong, "Award-winning lyricist Micki Grant talks about 'Don't Bother Me, I Can't Cope' at City Center," *New York Amsterdam News*, July 19, 2018. https://amsterdamnews.com/news/2018/07/19/award-winning-lyricist-micki-grant-talks-about-don/ Accessed May 21, 2022.

17 Eric Grode, "A Buoyant '70s Musical About Black Lives Lands in 2018," *New York Times*, July 20, 2018. https://www.nytimes.com/2018/07/20/theater/dont-bother-me-i-cant-cope-savion-glover-encores.html Accessed May 21, 2022.

18 Armstrong.

19 Grode, "A Buoyant '70s Musical About Black Lives Lands in 2018," *New York Times*, July 20, 2018. https://www.nytimes.com/2018/07/20/theater/dont-bother-me-i-cant-cope-savion-glover-encores.html Accessed May 21, 2022.

20 Armstrong.

21 Qtd in Grode.

22 Qtd in Grode.

23 Armstrong.

24 See Judith Sebesta, "Social Consciousness and the 'Search for New Directions': The Musicals of Gretchen Cryer, Nancy Ford, and Elizabeth Swados," in *Women in American Musical Theatre: Essays on Composers, Lyricists, Librettists, Arrangers, Choreographers, Designers, Directors, Producers and Performance Artists*, eds. Bud Coleman and Judith Sebesta (Jefferson, NC: McFarland, 2008), 200–220.

25 See Susan Faludi, *Backlash: The Undeclared War Against American Women*, NY: Crown, 1991.

26 See Lisa Levenstein, *They Didn't See Us Coming: The Hidden History of Feminism in the Nineties*, NY: Basic Books, 2020.

27 Adam Hettrick, "Women of *The Secret Garden* Talk Making History," *Breaking Character: A Concord Theatricals Publication*, January 7, 2016. https://www.breakingcharacter.com/home/2019/4/10/women-of-the-secret-garden-talk-making-history Accessed May 19, 2022.

28 Hettrick.

29 "Ch 36: *The Secret Garden*," *50 Key Stage Musicals* podcast. https://broadwaypodcastnetwork.com/fifty-key-stage-musicals-the-podcast/ch-36-the-secret-garden/

30 Frank Rich, "Review/Theater: 'Garden': The Secret Of Death And Birth," *New York Times*, April 26, 1991: C27+. https://www.nytimes.com/1991/04/26/theater/review-theater-garden-the-secret-of-death-and-birth.html Accessed May 20, 2022.

31 David Richard, "Only the Wind Should Sigh in This 'Garden,'" *New York Times*, May 5, 1991: H5. Alex Witchel recorded changes to the production after poor reception. "On Stage, and Off: Pruning 'The Secret Garden,'" May 3, 1991: C2. https://www.proquest.com/hnpnewyorktimes/docview/108793553/pageviewPDF/6DFC0AA0 5203448FPQ/1?accountid=13314

32 *50 Key Stage Musicals* podcast. Also see Anne Fliotsos, "'Open a New Window, Open a New Door': Women Directors Take the Stage," in Coleman and Sebesta, 190–93.

33 Elysa Gardner, "Julie Taymor on the Lasting Legacy of *The Lion King*," Broadway Direct, November 6, 2017. https://broadwaydirect.com/julie-taymor-lasting-legacy-lion-king/ Accessed June 17, 2022.

34 Gennaro, 187.

35 Mary Jo Lodge, "The Rise of the Female Director/Choreographer on Broadway," in in *Women in American Musical Theatre: Essays on Composers, Lyricists, Librettists, Arrangers, Choreographers, Designers, Directors, Producers and Performance Artists*, eds. Bud Coleman and Judith Sebesta (Jefferson, NC: McFarland, 2008), 240–41.

36 Lodge, 241. Also see Fliotsos, in Coleman and Sebesta, 174–99.

37 "Postfeminism, popular feminism and neoliberal feminism? Sarah Banet-Weiser, Rosalind Gill and Catherine Rottenberg in conversation," *Feminist Theory*, April 23, 2019. https://journals.sagepub.com/doi/full/10.1177/1464700119842555

38 Ben Brantley, "Review: 'Fun Home' at the Circle in the Square Theater," *New York Times*, April 19, 2015. https://www.nytimes.com/2015/04/20/theater/review-fun-home-at-the-circle-in-the-square-theater.html
39 Carly Erickson, personal email, June 6, 2019.
40 https://www.broadwayworld.com/shows/backstage.php?showid=331376
41 https://www.broadwayworld.com/grosses/WAITRESS
42 https://apnews.com/article/41abe3253a014a37af792694df4569b6
43 https://time.com/4285668/waitress-broadway-sara-bareilles/
44 https://time.com/4285668/waitress-broadway-sara-bareilles/
45 https://time.com/4285668/waitress-broadway-sara-bareilles/
46 https://time.com/4285668/waitress-broadway-sara-bareilles/
47 https://time.com/4285668/waitress-broadway-sara-bareilles/
48 https://time.com/4285668/waitress-broadway-sara-bareilles/
49 https://www.weseeyouwat.com/
50 https://american-rep-assets.s3.amazonaws.com/wp-content/uploads/2018/11/07142804/waitress-toolkit-final-8.19.pdf
51 https://time.com/4285668/waitress-broadway-sara-bareilles/
52 Laura Collins-Hughes and Alexis Soloski, "Broadway May Not Be So White, but It Is Woman Enough?" *New York Times*, May 31, 2016. https://www.nytimes.com/2016/06/05/theater/women-on-broadway-a-year-of-living-dangerously.html Accessed June 18, 2022.
53 Collins-Hughes and Soloski.
54 Collins-Hughes and Soloski.
55 Collins-Hughes and Soloski.
56 https://www.forbes.com/sites/jerylbrunner/2021/08/17/waitress-returns-to-broadway-next-month-starring-sara-bareilles/?sh=28e2a41c7541
57 https://www.nytimes.com/2020/03/12/theater/coronavirus-broadway-shutdown.html
58 https://www.npr.org/2021/09/14/1037194157/3-big-broadway-shows-reopen-with-covid-rules?t=1640881120877
59 https://deadline.com/2021/09/waitress-broadway-house-record-ticket-sales-1234827361/
60 https://www.hollywoodreporter.com/lists/tony-award-full-list-winners-2019-1214435/
61 Qtd in Leah Marilla Thomas, "How Anais Mitchell's Musical 'Hadestown' Is Making Broadway History for Women, *Bustle*, May 6, 2019. https://www.bustle.com/p/anais-mitchells-hadestown-is-making-broadway-history-for-women-but-she-wants-it-to-be-normal-for-the-next-generation-17130069 Accessed May 16, 2022.
62 Suzy Evans, "Our Favorite Moments from the 2022 Tony Awards, *TodayTix*, June 12, 2022. https://www.todaytix.com/insider/nyc/posts/our-favorite-moments-from-the-2022-tony-awards Accessed June 17, 2022.

RECOMMENDATIONS FOR ADDITIONAL RESOURCES

Coleman, Bud and Judith Sebesta, eds. *Women in American Musical Theatre*, Jefferson, NC: McFarland & Co, 2008.

This is a wide-ranging anthology with chapters on women creatives since the nineteenth century, including producer Hallie Flanagan, lighting designer Jean Rosenthal, orchestrator Trude Rittman, and many more.

Greenberg, Shoshana, compiler. "Maestra Timeline of Female and Non-Binary Composers." https://maestramusic.org/resources/timelines/female-composers-on-broadway/. https://maestramusic.org/resources/timelines/female-composers-on-broadway/. March, 2020.

Maestra launched in 2017 in person and in 2018 on the web as an organization for female musicians on Broadway. One resource their website provides is this detailed timeline starting in 1899 of female and nonbinary Broadway composers "from early revues to full-length scores."

Wolf, Stacy. *A Problem Like Maria: Gender and Sexuality in the American Musical*, Ann Arbor: U of Michigan Press, 2002.

This book examines the star personae of Mary Martin, Ethel Merman, Julie Andrews, and Barbra Streisand from a lesbian, feminist perspective.

Wolf, Stacy. *Changed for Good: A Feminist History of the Broadway Musical*, New York: Oxford UP, 2011.

This text is a study of women characters in relation to musical theatre's conventions from the 1950s to *Wicked*.

Timeline

@500-400 BCE   Ancient Greek Theater, including comedies by Aristophanes, flourishes. (Introduction)

1728   John Gay's *The Beggar's Opera*, the first ballad opera, premieres. (Introduction)

1840s–1870s   Minstrel shows, a racist form of musical entertainment that used white performers in black face, reach the peak of their popularity. (Chapter 1)

1866   *The Black Crook* premieres and becomes an early hit musical. (Introduction and Chapter 6)

1870s   Georg II, the Duke of Saxe-Meiningen, creates the position of the modern director. (Chapter 4)

1875   Vaudeville is launched in New York by impresario Tony Pastor, who cleans up Variety to create a popular entertainment suitable for families. (Introduction)

1878   Gilbert and Sullivan's first hit, *HMS Pinafore*, premieres in the US. (Chapter 2)

1903   *In Dahomey* premieres and is the first successful Black musical. (Chapter 1)

1907-1931   The *Ziegfield Follies* run yearly. These are the most successful of the Spectacular Revues, feature elaborate sets and costumes, and are created by impresario Florenz Ziegfeld. (Chapter 1)

1907   *The Merry Widow* premieres in New York. This early smash hit started a ballroom dance craze because of its focus on the waltz. (Chapter 2)

1913   The actors' labor union, Actors Equity Association, forms. (Chapter 1)

1914 The American Society of Composers, Authors and Publishers is founded to help composers and lyricists to secure the right to own and profit from their works. Composer Victor Herbert plays a major role in its creation, and battles to ensure interpolations by producers are not allowed in musicals. (Chapter 2)

1914 The Takarazuka Revue, the famous all-female theater company in Japan, is created as an alternative to the traditional Japanese all-male form of kabuki theater. (Chapter 9)

1920s The Harlem Renaissance, when Black culture and art flourished in New York City, occurs. (Chapter 1)

1921 *Shuffle Along,* the first successful musical written, directed, and acted by African-Americans, premieres. (Chapter 1)

1927 *Showboat,* the first musical drama, premieres. (Chapter 2)

1931 *Of Thee I Sing,* the first musical to win the Pulitzer Prize, premieres. (Chapter 2)

1934 Cole Porter, who had more hits in the 1930s than any other composer, premieres the hit musical *Anything Goes,* which was escapist fare during the Great Depression.

1937 *Pins and Needles,* the pro-union musical created by the members of the International Ladies Garment Workers Union, premieres. (Chapter 3)

1937 *The Cradle Will Rock,* the controversial, pro-union Federal Theatre Project musical is ordered to close but premieres anyway, in legendary fashion. (Chapter 3)

1943 *Oklahoma!,* the first collaboration of Richard Rodgers and Oscar Hammerstein II, premieres and breaks new ground in terms of structural integration and content. (Chapter 4 & others)

1946 *Annie Get Your Gun,* the most successful musical by composer Irving Berlin, premieres. Berlin composed twenty Broadway scores, and wrote numerous hit songs including "God Bless America" in 1938. (Chapter 10)

1949 Rodgers and Hammerstein's *South Pacific,* the second musical to win a Pulitzer Prize, premieres. (Chapter 2)

1956   *My Fair Lady*, by Lerner and Loewe, premiered. It was the most successful musical of the 1950s both on Broadway and world-wide, including in Japan where it premiered in 1963. (Chapter 9)

1957   *West Side Story*, which marks the start of the beginning of the Golden Age of the director/choreographer and introduces triple threat performers, but also includes harmful stereotypes of Latinx people, premieres. (Chapter 2)

1960   *The Fantasticks,* the longest running off-Broadway show, opens. (Chapter 6)

1964   *Fiddler On The Roof,* a major hit worldwide, premieres. (Chapter 6)

1968   *Hair,* billed as the first musical of the counterculture, brings rock music to Broadway. (Chapter 5)

1970   *Company,* the first concept musical, premieres. (Chapter 4)

1971   *Jesus Christ Superstar* premieres, after initially being created as a concept album by Andrew Lloyd Webber and Tim Rice, who used the money from the album release to fund the show. (Chapter 6)

1972   *Pippin,* a major work created by director/choreographer Bob Fosse, and the first show to create a TV commercial, pre-mieres. (Chapter 4 & Chapter 10)

1972   *Don't Bother Me, I Can't Cope,* which featured the first Black female composer, lyricist and librettist (Micki Grant) and the first Black woman director (Vinnette Carroll), premieres. (Chapter 10)

1975   *A Chorus Line,* the most successful musical created by director/choreographer/conceiver Michael Bennett, premieres. (Chapter 4 & 5)

1979   *Zoot Suit,* the only Chicano created and Chicanx-centered musical to have appeared on Broadway, premieres. (Chapter 8)

1982   The megamusical finds success with the premiere of Andrew Lloyd Webber's *Cats.* (Chapter 6)

1983   *La Cage Aux Folles,* the first musical to feature openly gay characters, premieres. (Chapter 3)

1987   *Les Misérables,* a megamusical which first introduced top ticket prices of $50, premieres. (Chapter 6)

1988   *The Phantom of the Opera*, the longest running musical on Broadway (as of 2023) premieres. (Chapter 6)

1991   *The Secret Garden*, the first Broadway musical created by an all-female team, premieres. (Chapter 10)

1994   *Beauty and the Beast*, Disney's first Broadway musical, premieres. (Chapter 6)

1996   *Rent*, the game changing rock musical by Jonathan Larson, premieres. (Chapter 5)

2006   *Spring Awakening*, the youth-oriented rock musical, premieres. (Chapter 5)

2008   *In The Heights*, with music and lyrics by, and starring Lin-Manuel Miranda, and which highlighted Latinx characters and culture, premieres. (Chapter 8)

2015   *Hamilton*, the Pulitzer Prize winning musical with music, lyrics and book by Lin-Manuel Miranda, which also starred Miranda and incorporated rap music, premieres. (Chapter 8)

2015   *Fun Home*, which centers on a lesbian graphic novelist and is the first Broadway show written by two women to win the Tony for Best Musical, premieres. (Chapter 10)

2016   *Waitress*, which features an all-female creative team, premieres. (Chapter 10)

2017   The #MeToo Movement, founded by Tarana Burke to speak out against sexual harassment of women, gained fame in connection with sexual harassment accusations against film and theater producer, Harvey Weinstein, and spread to a wider movement in which sexual harassment in other workspaces, including Broadway, was called out. (Chapter 10)

2020   "The We See You, White American Theater" movement originated as a letter and list of demands, and then a website and other actions crafted and disseminated by artists of color. It challenged racism in theater. (Chapter 10)

2022   *A Strange Loop*, the first musical by a Black creator (Michael R. Jackson) to be awarded the Pulitzer Prize (in 2020), premieres on Broadway. (Introduction)

Glossary

Burlesque   An early form of popular entertainment which spoofed and lampooned other creative works, but which was later was associated with unsavory elements including striptease.

Choreographer   The person who creates a musical's dances (originally called the dance director).

Composer   The person who writes the music or score of a musical.

Director   The person who supervises a musical and stages its action (and may create a concept to govern its production).

Director/choreographer   A person who both stages and creates the dances for a musical.

Dream ballet   A long, dance driven sequence in a musical, which often features ballet, but can use other styles of dance.

Eleven o'clock number   The last number in a musical that showcases the show's star before the final curtain.

Gesamtskunstwerk   A German term for a total or complete work of art popularized by composer Richard Wagner in his 1948 essays on performance.

Great White Way   A nickname for Broadway that emerged in the early 1900s which referred to the use of electric lighting in and on its theaters.

Interpolated songs   Using existing songs and repurposing them, sometimes with new lyrics, in musicals.

Kabuki Theater   A classical form of Japanese theatre which since 1629 has been an exclusively male art form.

Librettist   The person who writes the book of a musical.

Libretto   The book or story of the musical.

Lyrics   The words to a song.

Lyricist   The person who writes the words to a song.

Megamusical   A term for musicals that emerged in the 1980s that combine elaborate spectacle with operatic and pop influences.

Musical scene   A scene in a musical which is set to music and is usually a duet.

Overture   The first song of a musical, which occurs before the action of a show begins.

Producer   The person who provides the financial backing and sometimes the artistic leadership for a musical.

Refrain   The repeated portion of a song, often its most important part.

Reprise   The reappearance of a song later in a musical, usually in a shorter form and with different lyrics.

Revues   Early shows which feature musical numbers, scenes and even specialty acts, but include no libretto.

Score   The music for a musical, also the written musical notation of the music for a musical.

Spectacle   The scenery, costumes, lighting and special effects for musicals, which are sometimes associated with elaborate physical productions.

Triple Threats   Performers who are skilled in singing, dancing and acting.

Underscoring   The music that plays during spoken dialogue and is usually intended to heighten its emotional impact.

Verisimilitude   The appearance of truth or reality.

Additional Resources

Anderson, Virginia, "'Something Bad [Was] Happening': *Falsettos as an Historical Record of the AIDS Epidemic*," *Studies in Musical Theatre* 13, no. 3 (2019): 221–234. This essay argues for the importance of an often-overlooked aspect of *Falsettos*: the role of Dr. Charlotte, a character whose name is never spoken in performance. Her identities as a woman, a lesbian and a doctor—and the signification of each—unlock largely unspoken histories, reflecting and transforming broader histories of the AIDS epidemic.

Anne of Green Gables. 1969 London Cast Recording (1993). CD 53495. London: Sony West End. This is the only available recording of the full score.

Bernstein, Leonard, et al. "*West Side Story*: The New Broadway Cast Recording" New York: Sony Masterworks, 2009. This cast recording includes Spanish-language versions of "I Feel Pretty" ("Me Siento Hermosa") and "A Boy Like That" ("Un Hombre Asi") with translations by Lin-Manuel Miranda.

Blake, Eubie. *Sissle and Blake Sing* Shuffle Along, 2016. Noble Sissle. Harbinger Records HCD 3204, compact disc. Harbinger Records' album is the original 1928 archival record of Eubie Blake's score as it was performed by cast and crew on opening night. Although the album is not an "original Broadway cast recording," *Sissle and Blake Sing* Shuffle Along features performances by Blake, Sissle, and other participating artists.

Bloom, Ken, and Richard Carlin. *Eubie Blake: Rags, Rhythm, and Race.* New York: Oxford University Press, 2020. This is a recent, full-length study of James Hubert Blake and of his life and times as the composer of the 1921 musical comedy *Shuffle Along.* Bloom and Carlin won the 2017 GRAMMY Award for Best Album Notes at the 59th Annual GRAMMY Awards for the liner notes that accompany Harbinger Records' *Sissle and Blake Sing* Shuffle Along.

Carter, Marva. *Swing Along: The Musical Life of Will Marion Cook*. New York: Oxford University Press, 2008. This is a full-length study of Will Marion Cook and of his life and times as the composer of the 1903 musical comedy *In Dahomey*. Cook's experience at National Conservatory of Music of America and at Oberlin Conservatory of Music are addressed, as are his experiences in the Clef Club, for Black musicians, and in the Southern Syncopated Orchestra.

Chiemi, Eri. *Chiemi Show Time: My Fair Lady/Chiemi at the Coma*. CD. Tokyo: King Records, 2020. This remastered CD album, originally released as LP (1964), captures how Eri sang *My Fair Lady*'s songs. It is not the live recording of Tōhō's production due to mechanical rights issues, but her voice and the sound reveal a great deal about how Broadway sound was reproduced for Japanese audiences.

Coleman, Bud and Judith Sebesta, eds. *Women in American Musical Theatre*, Jefferson, NC: McFarland & Co, 2008. This is a wide-ranging anthology with chapters on women creative artist since the nineteenth century, including producer Hallie Flanagan, lighting designer Jean Rosenthal, orchestrator Trude Rittman, and many more.

Cote, David. *'Spring Awakening': In the Flesh*. New York: Melcher Media, 2008. This book recounts the process through which the musical was created.

Cramer, Lyn. *Creating Musical Theatre Conversations with Broadway Directors and Choreographers*. London: Bloomsbury Publishing, Bloomsbury Methuen Drama, 2013. In this book, Cramer interviews many of the leading directors and choreographers of the Broadway musical about their process. It includes profiles of Jerry Mitchell, Kathleen Marshall, and Andy Blakenbuehler, among others.

Decker, Todd R. *Show Boat: Performing Race in an American Musical*. New York: Oxford University Press, 2013. This is an overview of the show's creation with emphasis on both the music and the libretto, important productions and film versions of the show through the 1990s, and a fascinating consideration of the various roles of race in a landmark property involving that crucial lens in American life and history.

Eben, David and Meinhard Saremba. *The Cambridge Companion to Gilbert and Sullivan*. Cambridge: Cambridge University Press, 2009. This is a one-volume introduction to the topic with essays by numerous experts in the field providing considerations of the background to the operettas, focuses on the works in context and their librettos and music, and their reception in both professional and amateur productions.

Elisabeth. Live aus dem Theater an der Wien (2006). Directed by Sven Offen. DVD 6682527. Vienna: Hit Squad Records. This is a filmed record of the original 1992 production, re-staged in 2006; it includes English subtitles.

Gaines, Caseen. *Footnotes: The Black Artists Who Rewrote the Rules of the Great White Way*. Naperville: Sourcebooks, 2021. This is a cultural and social discussion of the authors of *Shuffle Along*, the relevant criticism, the script's production history, and the world of the musical. The original Broadway production of *Shuffle Along* is re-created from a treasure trove of audio recordings, clippings, financial and legal papers, personal correspondence, personal papers, printed ephemera, professional correspondence, and vertical files.

Gordon, Robert and Olaf Jubin (eds.) *The Oxford Handbook of the Global Stage Musical*. New York: Oxford University Press, 2023. This is an overview of the development of musical theatre as a global phenomenon; and it includes detailed analyses of other national and international hit shows.

Goldman, Harry Merton, "*Pins and Needles*: A White House Command Performance." *Educational Theatre Journal* 30, no. 1 (Mar., 1978): 90–101. With great detail, Goldman reconstructs the performance of *Pins and Needles* for President Roosevelt at the White House on March 3, 1938, offering insight into its development, staging, and reception.

Greenberg, Shoshana, compiler. "Maestra Timeline of Female and Non-Binary Composers on Broadway." https://maestra-music.org/resources/timelines/female-composers-on-broadway/. March, 2020. Maestra launched in 2017 in person and in 2018 on the web as an organization for female musicians on Broadway. One resource their website provides is this detailed timeline starting in 1899 of female and non-binary Broadway composers "from early revues to full-length scores."

Herrera, Brian Eugenio. *Latin Numbers: Playing Latino in Twentieth-Century U.S. Popular Performance*. Ann Arbor, MI: Univ. of Michigan Press, 2015. This text examines the influence of twentieth-century Latino stage and film actors on the American understanding of Latinos as a distinct racial and ethnic group.

Hoffman, Warren. *Great White Way: Race and the Broadway Musical*. New Brunswick, NJ: Rutgers University Press, 2020. This is a chronological study of how American musicals have reflected changing perceptions of race in America. This second edition includes a discussion of *Hamilton*.

Hunter, John. "Marc Blitzstein's *The Cradle will Rock* as a Document of America, 1937," *American Quarterly* 18, no. 2, Part 1 (summer, 1966): 227–233. Hunter's essay provides excellent contextualization for *The Cradle Will Rock*, offering insights into the cultural moment of the 1937 production as well as Blitzstein's craft and influences.

Jarrett, Gene Andrew. *Paul Laurence Dunbar: The Life and Times of a Caged Bird*. Princeton: Princeton University Press, 2022. This is a recent full-length study of Paul Laurence Dunbar and of his life and times as a musical theatre writer, a playwright, and a poet. Even though he made a living as a professional writer, the first US Black person to do so, Dunbar grew to resent the use of African-American Vernacular English that made him famous.

Kristina at Carnegie Hall. CD 2734981. New York: Universal Music/Decca Broadway/Mono Music, 2010. This is a live recording of the abbreviated English version of the musical.

Knapp, Raymond. *The American Musical and the Performance of Personal Identity*. Princeton: Princeton University Press, 2006. This thematic approach to musicals explores how they allow writers, performers, and audiences to explore personal identities, organized by categories and themes including operetta, gender and sexuality, relationships, and idealism.

Long, Robert Emmet. *Broadway, the Golden Years: Jerome Robbins and the Great Choreographer-Directors: 1940 to the Present*. London: Continuum, 2006. This book tracks the work of notable artists including Agnes de Mille, Robbins, Fosse, Champion, Bennett and Tune.

Lovensheimer, Jim. *South Pacific: Paradise Rewritten.* Oxford and New York: Oxford University Press, 2010. This is a consideration of the show's adaptation from Michener's collection of short stories, the creation of the score, the property's relation to and use of race, gender, and Western colonialism, the reception of the original production, and the show's performance history in subsequent versions.

Notre-Dame de Paris. Version Intégrale (1999). Directed by Gilles Amado. DVD 952509. Paris: Pomme Music. This is a filmed record of the Paris staging, with the original stars; includes English subtitles.

Pollack, Howard. *George Gershwin: His Life and Work.* Berkeley: University of California Press, 2006. This is a voluminous, chronological consideration of Gershwin's life and work with material on the creation and reception of each of his works, commentary on the music of each, and performance histories. There is an entire chapter on *Of Thee I Sing.*

Replogle-Wong, Holley Dawn. "Crossover and Spectacle in American Operetta and the Megamusical." University of California, Los Angeles, PhD dissertation, 2009. This is a cross-historical analysis of the reception of operetta and the megamusical in America through the lens of American cultural hierarchies, including extended discussions of *The Merry Widow* and *The Phantom of the Opera.*

Rich, Frank. "Discovering Family Values at *Falsettos,*" *The New York Times.* July 12, 1992. https://www.nytimes.com/1992/07/12/theater/theater-discovering-family-values-at-falsettos.html. Rich's essay about taking his children to see *Falsettos* offers another way in which the show serves as an activist musical. Rich contextualizes the show within vehement statements made by Dan Quayle concerning "family values" in which the then–Vice President denounced anything but a heteronormative nuclear family.

Rosenzweig, Josh, director. *Heart of Broadway: The Ensemble Behind Broadway Cares/Equity Fights AIDS* (film). Here Media, 2011. This documentary provides a comprehensive overview of the organization, its history, its creators, and three regular philanthroproductions.

Simon, Paul, et al. "The Capeman: Original Broadway Cast Recording." New York: Decca Broadway, 2006. This two-disc set features the entire score of the musical and includes performances by Ruben Blades, Marc Anthony, and Ednita Nazario.

Stempel, Larry. *Showtime: A History of the Broadway Musical Theater.* New York: W. W. Norton, 2010. This is a history of the Broadway musical from the 19th-century *The Black Crook* through the early twenty-first-century megamusical and "movical" (musicals based on films).

Sternfeld, Jessica. *The Megamusical.* Bloomington and Indianapolis: Indiana University Press, 2006. This pioneering treatment of megamusicals considers their musical and theatrical qualities alongside commercial concerns to illuminate their success and popularity.

Thelen, Lawrence. *The Show Makers: Great Directors of the American Musical Theatre.* New York: Routledge, 2002. This text features interviews about with many Broadway directors about their directorial processes, and includes the last interview given by Jerome Robbins before he died.

Warren, Michael John, dir. *Rent: Filmed Live on Broadway.* 2008; Culver City, Calif.: Sony Pictures Home Entertainment, 2009. DVD. Film versions exist of both *Hair* and *Rent*, which differ from their stage productions, as well as this version, which is a video capture of the Broadway performance.

Warren, Michael John, dir. *Spring Awakening: Those You've Known.* New York: Home Box Office, 2022. https://www.hbo.com/movies/spring-awakening-those-youve-known. This documentary follows the original company of *Spring Awakening* as they reunite years later for a concert of the show.

Wetmore Jr., Kevin J., Siyuan Liu, and Erin B. Mee, eds. *Modern Asian Theatre and Performance 1900-2000,* London/New York: Bloomsbury, 2014. This historical overview of modern drama in Asian countries and regions introduces where and how European and American musical theatre was produced in the region.

Wolf, Stacy. *A Problem Like Maria: Gender and Sexuality in the American Musical,* Ann Arbor, MI: University of Michigan Press, 2002. This book examines the star personae of Mary

Martin, Ethel Merman, Julie Andrews, and Barbra Streisand from a lesbian, feminist perspective.

Wolf, Stacy. *Changed for Good: A Feminist History of the Broadway Musical*, New York: Oxford University Press, 2011. This is a study of women characters in relation to musical theatre's conventions from the 1950s to *Wicked*.

Yamanashi, Makiko. *A History of the Takarazuka Revue Since 1914: Modernity, Girls' Culture, Japan Pop*. Leiden: Global Oriental, 2012. This English language book is a comprehensive historical survey of the Takarazuka Revue, one of the most important and long running Japanese musical theatre companies.

Yamanashi, Makiko, Sissi Liu, Gilbert C. F. Fong, Shelby Karyan Chan, Fan-Ting Cheng, Ji hyon (Kalya) Yuh and Caleb Goh. "Modern Musicals in Asia." In: *The Routledge Handbook of Asian Theatre*, edited by Siyuan Liu, 527–551, Abington/New York: Routledge, 2016. This country-by-country survey provides essential knowledge about how the American musical was introduced and has subsequently developed in Japan, China, Hong Kong, Taiwan, Korea, and Southeast Asia.

Index

Printed in Great Britain
by Amazon

40170012R00126